BILLY GRAHAM
Evangelistic Association
Always Good News.

Dear Friend,

I am pleased to send you this copy of Don Wilton's book *When God Prayed*. This insightful book began as a seminar at the Billy Graham Training Center at The Cove, where Don regularly teaches. He has been my father's pastor for several years.

As you read about Jesus' prayer from John 17, you will see foundational truths about salvation, the Christian's promise of future glory, and a call to unity for all those who know Him. "*I have given them the glory that you gave me, that they may be one as we are one*" (John 17:22, NIV). This prayer empowered the early disciples for what lay ahead and gave them direction for sharing the Gospel with others, and I pray you will find the same power as you explore the wonderful time when God prayed for *you*.

For more than 60 years, the Billy Graham Evangelistic Association has worked to take the Good News of Jesus Christ throughout the world by every effective means available, and I'm excited about what God will do in the years ahead.

We would appreciate knowing how our ministry has touched your life. May God richly bless you.

Sincerely,

Franklin Graham
President

If you would like to know more about our ministry, please contact us:

IN THE U.S.:
Billy Graham Evangelistic Association
1 Billy Graham Parkway
Charlotte, NC 28201-0001
billygraham.org
info@bgea.org
Toll-free: 1-877-247-2426

IN CANADA:
Billy Graham Evangelistic
  Association of Canada
20 Hopewell Way NE
Calgary, AB T3J 5H5
billygraham.ca
Toll-free: 1-888-393-0003

When GOD Prayed

DON WILTON

This *Billy Graham Library Selection* is published with
permission from B&H Publishing Group.

Nashville, Tennessee

©2008 by Don Wilton
All rights reserved
Printed in the United States of America

ISBN 978-1-59328-310-0
Previous ISBN 978-0-8054-4554-1

Published by B&H Publishing Group,
Nashville, Tennessee

Dewey Decimal Classification: 248.32
Subject Heading: PRAYER \ BIBLE. N. T. JOHN 17—
STUDY \ JESUS CHRIST—PRAYERS

This book is dedicated to my mother,
Rhodabelle Wilton

Mama prayed for me and God answered her prayers!!

Acknowledgments

I could not have written this book without the sustained love and encouragement of my wife, Karyn. My daughter, Shelley, most certainly must be thanked because she watched her dad with computer in hand and constantly provided him with the joy of life when the hours were long and hard.

I am deeply indebted to the Billy Graham Training Center at the Cove for continually allowing me the honor of teaching God's precious Word in such a special place. The invitation to teach on this subject provided the soil on which the initial seed was sown. My beloved congregation at First Baptist Church, Spartanburg, South Carolina, continues to be my essential foundation. They bless my heart with their continual encouragement in the ministry to which God has called me. They have become a strong tower of strength and light to many and have set a high standard of spiritual unity in the gospel of our Lord and Savior. Their sustained purpose is to encourage complete and courageous living in Christ. I also want to thank Jane Bateman and Cristie Wisecarver for their wonderful help in the compiling and editing of this manuscript.

Finally, I want to thank the Lord Jesus Christ for allowing me the privilege of preaching and teaching His Word.

Contents

Introduction

One of the great joys of my life has been my association with Dr. Billy Graham. The "hand of the Lord" is the first thing that comes to mind when I think about this dear man. My first visit to his home in Montreat is something I shall never forget. It was not, perhaps, the obvious things that embedded themselves in my heart and mind, and there have been so many over the years; it was the profound humility that flowed from the heart of this precious man of God. He has always spoken to me as though I was the master and he was the slave. Can you believe that? On one occasion I knelt before Dr. Graham as he placed his hands on me and prayed for me. On a human level it was like I was hearing God pray!

Of the many things the Lord has commissioned His servant to do, one assignment in particular has produced remarkable blessings for thousands of people from all over the world. The Billy Graham Training Center at the Cove, situated between Black Mountain and Asheville, is a retreat center that stands on gorgeous land and sparkles with the magnificent beauty of the Blue Ridge Mountains of North Carolina. Every time I am at the Cove, I hear God speak!

God speaks through the incredible men and women who know the true meaning of servanthood in that place. God speaks through speakers who are prayerfully selected to deliver a fresh word from the Word of God. God speaks as you meander down the hallways and find yourself being drawn into the wonder of it all. God speaks as you soak up the awesome extent with which the Lord Jesus used the Billy Graham team to reach millions of people for our Savior. God speaks when you gather in the dining room to feast on the most wonderfully prepared meals you can ever imagine. God speaks when new friendships are made and when you meet other believers from every walk of life and every place imaginable.

God speaks when you put on your hiking boots, take a walking stick, and abandon yourself to the beauty of God's creation. God speaks when you enter the chapel and find yourself standing in the presence of a mighty God who loves you. God speaks when you just listen. It's as though you can hear God praying!

And so it was when I was given the great honor of teaching another seminar at the Billy Graham Center at the Cove. My subject: When God Prayed.

No person can truly describe exactly what happened. It certainly was not the preacher. It was not the organization of the material. It was not the thoroughness with which the subject was covered because there was too much else to say. But somehow, God spoke. Deep down in our hearts, we heard God pray!

Jesus was about to go to the cross. His life and ministry had exhausted Him. Everywhere He went the people followed Him. The crowds pushed down on Him. They demanded of Him. They jeered and criticized Him. They accused Him of the worst kinds of blasphemy and they even threatened to kill Him. But He was not deterred; He was on mission. He knew what He was doing and where He was going.

He had felt tears, like drops of blood rolling down His face. He had tried time and time again to warn His disciples He was going to leave them. He had stood and cried out to the Father asking that the cup of His impending suffering be removed. Unlike all of us, Jesus did not have to suffer and die in order to know what suffering and dying were all about. But His hour had come. It was time to complete the mission. It was time to go all the way, even to His death on a cruel Roman cross. Fully and completely aware of His destination, Jesus took the cup and started the long journey to the cross.

Jesus looked up to heaven and spoke. Yes, He spoke in His capacity as the Son of Man, but He was also God. When He came down to this earth and took on the flesh of sinful man, He did not relinquish His glory as God. He did not abdicate the throne! He simply laid aside the privilege that was rightfully His with one purpose in mind: to fulfill God's eternal plan for the redemption of sinful man.

And so this prayer! Yes, Jesus, the Son of Man, is having a conversation with God. On the human level it is a monologue. We hear the Son talking to the Father. There is no doubt about it! In this sense this prayer is about Jesus having a conversation with Himself. Perhaps we may try to define this prayer as a soliloquy of sorts. In speech and drama we understand a soliloquy to be the act of talking while alone. Macbeth did it! Juliet did it! A soliloquy finds a character disclosing his innermost thoughts out loud. The conversation becomes the window to the soul. What comes out of the mouth is actually what lies hidden in the heart. Was Jesus simply having a conversation with Himself? Was He simply bringing to the surface His own agenda as the Son of Man? Was He speaking independently of the Father? Was He even capable of doing anything independently of the Father?

Well, yes, He was. But, then again He wasn't. How could the Son be independent of the Father?

It's like our effort to describe the earnestness and intensity of this prayer. Was Jesus praying with tension or intensity? Tension could justifiably be used to describe the human side of Jesus' prayer. He was praying as the Son of Man who absolutely knew and understood the agony of the cross that waited to pounce on Him like a roaring lion seeking to devour the flesh of a bloodied victim. Jesus knew Satan was waiting for the chance to finally get his hands on the Son of God and tear Him to pieces! Yes, tension must have been all over the Lord Jesus who understood the horrors of the cup of His pending suffering. Yes, He was becoming sin for us even though He knew no sin Himself. Yes, the appointed hour at which the Father would turn His face from His beloved Son was rapidly approaching. And the closer Jesus came to the cross, the more strained the relationship. When Jesus uttered these words to the Father, there must have been major tension, because the Lord Jesus must have been stretched and strained in His human capacity with all the mental and emotional issues He had facing Him.

You can feel the tension! To deny it is to deny that Jesus became flesh and dwelt among us. You can't have it both ways. He is not simply informing God about His agony. *Besides, God does not need to be informed. He knows.*

Our Savior prays with intensity. While the word *tension* describes the inner struggle, *intensity* describes the connection. *Intensity* speaks to the content of the conversation. Tension describes *how* He spoke, intensity describes *what* He spoke. Every word uttered is loaded with meaning and purpose. Every word spoken by the Lord is intensely personal because it comes from the heart of the Savior in His capacity as the Son of Man. Every word spoken by the Lord is intensely theological because it connects the Son and the Father, provides more insight into this triune God, and teaches us about the nature and character of God. Every word said by our Savior is intensely practical because it provides the prerequisites and practices for Christ's disciples. Every word spoken by our Savior is intensely emotional because it reminds us about the vast extent of His love, the deep dimensions of His grace, the spiritual significance of His sacrifice on the cross, the practical demand of Christian discipleship, and the imperative call to share the good news with all the nations of the world.

The intensity with which the Son speaks to the Father is the hallmark of the high regard the Father has for His beloved Son. The manner with which this conversation takes place is the most eloquent confirmation of the force that lay behind the cross; it is the greatest testimony to the concentrated strength with which the Son obeyed the Father, even to His death on the cross.

So, yes, we will find our Savior pleading with the Father, but not to be delivered from the inevitability of His unquestioning obedience. He was not pleading for His life to be spared. He had settled that issue once and for all. This prayer is not about settling an issue. The issue at hand was the hour of Jesus' sacrifice on the cross, an issue that had been settled from before the foundation of the world. Nothing was going to change the mind of God regarding His plan for the redemption of sinful man.

This prayer is the affirmation of an issue that had already been settled. Perhaps we will overhear God speaking in concert with His Son as together they affirm, once and for all, the issue of the reconciliation of an unrighteous people with a holy and righteous God.

To settle something means to resolve definitively and conclusively a pending state or decision. There was nothing pending as to the means by which God would reconcile man to Himself. The decision had been made. For that matter the word *settle* could even be construed as the need to terminate a pending activity or action. There is not even the slightest possibility that Jesus spoke these words in an effort to alter the course of the sovereign will of Almighty God.

I am not trying to play a semantics game here. Words are simply the means by which we express an understanding to one another—I realize this—but in the context of this remarkable conversation, it will help us to have a clearer understanding and grasp of what is said if we split and dissect our understanding of the verbs "to settle" and "to affirm." In this prayer the Son is affirming the Father, and the Father is affirming the Son. The assertion made here concerns the fact that God's love is true, and the means by which God is demonstrating His love is true. God is true and His actions and activities are true, and the fact that man can be reconciled to God through the sacrifice of the Son is true.

This prayer is the ratification of God's prior decision and judgment concerning the desperate plight of man.

Now that's an affirmation and not a settlement! God the Father and Jesus Christ the Son are expressing agreement about the giving of God and the willing obedience of the Son. The sovereign act of giving and the willing act of obedience come together in this wonderful prayer. Remember, God was in Christ Jesus "reconciling the world to Himself" (2 Cor. 5:19).

When my three children were growing up, I would often get down to their level, eyeball to eyeball. These were always wonderful times. The picture presented would be of Dad rolling around on the carpet or hiding in the closet listening to them scouting out the entire house in an effort to find out where he was hiding. We would screech and hoop and holler like a bunch of wild little kids having the fun of our lives. On beautiful beaches from Australia to South Africa and from Gulf Shores, Alabama, to Litchfield, South Carolina, we would run and romp to our heart's content. Every time I played with my children, I became a child. I did so because I loved my children so very much. My world had to become their world; my level had to be reduced to their level. I had to connect with them. They had to see me on a level at which they would know I understood them. By doing this, I was communicating to them that I cared for them, and that I identified with them, and I would die for them.

But never once did I cease being Dad. Never once did I relinquish my authority. Never once did I cease being their father. My childlike actions and activities were never an indicator that I had relinquished my adulthood. They were never a sign that I had abdicated my fatherhood. My behavior meant I was willing to do whatever was necessary to let them know just how much I loved them and how much I always will love them.

And so here we hear the Lord Jesus at the hour of His accomplishment. His work was about to run its course although His ministry would never run out.

The subject of this book takes us deep into one of the most incredible accounts in the Bible. The book of John is considered by some to be the Magna Carta of the life and ministry of the Lord Jesus Christ. There are many reasons for this, of course, not the least of which is the inclusion of this most remarkable conversation between the Son and the Father just a few days before Jesus' sacrifice. The words uttered by our Savior have lasting significance in that they establish the absolute truth of many major issues of the Christian faith. The Son of Man speaks with the authority given Him by the Father "over all flesh," and its timeless message heralded the dawning of a new and blessed hope for all mankind. God's eternal plan for the redemption of man was a few short steps away from the Kidron Valley and the Son of Man's betrayal. As the hour of His willing obedience closed around His heart and presented His soul with the insufferable cup of His pending death on the cross, Jesus prayed.

As the dark shadow of man's hatred slowly spread its deadly tentacles around the spotless Lamb of God, we listen in on what sounds like one of Shakespeare's soliloquies. We only hear the voice of the Son, but then upon further reflection we realize that the restoration of the glory He once had with the Father from before the world existed served to unite them in one common sound that came forth from the heart of God. Yes, indeed, God is at prayer!

The work He was about to complete, combined with the words that came from His precious mouth, collided with His presence to reveal the name of God to all who would believe in the one true God. When Jesus worked, God was at work. When Jesus loved, God loved. When the Son of Man spoke, God spoke! For "the one who has seen Me has seen the Father" (John 14:9).

I heartily recommend that you have your Bible open to John 17 as you read this book. I constantly refer to the text itself because it is important to stick with the content of Jesus' words. No effort is made to suggest that all the salient issues are adequately covered. I pray that this book will stir your soul and move your heart to a fresh realization of the wonderful work of our Lord and Savior as He came in obedience to the Father even unto death. I pray that you will discover just how much we have not discovered and just how far-reaching the mind of Christ really is. I pray that we will all be driven to our knees in gratitude to God, the God and Father of our Lord Jesus Christ.

Part I

The Inner Prayer

Chapter 1

The Look

As a little girl, Chloe visited a neighbor's church for the first time. The neighbor pointed to a box in the sanctuary and whispered, "See that large box? God is in there." The little girl could not take her eyes off the box. She was afraid God would either come out of the box and scare her half to death or stay in the box leaving her wondering what He might look like or what He might say. This little girl was not sure exactly which of the two options she desired most.

Throughout the ages man has tried to fathom God. Think about this for a moment. Who is He, really? And if we figure Him out for who He really is, how is it remotely possible for us to have any access to Him at all? When this lady was just a little girl, she was grappling with matters of theology without even knowing what she was grappling with or why. Sounds like the trivial pursuit of countless thousands of well-intentioned men and women who have spent countless thousands of hours of time and effort in an attempt to approach an unapproachable God. The bottom line is that man cannot approach God in any way in and of himself.

The enthralling stories we find recorded in the annals of history bear testimony to every conceivable effort on the part of sinful man to find a special place of favor in the eyes of a righteous and holy God. Some of the great church fathers of the ancient world lived lives of extreme denial in an effort to find this favor. One monk lived in a cave for forty years, and another lived on top of a platform for decades. These dramatic efforts to reach out and touch our heavenly Father have, by no means, been limited to the poor and depraved. Pages of history books present heart-wrenching accounts of many well-known and highly regarded people, like Francis of Assisi. This extraordinary man must be admired for the way in which he literally cast his earthly possessions aside in a wonderful pursuit of a holy and righteous God. Great men, like Origen, mutilated themselves in the most horrid ways possible in order to remove anything physical or otherwise that would distract them from their relentless desire to have an intimate and personal relationship with a God so pure and lovely. Man knows nothing about God on his own. And this despite all the people like Joseph Smith, Mary Baker Eddy, Sun Yung Moon, Jim Jones, and even Buddha himself.

Hence the significance of this moment in human time just moments before the cross. No wonder the hour had come. The great climax was about to arrive, and God's eternal and sovereign plan for the redemption of mankind was about to unfold.

The book of Hebrews establishes and affirms the magnificence of God's sovereign plan for mankind beginning long ago.

> Long ago God spoke to the fathers by the prophets at different times and in different ways. In these last days, He has spoken to us by His Son, whom He has appointed heir of all things and through whom He made the universe. He is the radiance of His glory, the exact expression of His nature, and He sustains all things by His powerful word. After making purification for sins, He sat down at the right hand of the Majesty on high. So He became higher in rank than the angels, just as the name He inherited is superior to theirs. (Heb. 1:1–4)

God has chosen to reveal Himself in specific ways. In times past He accomplished this task "by the prophets." And many there were indeed! From Moses we learn that God keeps His word. From Abraham we learn that God is covenant. From Joshua we learn that God is with us. From Gideon we learn that God wants our worship. From Samuel we learn that God is Spirit. From Elijah we learn that God is approachable. From Jehosophat we learn that God wins battles. From Isaiah we learn that God is holy. From Daniel we learn that God is always in total control! And the list goes on.

I really want us to remain connected to this God-moment because of the unbelievable significance of what this conversation is all about. In other words do not lose sight of Jesus looking up to heaven because He is standing there as our high priest.

Try to imagine this incredible moment frozen in time, the dispensation of God's eternal time line at this point. Fast-forward with me from the age of the prophets to the time the Lord Jesus healed the blind man at the pool of Siloam in John chapter 9. The life and ministry of Jesus produced conflict in the religious beliefs and practices of the Pharisees. To them, an upstart had arrived on the scene!

The man Jesus had healed was brought before the Pharisees. Another major issue had arisen because the day that Jesus took the mud to open his eyes was the Sabbath. In order to press the issue, the Pharisees asked him how he received his sight.

"He put mud on my eyes," he told them. "I washed and I can see."

Therefore some of the Pharisees said, "This man is not from God, for He doesn't keep the Sabbath!" But others were saying, "How can a sinful man perform such signs?" And there was a division among them.

Again they asked the blind man, "What do you say about Him, since He opened your eyes?"

"He's a prophet," he said.

The Jews did not believe this about him—that he was blind and received sight—until they summoned the parents of the one who had received his sight.

They asked them, "Is this your son, the one they say was born blind? How then does he now see?"

"We know this is our son and that he was born blind," his parents answered. "But we don't know how he now sees, and we don't know who opened his eyes. Ask him; he's of age. He will speak for himself." His parents said these things because they were afraid of the Jews, since the Jews had already agreed that if anyone had confessed Him as Messiah, he would be banned from the synagogue. This is why his parents said, "He's of age; ask him."

So a second time they summoned the man who had been blind and told him, "Give glory to God. We know that this man is a sinner!"

He answered, "Whether or not He's a sinner, I don't know. One thing I do know: I was blind, and now I can see!"

Then they asked him, "What did He do to you? How did He open your eyes?"

"I already told you," he said, "and you didn't listen. Why do you want to hear it again? You don't want to become His disciples too, do you?"

They ridiculed him: "You're that man's disciple, but we're Moses' disciples. We know that God has spoken to Moses. But this man—we don't know where He's from!" (John 9:15–29)

Jesus had arrived, and they just did not get it! The skeptics had even been given a practical demonstration when Jesus was baptized in the Jordan River. They had heard the Baptist preach, "Here is the Lamb of God, who takes away the sin of the world" (John 1:29). They had witnessed the dove that descended on Him and the voice that made the pronouncement concerning Him.

"We don't know where He's from!" Can you believe such a statement? God had spoken through the prophets, most of whom were revered by the Pharisees; and yet those same people who were such proponents of righteousness, adhered to the law, and obeyed the prophets and taught them not to believe the words they had heard! Perhaps they knew their treasury was about to be threatened. Their status quo was about to be turned upside down!

The prophets spoke at different times and in different ways. It seems the Lord God came to humankind from every conceivable angle. Just consider the extent to which God revealed Himself through the thirty-nine books of the Old Testament alone. In Genesis 1:1 we are told that God has always existed. In Exodus 8:10 we are told God is unique. In Leviticus 8:35 we are told God demands obedience. In Numbers 11:10 we learn that God actually gets angry. In Deuteronomy 6:4 we discover that God is one person. In

Joshua 3:9 we hear that God is a real presence. In Judges 6:11 we discover that God has an angel. In Ruth 6:11 we are comforted to know that God blesses people. In 1 Samuel 12:19 we discover that man can talk to God. In 2 Samuel 12:1 we learn that God commissions people and sends them out into the world to do His business. In 1 Kings 2:3 God praises those who keep His commandments. In 2 Kings 5 God heals the sick. In 1 Chronicles God is a victorious commander of the battlefield. In 2 Chronicles 10:15 we are comforted to know that God keeps His word. In Ezra 3 God inhabits His temple. In Nehemiah 1:5 we hear a man pleading with God. In Esther, God is in control of the affairs of His people. In Job 11:16 we read of a God who will forget our sin. In Psalm 6:2 we see a merciful God. In Proverbs 22:12 we feel the eyes of God on His people. In Ecclesiastes 11:5 God is the maker of all things. In the Song of Solomon God is love. In Isaiah 6:1 God is high and lifted up. In Jeremiah 7:3 He demands repentance.

In Lamentations 3:61 God hears our cry. In Ezekiel 3:27 God is sovereign. In Daniel we discover that God controls the affairs of all people. In Hosea 12:6 the Lord wants us to wait on Him. In Joel the Lord thunders ahead of his army. In Amos 4:13 we find God revealing His thoughts. In Obadiah 21 we understand the kingdom will be God's. In Jonah we learn God means business when He calls. In Micah 4:5 we receive the news that we will live with the Lord forever. In Nahum 1:3 the Lord is slow to anger and great in power. In Habakkuk 1:12 God is holy. In Zephaniah 1:14 the great day of the Lord is near. In Haggai 1:13 God is with us. In Zechariah 3:2 we find God rebuking Satan. And in the last book of the Old Testament, Malachi 3:6, we celebrate the fact that God never changes!

There it is! Some of the many ways and times God chose to speak through the prophets. Think of the many visions and dreams that painted a picture of our God; think of the stories that presented our God; think of the epic battles won by our God! And we haven't even begun to scratch the surface of the Scriptures in terms of the law, prophecy, and doctrine—all of which were a vital means by which God spoke in times past—let alone matters pertaining to style in the Bible, combined with beautiful poetry, captivating narratives, spoken dialogues, and insightful monologues—all of which were used in significant ways to make God known to man. Jesus came and fulfilled all of this!

As our Savior stood up, lifted His head, and looked toward heaven, everything was being brought together and made whole.

"Father," Jesus said.

Chapter 2

The Hour

I think it is very important to understand the significance of this specific moment in the life and ministry of the Lord Jesus. This was no ordinary time.

In John 17:1 Jesus prayed, "The hour has come."

The time had arrived to bridge the gap between sinful man and a righteous and holy God. One of the greatest disasters in recent memory provides a good illustration of the moment in time when the floodgates of sin were unleashed.

In August 2006, my two sons, Rob and Greg, invited their dad and a group of men to join them for an evening of prayer on the Gulf Coast of Mississippi. I remember the day quite well. After meeting my brother, Murray, in Mobile, Alabama, we drove down to the Gulf Coast, passing through Biloxi, Gulfport, and Long Beach on our way to meet the gentlemen. The evening was spectacular, to say the least. We even crossed the bridge into Bay Saint Louis and enjoyed a fine meal of seafood before gathering together to pray through the night. The news we were listening to was ominous. A massive hurricane was rearing its ugly head in the Gulf of Mexico and seemed destined for a potential head-on collision with the great city of New Orleans. It just could not be, we thought! Impossible and unlikely, we determined. Nothing could happen to New Orleans, the city I had grown to love and the home of my beloved seminary. This was the place where all three of our children had been born.

The old guys finally capitulated at about midnight, leaving the all-night praying up to the young bucks. At about three in the morning, they all arrived at my door to announce that they were heading back to their wives and loved ones in New Orleans because the news was not good at all.

By early the next morning, my brother and I headed back to Mobile to catch our flights back home. And the rest is history!

We all know the story. Hurricane Katrina was one thing, but the breech of the wall was another! Judging by all that has been said, New Orleans actually survived the hurricane, at least to some lesser degree of damage. But the wall was breeched! And when the levee broke, the city drowned. What a tragedy it became!

Since that fateful series of events, I have often found myself thinking about the tragedy caused by man's separation from God because of willful sinfulness. When Adam and Eve sinned against God, the levee was breeched. The wonderful relationship that had existed between God and man, seen so magnificently in God's fellowship with His creation in the garden of Eden, was ruptured and rendered useless. Prior to that hour, death was unheard of because there were no wages to pay. But after the breech the floodgates opened, and from then on death became the persistent drumbeat of every person born who is to die. The wages of sin had been set in motion.

Until this moment! The moment that Jesus sat in the garden and prayed to the Father.

"The hour has come," Jesus announced.

The floodgate was about to be closed once and for all. What, exactly, did Jesus mean when He spoke of "His hour"? We will consider this hour from four perspectives.

It Was an Eternal Hour

So much can be said about the hour of Jesus' appointment with death. For one thing it was an eternal hour because it pointed not to any human understanding of time and space but rather to the sovereign action of a sovereign God who acted before time began. When Jesus announced to the Father that "the hour has come," He was not informing God about something He did not already know. This is why we are hearing God pray! This was not a conversation about information. God already knew because He was hearing from Himself in the flesh!

Yes, Jesus is speaking to the Father in His role and capacity as the Son of Man, but He had not capitulated His nature. Jesus Christ had changed His state, but He had not exchanged His existence! When Jesus became flesh, He willingly entered a human time zone. As such, this was a human hour. But He did not cease to exist as God in the fullest sense, including God's eternal timelessness.

This moment most certainly pinpointed a human element of time and space. While some of Jesus' activities as a boy established the discrepancy between His earthly mission and His heavenly status, the wedding feast at Cana in Galilee was where the differential was clearly seen for the first time in His earthly life and ministry. The biblical account in John 2 tells us that Jesus' mother approached her son immediately when the news was announced that the wedding wine had begun to run out.

The predicament was obvious. Back in their day, wine cellars were unheard of, let alone refrigeration! The fruit of the vine was not only in short supply, but, when harvested, was served with great haste. It followed logically that the best wine would have been served at the front end of the wedding, not the least of reasons because it could spoil. It also was not uncommon to water down the wine in order to offset the sharpness of the taste. And yet as time progressed, the best wine began to run out. The master of ceremonies was entrusted with the responsibility of gradually introducing more and more water so that the supply of wine would last for the duration of the feast.

Note that the Lord Jesus did not treat His mother with contempt or rudeness in His question of her: "What has this concern of yours to do with Me, woman?" (John 2:4). He was establishing His hour that had not yet come within the context of the unfolding of His purpose on earth in application to a human time frame. In this context Jesus was reminding His mother that everything He was doing was subordinate to His mission. As such He could have been conversing with the only person who truly recognized Him—not as the boy she had raised but as the promised Messiah and Son of God. After all, His mother had pondered all these things in her heart.

Jesus' phrase "My hour has not yet come" (v. 4) was a constant reference to His pending death and ultimate exaltation to the right hand of God that we read so often about in the life and ministry of the Lord Jesus (John 7:30; 8:20; 12:23, 27; 13:1; 17:1). This was the reason no one laid a hand on Him, because His hour had not yet come. God's sovereign plan and timetable for the Lord Jesus would not allow them to touch Him until God's appointed time for His Son to go to the cross.

Later on, Andrew and Philip heard Jesus say, "The hour has come for the Son of Man to be glorified" (John 12:23). Here again He was referring to His death and resurrection, but this time He was not speaking of the future as He had always done in the past. And He referred to Himself as "the Son of Man," which was His favorite designation for Himself. Every time He referred to Himself as such, He was associating Himself not only with the themes of death and resurrection but also in His capacity as the full revelation of God. In John 6:27 He directs the disciples toward "food that lasts for eternal life, which the Son of Man will give you, because God the Father has set His seal of approval on Him."

This is exactly what we hear the Savior say when God prays. "For You [the Father] gave Him [the Son] authority . . . so He [the Son] may give eternal life" (John 17:2).

The hour had arrived!

It Was a Human Hour

God has always been the God of order, not chaos. From the beginning of time our Father has orchestrated events and happenings according to His purpose. He works all things together in order to conform us to His plan of action (see Rom. 8:28). So, while this was most certainly an eternal hour, it was a human hour as well. The unfolding events were chronological. From the time Jesus was born in Bethlehem, He walked the chronology of God's timetable in the footsteps of a man.

Every time we visit the land of Jesus' birth we follow the way of the cross, step-by-step, station by station, moment by moment. We feel His pain and experience His agony as He prays in the garden. We all hurt because His disciples fell asleep and could not wait for Him.

And now the hour had come!

It Was a Sacrificial Hour

This moment in time also represented the hour of Jesus' greatest sacrifice. Most certainly He had sacrificed to an extreme by laying aside His glory. Most certainly He had sacrificed to an extreme by becoming human flesh. But the climactic moment of His sacrifice was approaching and He knew it. When He prayed, we are listening to the heart cry of the Son of Man being confronted with the reality of His impending agony. Much earlier Jesus set the stage.

> Jesus replied to them, "The hour has come for the Son of Man to be glorified.
>
> "I assure you: Unless a grain of wheat falls into the ground and dies, it remains by itself. But if it dies, it produces a large crop. The one who loves his life will lose it, and the one who hates his life in this world will keep it for eternal life. If anyone serves Me, he must follow Me. Where I am, there My servant also will be. If anyone serves Me, the Father will honor him.
>
> "Now My soul is troubled. What should I say—Father, save Me from this hour? But that is why I came to this hour. Father, glorify Your name!" (John 12:23–28)

Wow! The hour of sacrifice was approaching when Jesus replied to His disciples in this context; but now, as He prayed, it was here! In the former encounter we find our Savior connecting the fact of His impending death to the principle of Christian discipleship. For just as the sown kernel dies to bring about a rich harvest, so the death of the Son of God will result in the salvation of many. But as the application of the fact of His death is made, so, too, is the application to all who follow Him in willing obedience. They may have to be willing to lose their lives for His sake, in both service to Him and witness for Him.

Remember His words shortly after His formal commissioning of the disciples.

"Therefore, everyone who will acknowledge Me before men,
I will also acknowledge him before My Father in heaven. But whoever denies Me before men, I will also deny him before My Father in
heaven. Don't assume that I came to bring peace on the earth. I did
not come to bring peace, but a sword. For I came to turn
a man against his father,
a daughter against her mother,
a daughter-in-law against her mother-in-law;
and a man's enemies will be the members of his household.
The person who loves his father or mother more than Me is not
worthy of Me; the person who loves son or daughter more than Me is
not worthy of Me. And whoever doesn't take up his cross and follow
Me is not worthy of Me. Anyone finding his life will lose it, and anyone losing his life because of Me will find it." (Matt. 10:32–39)

Implicit in Jesus' explanation of Christian discipleship is the heart cry of
His troubled soul. The term He used, "Now My soul is troubled," provides a key
insight into our Savior's emotional dilemma as He looked to the heavens in this
sacrificial hour. The term itself is strong and indicates horror, anxiety, and even
agitation. The mere thought of having to endure the suffering and shame of the
cross was enough to cause the Son of Man severe pain and anguish.

It was the overriding purpose of the hour that sustained the Lord Jesus.

It Was a Sovereign Hour

While I would never try to line up an order of priority as to the meaning
of Jesus' words, for they are all vital to our understanding of this conversation,
I do believe we cannot ignore the significance of the sovereignty of God that
was at work as Jesus prayed. In short, God, in His sovereign wisdom, con-
structed the ministry of reconciliation because of His divine love and by His
matchless grace.

The biblical account of the events and circumstances surrounding Jesus'
trial and execution definitively present a picture of marauding crowds clamoring
for His blood. The rulers of the Jews must have thought they had accomplished

much when they forced Pilate to acquiesce to their pitiful demands. Had the Roman authorities empowered them to order the execution of whomever they chose to execute, Pilate would hardly have been necessary. And yet despite all of this, they were still marching to the drumbeat of God. Although those who screamed for the blood of the Savior probably went home after Jesus' death and bragged to their friends and families about how successful they had been in bringing Jesus to justice, they were right in line with God's perfect timing. In reality, they were irrelevant!

Years later Paul contextualized this issue. The Corinthian Christians were given a stark reminder of their own human irrelevancies when Paul put it like this:

> From now on, then, we do not know anyone in a purely human way. Even if we have known Christ in a purely human way, yet now we no longer know Him like that. Therefore if anyone is in Christ, there is a new creation; old things have passed away, and look, new things have come. Now everything is from God, who reconciled us to Himself through Christ and gave us the ministry of reconciliation: that is, in Christ, God was reconciling the world to Himself, not counting their trespasses against them, and He has committed the message of reconciliation to us. Therefore, we are ambassadors for Christ; certain that God is appealing through us, we plead on Christ's behalf, "Be reconciled to God." He made the One who did not know sin to be sin for us, so that we might become the righteousness of God in Him. (2 Cor. 5:16–21)

Ultimately this was the hour to which Jesus referred. It was God's hour—planned by God, designed by God, carried out by God through the person and work of His Son, the Lord Jesus Christ!

This was the moment of sovereign power when alienated man would be permitted to full reconciliation with God in Christ. This "hour" was the "in Christ" moment, two words that carry the entire redemptive plan for man. Herein lies ultimate security for all believers because the Lord Jesus Christ bore in His body the judgment of a righteous God on sinful man. This is the only means by which all believers are accepted by God. Furthermore, "the hour" had come whereby God would guarantee passage into heaven for eternal life. And let's not underestimate the unbelievable acquisition involved in becoming a new creation in Christ!

In a sense, we hear God the Father speaking forth from the throne of His righteousness, "From this hour on, all people for whom My Son will die, will be totally forgiven of all sin, will be guaranteed a place in heaven with Me forever, and will be granted all the rights and privileges I have conferred upon the One in whom I am well pleased!"

The key, of course, to Jesus' hour of death lies in these verses because they summarize the heart of the gospel message in two ways: God's imputed righteousness and Jesus' substitutionary death.

GOD'S IMPUTED RIGHTEOUSNESS

This was the hour at which God would no longer count the sins of man against him. The hour He was speaking of not only pointed to the actual activity related to His death on the cross but also to the resultant action it produced. Herein lies the heart of the doctrine of justification, which basically tells us that when we repent of our sins and place our faith and trust in the Lord Jesus Christ, God declares the repentant sinner righteous because he has been covered by the sacrifice of Jesus. This is how we become reconciled to God.

JESUS' SUBSTITUTIONARY DEATH

Even though Jesus Himself knew no sin, He took on Himself the sin of the world and became sin for the world. Here we see God the Father using the principle and action of imputed righteousness in treating His Son as though He were a sinner even though He was not. That is why "He made the One who did not know sin to be sin for us" (2 Cor. 5:21).

The hour to which Jesus referred was a sovereign hour because God made it that way according to His plan from before the foundation of the world. The hour of His death saw God the Father regarding Jesus, His Son, as if He were a sinner even though He was not. As a result, He had Jesus die as a substitute in order to pay for the sins of all who would come to place their faith and trust in Him as their personal Lord and Savior. In that very moment of that very hour

God exhausted His anger against sin by taking it out on His beloved Son on the cross. And because of Jesus' substitutionary role in paying the price for our sin, the righteousness that is credited to the believers' accounts is the righteousness of the Lord Jesus Christ who bore their sins so they could bear His righteousness!

This is why Jesus asked the Father to glorify Him.

Chapter Three

The Glory

"Glorify Your Son so that the Son may glorify You" (John 17:1).

"I have glorified You . . . before the world existed" (John 17:4–5).

Some time ago I heard the story of a man who had been convicted of a serious crime. For some twenty-five years he languished in jail while his children grew up without him, his wife divorced him, and the rest of his family disowned him. Then one day, out of the blue, another man was found to have DNA matching him to the crime. It must have been quite a day in the life of the man originally convicted of a crime he did not commit. Many of the news media were present when he was set free and declared innocent of the crime. One television reporter shoved a microphone in front of the man as he was leaving the prison for the first time in so many years and asked him, "What do you plan to do with your life now that you're free?"

"Restore my honor," he replied before walking off without further comment.

Jesus was convicted by a sinful world and sentenced to death—even though He was totally innocent of all the charges against Him. But He stood trial willingly because He was obedient to the Father, all the way to His death on the cross. Now was the time, through His death, burial, and resurrection from the grave, for Jesus to be glorified in the presence of the Father "with that glory I had with You before the world existed."

His willing obedience was at a climactic moment when He stood before the Father and announced, "The hour has come" (John 17:1). And as He went willingly down that shameful road to the cross, He had but one request of the Father. Glorify Your Son so that Your Son may glorify You!

The matter of the restoration of the privilege He had laid aside rested in the heart of a great and wonderful God. And only the Son of Man could have had any earthly idea of the splendor of God's glory! Only the Lord Jesus Christ could have really known the glory of God, because He *is* God!

God is beyond human comprehension. He is more majestic than majesty. He is more loving than love. He is more just than justice. He is more gracious than grace. He is more righteous than righteousness. He is more magnificent than magnificence. He is more powerful than power. He is more holy than holiness. In other words, our words and our understanding of our words can never do justice to the essence of who God is!

When we read the prayer of God, we find ourselves looking into the heart and holiness of our heavenly Father. And how can we describe or explain Him? Eternal. Holy. Just. Righteous. Creator. All knowing. All wise. Ever present. Wonderful. Counselor. Mighty King. Lion of Judah. Everlasting Father. Prince of peace!

How does one reconcile these truths? Holy, yet He longs for deep and abiding intimacy with the same fallen creatures who have hearts that are exceedingly wicked. Eternal, yet interested in the minutest details of every individual's life. Righteous, yet the friend of every sinner for whom the Lord Jesus Christ died! So mighty that He rules this incredible universe and yet so small that He has the capability, capacity, and care to live within each heart and life in the most personal and intimate way.

These truths are real and attainable because in Jesus Christ the radiant splendor of God's glory is made available to all who believe on His name. And this was the moment. His hour had come!

Having made His declaration to the Father, Jesus then asks the Father to "Glorify Your Son so that the Son may glorify You" (John 17:1). In other words, Jesus was asking the Father to glorify Himself by glorifying the Son on the cross.

Evidently an exchange was taking place! Perhaps Jesus was making His rightful claim!

Why was this exchange of glory to take place? And why was His claim rightfully His to make? What exactly qualified the Son of Man to request a splendor that could only belong to God? The Lord Jesus had alerted the disciples as to His impending glorification through His death, burial, and resurrection. In John 12, while predicting His crucifixion, He told them, "The hour has come for the Son of Man to be glorified" (v. 23). And then He cried out, "Father, glorify Your name!" (v. 28). This request embodied the principle that the Lord Jesus lived by. In fact, it was the same principle He would die by!

This earlier request for the Father to glorify His name is one of only three instances during Jesus' ministry when the Father actually answered the Son. The first answer came after Jesus' baptism when the Spirit of God descended on Him like a dove "and there came a voice from heaven: This is My beloved Son. I take delight in Him!" (Matt. 3:16–17).

My daughter Shelley has been blessed with a beautiful singing voice. On a number of occasions her mother and I have found ourselves seated in a concert hall at Converse College listening to many gifted girls presenting their voice recitals on stage. The hall is usually filled with family members and supporters who join together in applauding every effort. But I must confess I am extremely biased! Every parent and every grandparent knows exactly what I mean. We all take particular delight in our own flesh and blood. To be quite frank, I do not believe there is another soul out there who is more beautiful than my daughter. I take great delight in her!

And so it is with the Father as He glows with delight in the presentation of His Son. "This is My beloved Son," He exclaimed, "because He shows forth the same glory of which I am!" The Father's second verbal response to His Son took place on the Mount of Transfiguration.

> After six days Jesus took Peter, James, and his brother John, and
> led them up on a high mountain by themselves. He was transformed
> in front of them, and His face shone like the sun. Even His clothes
> became as white as light. Suddenly, Moses and Elijah appeared to
> them, talking with Him.

Then Peter said to Jesus, "Lord, it's good for us to be here! If You
want, I will make three tabernacles here: one for You, one for Moses,
and one for Elijah."

While he was still speaking, suddenly a bright cloud covered
them, and a voice from the cloud said: "This is My beloved Son.
I take delight in Him. Listen to Him!" When the disciples heard it,
they fell facedown and were terrified. (Matt. 17:1–6)

Here we find Jesus undergoing a dramatic change in appearance so that the
disciples could see Him in all His radiant glory! One of the privileges the Son of
Man had to lay aside in order to fulfill the Father's plan of redemption was the
privilege of looking like God. Now I am sure that those who walked and talked
with Him on this earth would have said the most wonderful things about the
physical attractiveness of the Lord Jesus. Perhaps they would have talked about
how kind His face was, or how personable and sweet His smile was. Perhaps
they would have all agreed that He was pleasing to look at, and some might have
commented on many other admirable features of His personality and counte-
nance. But He had become man. His body was deteriorating. There had to have
been the odd wrinkle, and when they saw Him get so angry in the temple, the
scowl on His brow must have been noticeable. This dramatic change on the
Mount connected the Son of Man with the Son of God in terms of the glory
of God. The glory the Son was asking to be restored was nothing short of the
splendor He had laid aside to make the journey to earth. It was mission driven.
He laid His radiance down as God and took on the form of man. Through His
death on the cross and His glorious resurrection was about to be exalted to the
seat where He sits in all His radiant splendor as God.

In this instance, Peter makes the terrible error of putting Moses and Elijah
on the same level of glory and splendor as the Lord Jesus. This is why God's voice
boomed out of the heavens and interrupted Peter "while he was still speaking."
The glory of God cannot even remotely be equated with that of man. Peter just
didn't get it and certainly did not listen to his teachers too well. They would
have told him the account of Moses going up into the mountain and being
tucked away in the cleft of a rock because the glory of God was passing by. So
magnificent indeed was the face of God that Moses' face shone when he came

down from the mountain, and he hadn't actually looked on the face of God! On the other occasion, Moses had had to take off his shoes in the presence of the Lord because God's glory had transformed even the ground upon which he stood into holy ground!

No wonder God spoke up and interrupted Peter!

The Four Elements

Four elements are manifestly evident in this dramatic request of the Son. The willingness with which the Lord Jesus laid aside His rightful privilege took place for a specific reason, as a specific event, for a specific purpose, and by a specific design.

A SPECIFIC REASON

God, in His divine providence, had a number of specific reasons He chose His Son to fulfill His program of redemption, thereby requiring the laying down and picking up of His glory.

He Is the Only One

This first reason finds its point of origin in the heart of God from before the foundation of the world. Jesus is the Son of God, the only One of His kind. Consider the all-time favorite verse of Scripture: "For God loved the world in this way: He gave His One and Only Son, so that everyone who believes in Him will not perish but have eternal life" (John 3:16).

Jesus Christ was the top qualifier. God chose His Son because the Son was the only one who met all the requirements of substitution.

Most Americans are familiar with the television show *American Idol*. Millions of people became mesmerized by the plight of those who would be crowned America's idol. Hundreds, if not thousands, made application to be considered by Simon's panel of experts. The first phase eliminated scores of potential wannabees even before they had been given the first opportunity to be heard, let alone actually seen! Then those who made it to the initial rounds were put through a grueling public display in front of the cameras. Millions of people laughed at them, jeered, cried, and squirmed as the hopefuls stood before their judges and literally begged to at least be given the opportunity to be heard. One young lady, upon hearing she was not fit to be heard by Simon, broke down sobbing and pleaded her case before the panel: "I know they [the American people] will love me if they just can hear me!" she wept. The efforts were to no avail, of course.

The process is simple really. Chip away at the mountain until only a hill remains. Then chip away at the hill until only a mound remains. Then chip away at the mound until only a few ants, who lived in the mountain but could not be seen, remain. Then finally, select only one ant and crown her the queen of the universe or king of the mountain!

Nothing like this happened when it came to Jesus being selected by God for His mission. There was no mountain to begin with and certainly no mound. In fact, there were no other ants that could ever remotely qualify to become the king of the hill because Jesus was already King of kings and Lord of lords. The selection of the Lord Jesus as the only means by which man could ever be reconciled to the Father required neither a process nor an application; it was based on a plan—an eternal, sovereign plan!

Here we have the Son's mission bound up in the supreme love of God toward a hateful world and validated through His uniqueness as "the One and Only Son" (John 1:14). Because Jesus Christ was uncreated in terms of His being "with God in the beginning" (John 1:2) and as God, the specific reason for His coming made His willingness to be reduced to human flesh all the more unique. As He laid aside His heavenly glory, the eternal Son of God became time restricted as the Son of man. The supernatural One allowed Himself to become natural but never ceased being God. He simply put on human flesh and came and lived among fallen men.

Because Jesus was unique in that He was God's only Son, man was able to observe "His glory, the glory as of the One and Only Son from the Father, full of grace and truth" (John 1:14).

When we hear God pray, we more fully understand how Jesus asked the Father to restore to Him the glory He had before time began. The specific reason was that Jesus was the only One who could have laid this glory aside in order to fulfill the Father's plan of redemption.

He Is the Sent One

The second reason Jesus was chosen was because He is the One sent by God to fulfill His mission and lay down His glory. Jesus was dispatched to earth because He was the only one who had the authority of God to carry out God's plan for the giving of "eternal life to all You have given Him" (John 17:2). (I will be dealing with the statement by Jesus that "You gave Me authority" in a later section.)

Jesus was chosen because of His functional designation as both apostle and high priest. The letter to the Hebrews explains this more clearly in the context of a people who had been taught that the only way to God was through their high priest. This was the old covenant. Only the high priest could enter the holy of holies. This all changed when Jesus laid down His glory.

> Therefore, holy brothers and companions in a heavenly calling, consider Jesus, the apostle and high priest of our confession; He was faithful to the One who appointed Him, just as Moses was in all God's household. For Jesus is considered worthy of more glory than Moses, just as the builder has more honor than the house.
> (Heb. 3:1–3)

Remember that the Jewish people had a series of major heroes in their religion. Our understanding of an apostle is of one who was "sent out" by the only one who had the authority to do so. This carries with it the logical accompanying idea that such a "sent out" one would carry with him all the rights, power, and authority of the one who sent him. While Moses was sent out to deliver the children of Israel from bondage (see Exod. 3:10), Jesus was sent out by the Father to deliver humankind from his or her spiritual Egypt and sinful bondage with the complete accompanying authority from the Father who sent Him. The sending out of the Lord Jesus, therefore, has to do with the supremacy of Christ in that He was greatly superior to Moses, Elijah, and all the prophets.

It is no wonder the Lord Jesus lovingly answered Thomas's million-dollar question, "How can we know the way?" (John 14:5) with a direct and unapologetic reference to His chosen status.

Jesus told him, "I am the way, the truth, and the life. No one comes to the Father except through Me" (John 14:6).

And the fact that He was sent out by the Father, Jesus continued, was in order to reveal who God is and to bring glory to His name. Read how Jesus stated this timeless truth, which, on the eve of His journey to the cross, helps us to understand why He made so much of the glory He laid aside by coming to this earth, the glory He gave to the Father by dying on the cross, and the glory He was destined to reclaim because He had completed the work "You gave Me to do."

> "If you know Me, you will also know My Father. From now on you do know Him and have seen Him."
>
> "Lord," said Philip, "show us the Father, and that's good enough for us."
>
> Jesus said to him, "Have I been among you all this time without your knowing Me, Philip? The one who has seen Me has seen the Father. How can you say, 'Show us the Father?' Don't you believe that I am in the Father and the Father is in Me? The words I speak to you I do not speak on My own. The Father who lives in Me does His works. Believe Me that I am in the Father and the Father is in Me. Otherwise, believe because of the works themselves.
>
> "I assure you: The one who believes in Me will also do the works that I do. And he will do even greater works than these, because I am going to the Father. Whatever you ask in My name, I will do it so that the Father may be glorified in the Son. If you ask anything in My name, I will do it." (John 14:7–14)

He Is the Sacrificed One

A third reason the Father chose the Son to lay down His glory was because of His once-for-all sacrifice. God knew He was not leaving a single stone unturned when He sent the Lord Jesus to become the sacrifice for the sin of man. And it would require the radical measure of laying down His rightful glory with the Father in heaven in order to accomplish "such a great salvation" (Heb. 2:3). No wonder we will never escape condemnation for sin and the just punishment due to those who reject Him if we "neglect" the sacrifice of the Lord Jesus Christ.

Nothing else could suffice! Jesus had to set His glory aside because all other means had failed.

> Since the law has only a shadow of the good things to come, and not the actual form of those realities, it can never perfect the worshipers by the same sacrifices they continually offer year by year. Otherwise, wouldn't they have stopped being offered, since the worshipers, once purified, would no longer have any consciousness of sins? But in the sacrifices there is a reminder of sins every year. For it is impossible for the blood of bulls and goats to take away sins.

> Therefore, as He was coming into the world, He said:
> You did not want sacrifice and offering,
> but You prepared a body for Me.
> You did not delight
> in whole burnt offerings and sin offerings.
> Then I said, "See, I have come—
> it is written about Me
> in the volume of the scroll—
> to do Your will, O God!

> After He says above, You did not desire or delight in sacrifices and offerings, whole burnt offerings and sin offerings, (which are offered according to the law), He then says, See, I have come to do Your will. He takes away the first to establish the second. By this will, we have been sanctified through the offering of the body of Jesus Christ once and for all. (Heb. 10:1–10)

There it is! I can hear the Lord Jesus saying, "Father, You selected Me because I am Your only Son. You sent Me because I accepted Your commission and plan to redeem all people. I am about to lay down My life as the full, atoning sacrifice for all those that believe on Your name. I have come with Your complete authority over all flesh in order that I may give eternal life to all. I am completing the work You gave Me to do. So please, Father, glorify Me in Your presence with that glory I had with You before the world existed."

I wish I could write these eternal truths with the biggest, boldest print there is. We have a high priest who loves us. Imagine that! We can now enter the holy of holies. Why? Because the impenetrable curtain that separated sinful man from God's presence was about to be torn in two. Ripped asunder from top to bottom. And because it would be ripped top to bottom, it signified that this was all of God and none of man. The old covenant was about to be replaced with the new covenant. When was this curtain torn in two? At the crucifixion. There, on the cross, Jesus would groan to the Father, "Why have You forsaken Me?" (Matt. 27:46) because the Father was going to turn His back on our sin *and* His Son. This is how Jesus would glorify the Father. This is how He would complete "the work You gave Me to do" (John 17:4). The price would be paid. All who believe by knowing You, "the only true God" (v. 3), would do so through "the One You have sent—Jesus Christ." What a guarantee!

I love that old-time song that tells it all:

> *At the cross at the cross where I first saw the light*
> *And the burden of my heart rolled away,*
> *It was there by faith I received my sight*
> *And now I am happy all the day!*
> —Isaac Watts

A Specific Event

If the first element centered in a specific reason, then the second element found its core value in a specific event.

Note, again, what Jesus said to the Father: "I have glorified You on the earth by completing the work You gave Me to do" (John 17:4).

The Son made an inextricable connection between the glory He brought to the Father while He was on the earth and the completion of the work God had given Him to do. I believe Jesus' entire life and ministry constituted the work assignment He was assigned to do!

Everything the Lord Jesus did was a vital and necessary part of God's plan. Nothing happened by mistake in God's economy and chance never has and never will have even the remotest place in the heart of God.

Many years ago I worked for a farmer in Africa during my university vacations. This family had a beautiful and extremely large farm in the Orange Free State, situated in the heart of the wheat lands of the country in which I lived. Mr. Odendaal, for some reason, trusted me with the care of his farm while he and his family traveled up north for three weeks at a time to hunt large game. On one occasion my younger brother, Murray, hitchhiked hundreds of miles to join me on the farm. I was delighted for the company, and soon we settled into a work routine that ensured we would carry out all the assignments we had been given by the farmer before he left for the bushveld. We had to help inoculate thousands of sheep, ride the fences to make certain animals had not entered or decided to leave restricted areas, offer general supervision to labor crews, and do many other things that have to be done on a farm of that magnitude.

One assignment was more important than all the others. We had to get up at 2:45 in the morning to start the engines so vital to milking a herd of about three hundred head of cattle. After religiously carrying out our assignment for some two weeks, my brother and I came up with a "brain wave." Quite simple, really. I would get up one day; he would get up the next! That way we both got to sleep in at least every second day until about five every morning!

The plan worked well until early one morning I was rudely awakened by the slamming of Land Rover doors and the voices of many people. I sat bolt upright in my bed, looked around in panic, saw that Murray was still soundly asleep, and looked at my watch. It was five a.m.! Horror upon all horrors! We had overslept for the first and only time in three weeks, and this was the day the family decided to come back home!

It was not like this at all when it came to the work the Father assigned to the Son. And He never overslept while on duty. Not one time. Ever! Everything He did was vitally connected to God's plan and purpose for you and me. The life and ministry of the Lord Jesus was vast. He was born in a manager, baffled the scribes and Pharisees in the temple, and learned carpentry from Joseph. He healed the sick, walked many miles, calmed the sea, and fed five thousand people on a hillside. He cast out demons, called the hand of the legalists, confronted His critics, and challenged His disciples.

Everything He did pointed to His death, burial, and resurrection from the grave. This was the supreme reason He had a rightful claim to reclaim the glory He had from before the world existed.

When God prayed, we not only hear the Son's claim to the restoration of His rightful glory because of a specific reason but also because of the specific event that was about to take place. And so, having taken a good look at the Son's work assignment in general, we now look at the pivotal point of that assignment. Jesus was headed to Calvary! Look at what happened immediately following His prayer:

> After Jesus had said these things, He went out with His disciples across the Kidron Valley, where there was a garden, and He and His disciples went into it. Judas, who betrayed Him, also knew the place, because Jesus often met there with His disciples. So Judas took a company of soldiers and some temple police from the chief priests and the Pharisees and came there with lanterns, torches, and weapons.
>
> Then Jesus, knowing everything that was about to happen to Him, went out and said to them, "Who is it you're looking for?"
>
> "Jesus the Nazarene," they answered.
>
> "I am He," Jesus told them. (John 18:1–5)

Here we see the supreme courage of our Savior as He determines to go to the cross. On the cross His purity and perfection would be violated as He bore the wrath of God for the sins of the world. This was the specific event for which Christ had laid aside His glory. This was the moment when "the light of men . . . shines in the darkness, yet the darkness did not overcome it" (John 1:4–5).

The parallel thought here directs us to the obvious effect a single light has on a room enclosed by total darkness. Just as that single spark of light has the power to overcome the overwhelming percentage of darkness, so the presence and power of evil and sin are overcome by the person and work of the One who was about to fulfill His mission on earth by going to the cross.

This was the specific event that led our Savior in His obedience to the Father. It was the goal for which He strived. It was the reason He laid aside

His rightful glory as God, and it was the fundamental and rightful claim He made to be restored with the "glory I had with You before the world existed" (John 17:5).

A SPECIFIC PURPOSE

The third element also sheds light on the fact that the Lord Jesus was going obediently to the cross, thereby justifying His right to reclaim that same glory from the Father.

Jesus came to this earth for a specific purpose.

And this purpose was tied into the glory and honor brought by the Son to the Father. Because the Lord Jesus became totally obedient to God all the way to His death on the cross (see Phil. 2:8–9), God highly exalted Him and gave Him a name that is above every name! By virtue of what Jesus was about to do on the cross, He fulfilled all the requirements demanded by a holy and righteous God. In other words, the Lord Jesus became the supreme representative of mankind when He willingly became obedient. Through His incarnation, substitutionary sacrifice, and complete victory over sin and death, He was due glory and honor "so that at the name of Jesus every knee should bow—of those who are in heaven and on earth and under the earth—and every tongue should confess that Jesus Christ is Lord, to the glory of God the Father" (Phil. 2:10–11).

Did you get that? Read this passage carefully, and it will put all of this in its proper perspective.

But one has somewhere testified:
What is man, that You remember him, or the son of man, that You care for him?
You made him lower than the angels for a short time;
You crowned him with glory and honor and subjected everything under his feet.
For in subjecting everything to him, He left nothing not subject to him. As it is, we do not yet see everything subjected to him. But we do see Jesus—made lower than the angels for a short time so that by God's grace He might taste death for everyone—crowned with glory and honor because of the suffering of death.

For it was fitting, in bringing many sons to glory, that He, for whom and through whom all things exist, should make the source of their salvation perfect through sufferings. For the One who sanctifies and those who are sanctified all have one Father. That is why He is not ashamed to call them brothers, saying:

I will proclaim Your name to My brothers; I will sing hymns to You in the congregation.

Again, I will trust in Him. And again, Here I am with the children God gave Me.

Now since the children have flesh and blood in common, He also shared in these, so that through His death He might destroy the one holding the power of death—that is, the Devil—and free those who were held in slavery all their lives by the fear of death. For it is clear that He does not reach out to help angels, but to help Abraham's offspring. Therefore He had to be like His brothers in every way, so that He could become a merciful and faithful high priest in service to God, to make propitiation for the sins of the people. For since He Himself was tested and suffered, He is able to help those who are tested. (Heb. 2:6–18)

Do you remember that wonderful hymn, "He Is Able to Deliver Thee"? It was penned by William A. Ogden in the eighteen hundreds:

'Tis the grandest theme thro' the ages rung;
'Tis the grandest theme for the mortal tongue;
'Tis the grandest that the world e'er sung:
Our God is able to deliver thee.
He is able to deliver thee,
He is able to deliver thee;
Tho' by sin opprest,
Go to Him for rest;
God is able to deliver thee.

And that's just the first verse! The hymn writer has captured it all!

Were it not for the divine purpose of God, in Christ Jesus, we would be lost in our trespasses and sins forever. While angels are given supernatural powers by God, have continual access to God, and are not subject to death, the original administration of the earth was placed in human hands (see Gen. 1:26–28). The fall of man in the garden of Eden rendered him incapable of carrying out God's original plan. Our Redeemer came so that man's original purpose could be fulfilled. Therein lies His glory, and therein lies the honor which was rightfully His to claim just hours before He began His long and agonizing walk to the cross.

The above passage tells us three things about the means by which the Son fulfilled this divine purpose.

He Became the Taster of Our Death

One cannot help but be reminded of the historical accounts of great kings and queens of the past, many of whom had slaves who served them by tasting their food before they, themselves, ate it. Basically these (unfortunate) people were assigned to make certain the one to whom they were subject to not harm in any way. Sadly, there are numerous accounts in which poison was placed in a cup or introduced to a plate of food in an effort to assassinate and remove royalty. The job of the taster was simply to put himself in harm's way even to the point of death on behalf of the one he served.

When Jesus laid aside the glory He had with the Father from before the world existed, He put Himself in harm's way. The harm that came to all of fallen humankind because of sin was death. This was a terminal harm because "the wages of sin is death" (Rom. 6:23). Jesus, however, became sin for us, even though He, knew no sin! It was an intentional and purposeful act of obedience. It was designed that way—to bring "many sons to glory" and to "sanctify," or present them as holy in the presence of a righteous God. This was God's gift of eternal life through the Lord Jesus Christ.

But this precious gift of Jesus as the taster of our death finds even further significance.

He Became the Author of Our Salvation

As we listen in and overhear the Godhead in conversation, we find the Son asking the Father to commence the plan—the plan Jesus laid aside this glory to fulfill. If you would allow me to be a little forward with the words of the Lord Jesus, His prayer could read something like this:

> *My Father, I am now standing here on this earth having just completed some thirty years of life and ministry. I came in full and complete obedience to You because of Your plan to reconcile sinful mankind to Yourself from before the world began. I realize that I am the only One who can make satisfaction to You for the sins of man because I am Your beloved Son. I have been extremely busy doing Your business here on earth. Everything I have done has been designed to bring glory to You alone. Now it is time for Me to complete My work by going to the cross. It pains Me greatly to think about all the ways in which I am going to suffer in My human body, and I wish You could spare Me from this. Nevertheless I am pledged to go to My death on the cross, and I am willing to suffer shame and humiliation in order to accomplish the reconciliation of man to You.*
>
> *So, Father, please let Me get on with it now! My time has come, and this is My purpose. I desperately want to come back to heaven and be reunited with You. When I took on this human flesh, You know that I had to lay aside My glory as God. And the only way I will be able to become reclothed in this glory is when I give up My Spirit on behalf of sinful man. This will happen to Me when I die on the cross, as I carry all the sin of the world to the grave. But when You raise Me up on the third day, then I will ascend back into the heavens to be one with You again forever. My death, burial, resurrection, and exaltation at Your right hand is the only means by which You will give Me back the glory I had with You from before the world existed.*
>
> *So, Father, let's get on with it!*

In His capacity as the author of our salvation, Jesus fulfills three functions:

1. He functions as the captain of our salvation. In this sense the Lord Jesus became a pioneer for us, blazing a trail for all to follow. This carries with it the idea of an initiator or determiner because of the way in which He involved the whole world in His endeavor.

2. He functions as the carrier of our salvation. The means by which the Lord
Jesus carried or transported our salvation was though His suffering. In His
divine nature as God, He was perfect. He was already so before He came to the
earth, and, as we have already discussed, He did not relinquish His perfection
at any time during His earthly life and ministry because He remained sinless.
He knew no sin even though He became sin for us. His human nature, rather,
was perfected through His obedience, which meant He would suffer in order to
become an understanding high priest for believers. In this capacity Jesus carried
our salvation through His sufferings because, in so doing, He established the
perfect righteousness to be imputed to those who professed Him as Savior and
Lord.

3. He functions as the completer of our salvation. By virtue of His death on
the cross, Jesus was able to cry out, "It is finished." This cry from His agonized
heart signaled the completion of all that was necessary to appease the wrath of a
righteous God toward an unrighteous people. In short, His cry marked the end
of His mission.

When President George W. Bush stood proudly on the deck of a United States
aircraft carrier and announced "Mission complete" in Iraq, he was speaking only
from the perspective of his limited understanding as the commander in chief of the
United States of America. The picture we have of the Lord Jesus in this prayer is
entirely different. When the Son of God cried out from the cross, "Mission complete," He was speaking from His capacity as the God of the universe.

Remember what John had to say in his prologue: "In the beginning was the
Word, and the Word was with God, and the Word was God. He was with God
in the beginning. All things were created through Him, and apart from Him not
one thing was created that has been created" (John 1:1–3).

Jesus' ability to complete our salvation was absolute because "You gave Him
authority over all flesh; so that He may give eternal life to all You have given
Him" (John 17:2). It was guaranteed!

God's fundamental attributes had rendered Him inaccessible up to this
point. And man's fundamental problem with sin rendered him incapable of ever
having communion with God. Now, however, access to the Father has been
granted. You and I have been invited directly into His presence because the Son
acted before us as Savior. The Lord Jesus Christ has completed the whole process

by going from life (which He is) to death (which we are) to life (which we all can have). "For God loved the world in this way: He gave His One and Only Son" (John 3:16). All of God and none of man. Praise His name.

The door was opened to all who would believe on His name. By doing so, Jesus functioned as the author of our salvation. He became the captain, the carrier, and the completer of all that was necessary to reconcile us to God. No wonder He wanted the Father to get on with it so He could reclaim His glory!

He Became the High Priest for Our Intercession

The specific purpose for which Jesus died meant He became the taster of our death and the author of our salvation. But it also meant He became our high priest, the One who now is able to intercede for all of us!

The Son had to be made like His people in order for Him to satisfy God's righteous requirement for reconciliation. And His "work" would only be complete by His demonstrated mercy to mankind and His parallel faithfulness to God. In short, Jesus' hour was the moment He went to the cross, thereby satisfying God's requirement for sin and His offer of full and complete forgiveness.

This was His high priestly ministry, which, after He was exalted to be seated at the right hand of God (His glory now restored), He was able to continue His ministry of intercession.

And this is how it happened. First, He shared in our humanity. Second, He destroyed the power of death. Third, He delivered man from slavery to sin. Fourth, He made atonement for our sins. And fifth, He served only God!

"Father," He prayed, "it's time for Me to become high priest!"

Because Jesus is our high priest, we are not only able to enter the holy of holies, but we can also listen in on this extraordinary conversation between the Father and the Son. I alluded to this earlier. We are talking holy ground here! The Old Testament believers would not have believed that you and I could stand on holy ground. Bask in the awe of this. Take off your shoes.

A SPECIFIC DESIGN

The fourth element has to do with the specific design of God's plan for the redemption of mankind. What was it about the way in which the Father designed the cross that enabled the Son to become the substitute for our sin?

When Jesus told the Father it was time to go to the cross, He knew He was following the Father's specific design. And the bottom line meant Christ's death would fulfill God's will according His specific design. In Hebrews 10, the writer answers the question of God's eternal design by establishing why the Lord Jesus had to go to a cross, specifically designed to bring Him (the Father) glory.

> By this will, we have been sanctified through the offering of the body of Jesus Christ once and for all. Now every priest stands day after day ministering and offering time after time the same sacrifices, which can never take away sins. But this man, after offering one sacrifice for sins forever, sat down at the right hand of God. He is now waiting until His enemies are made His footstool. For by one offering He has perfected forever those who are sanctified. The Holy Spirit also testifies to us about this. For after He had said:
> "This is the covenant that I will make with them after those days, says the Lord: I will put My laws on their hearts, and I will write them on their minds."
> He adds: "I will never again remember their sins and their lawless acts."
> Now where there is forgiveness of these, there is no longer an offering for sin. (Heb. 10:10–18)

Although I am by no means a designer of buildings, I still can appreciate the importance of the foundation and cornerstones. I have often watched houses being built and always note the way in which the design follows a specific procedure. The concrete is poured, the foundation pillars are erected, floors are laid, and the corners are established. More important, however, each room or component of a building is usually designed to fulfill a functional purpose.

Some years ago my wife and I realized I needed a home study. We set about designing a room in our house just for that particular purpose. At this very moment I happen to be seated at my desk in this study. My computer has a special place, and I am surrounded by bookshelves and the various means by which I am able to maximize the essentials of study.

The way God designed the cross can be more clearly understood if we analyze it in six ways. These six features fulfill the functional nature of the purpose for which our Savior died. There are several others, of course, but these lie at the cornerstone of God's design.

To Make Perfect

The law had failed in its ability to provide man with the means whereby he could be reconciled to God because "it can never perfect the worshipers by the same sacrifices they continually offer year after year" (Heb. 10:1). A walk through the Old Testament will confirm this rather clearly. One struggle after another is recorded in narrative detail! And now we see the Lord Jesus Christ, the perfect Son of the living God, making it possible for an imperfect man to be made perfect through His perfect sacrifice for sin on the cross! God's perfect design was made possible through His perfect Son, who by one offering has perfected forever those who are sanctified.

No wonder Jesus was insisting that His hour had come to go to the cross! Think about this for a moment. Spiritual perfection is the only means by which man can (possibly) have access to God. Furthermore, spiritual perfection is the only means by which we have the ability to attain spiritual perfection. And, to add to all of this, spiritual perfection is the only means by which we are declared complete in our salvation!

To Remove the Burden of Sin

The picture presented here is one of desperation caused by the burden of sin. The Jews not only sacrificed animals, one at a time for one sin at a time, but they also had to come back time after time in a vain effort to remove the stain and guilt of sin. The repeated sacrifices offered every year were, in and of themselves, "a reminder of sins every year" (Heb. 10:3). "For it is impossible for the blood of bulls and goats to take away sins" (Heb. 10:4). Continual repetition reminded them continually of just how sinful they really were. As a result, the Old Testament Jews were never freed, not only from the presence and awareness of sin but from the guilt of sin. Now, however, because of the Lord Jesus Christ and His death on the cross, Christians are delivered from the burden of sin.

Isaac Watts put the matter of our burdens squarely on the sacrifice of the Lord Jesus in his timeless hymn "At the Cross."

Alas, and did my Savior bleed, And did my Sovereign die?
Would He devote that sacred head, For sinners such as I?

Was it for crimes that I had done, He groaned upon the tree?
Amazing pity, grace unknown, And love beyond degree!

Well might the sun in darkness hide, And shut His glories in,
When Christ the mighty Maker died For man, the creature's sin.

Thus might I hide my blushing face, While His dear cross appears,
Dissolve my heart in thankfulness, And melt mine eyes to tears.

But drops of grief can ne'er repay The debt of love I owe;
Here, Lord, I give myself away, 'Tis all that I can do.

At the cross, at the cross where I first saw the light, And the burden
of my heart rolled away, It was there by faith I received my sight, And
now I am happy all the day!

The question is: What is at stake here? Jesus was insistent about bringing the Father glory through the cross because the removal of the burden of sin would have three results:

1. It would remove sin.
2. It would redeem man.
3. It would satisfy the Father, who is holy.

When Jesus removed this terrible burden of sin from all of mankind, He removed their lack of freedom because they had been bound by endless repetition. He removed their lack of joy because they had been so bound by the burden of legalism. And He removed their lack of peace because they had been so burdened by their inability to gain total and absolute forgiveness.

To Give His Body

A third feature of God's design for the cross had to do with the giving of the body of Christ. It carried major significance in the context of the Son's conversation with the Father as He looked up to heaven.

The prophet, Isaiah, put it like this:

> Yet He Himself bore our sicknesses,
> and He carried our pains;
> but we in turn regarded Him stricken,
> struck down by God, and afflicted.
> But He was pierced because of our transgressions,
> crushed because of our iniquities;
> punishment for our peace was on Him,
> and we are healed by His wounds.
> We all went astray like sheep;
> we all have turned to our own way;
> and the LORD has punished Him
> for the iniquity of us all.
> He was oppressed and afflicted,
> yet He did not open His mouth.
> Like a lamb led to the slaughter
> and like a sheep silent before her shearers,
> He did not open His mouth. (Isa. 53:4–7)

Why was the giving of His body so much a part of God's perfect design in the carrying out of His divine plan for our redemption? Simply stated it was because His body "bore our sicknesses" (Isa. 53:4). In so doing Christ Jesus holds up and supports our grief because He accepted His obligation to do this. In His body He carried our sorrows, and the Lord "punished Him for the iniquity of us all" (Isa. 53:6). As Servant, the Lord Jesus suffered as the substitute for our sin. In other words, He was the substitute recipient of God's wrath on sinners. Peter confirmed this when he said, "He Himself bore our sins in His body on the tree, so that, having died to sins, we might live for righteousness; by His wounding you have been healed. For you were like sheep going astray, but now you have returned to the shepherd and guardian of your souls" (1 Pet. 2:24–25).

The word *wounding* is even better translated "stripes." This word gives us a clear picture of the design of the cross in that the stripe that caused His death is the stripe that brought salvation to those for whose sins He died!

In this prayer Jesus is demanding His hour on the cross because the giving of His body, by design, is the literal shouldering of the consequences of sin and the righteous anger deserved by sinners. God designed the cross in such a way that He (the Father) laid man's iniquity on the Son, thereby treating Him (the Son) as if He had committed every sin ever committed by every person who would believe. And this treatment would occur despite the fact that the Lord Jesus was perfectly innocent of any sin Himself.

This is one essential element of the Lord's Supper or Communion, as some call this wonderful ordinance. When the Lord Jesus took the Twelve into the upper room on the night before He was betrayed, He took bread, gave thanks, broke it, and said, "This is My body, which is [broken] for you. Do this in remembrance of Me" (1 Cor. 11:24).

The carrying of our sorrows and the bearing of our sins through His broken body speak, essentially, of three important functions:

1. It speaks of His unique capability. Only the Lord Jesus was capable of doing what only He could do as the Son of God. Classic humanism declares the unique capability of man in the accomplishing of anything he chooses to accomplish. And God has certainly gifted His human creation in many wonderful ways. We can send a man to the moon and even discover the secrets of medical wonders. But no one is capable of bearing the guilt of his own or another persons sin in his own body. Only the Lord Jesus could have done this for us.

2. It speaks of His unique containing ability. Here we find the Savior imploring the Father for His hour because His human flesh was the only human flesh that could contain all that was necessary to absorb the wrath of God against all human flesh! When Jesus became flesh, His body became the vehicle structured to contain or house all the sinfulness of man yet without becoming sin Himself. This is one of the most difficult things for us to grasp. Perhaps an illustration might help.

Some years ago I was privileged to travel on a mission to China and Mongolia with Johnny Hunt, the senior pastor of Woodstock Baptist Church, in Woodstock, Georgia. My friend Steve Gaines (now the pastor of Bellevue Baptist Church in the Memphis area) and I found ourselves in the northern Mongolian city of Dachan with some of the most dedicated people I have ever been around. There was not much to see in that desolate area just below Siberia, but one thing fascinated me. Big shipping containers were parked all over the place. They seemed to be everywhere. "What are they there for?" I asked. I have never forgotten the answer I received. "Oh, those containers house an entire family's possessions!" "All of it!" I exclaimed with disbelief. "Surely not everything a person owns in this life?"

But it was true. Evidently the unbelievable crime rate forced many families to put most of their possessions into one of these containers and lock it up. They became impenetrable fortresses that contained everything they owned in this life. The more fortunate members of the community who had motor cars also used these containers to lock up their vehicles for ultimate protection.

And so it was with the giving of His body. Contained within the framework of His human flesh was the willing obedience of the Son of God who became flesh for us (see John 1:14).

3. It speaks of His unique conveying ability. Paul understood the unique conveying ability of the cross like this: "For to those who are perishing the message of the cross is foolishness, but to us who are being saved it is God's power" (1 Cor. 1:18).

In other words, through the giving of His body, the Lord Jesus Christ was uniquely able to convey man to God. This is the action of conversion. The apostle John synopsized this spiritual transformation when he stated, "We know that we have passed from death to life" (1 John 3:14) in the context of the litmus test of love, one of the practical means by which a person can know they are totally secure in Him forever.

When the Lord Jesus comes into the heart and life of those who repent of their sins and trust in Him as their Lord and Savior, a dramatic conveying takes place. The Spirit of God, through the righteousness of the Lord Jesus and by virtue of His death on the cross, passes the sinful person from death to life. The individual is spiritually saved from death and hell unto life and heaven and is subsequently freed from any condemnation of sin (see Rom. 8:1).

Not only does the giving of His body signify the bearing of our grief and the carrying of our sorrows but also the piercing for our sin. This was the means by which the Lord Jesus, through the giving of His body, made a way possible, despite the impossibility, of a sinful person to be reconciled to a righteous God.

Many years ago a group of my close friends and I decided to travel down the wild coast of South Africa. It was a grand experience. Tony's father was a frontier trader just south of the small town of Butterworth in the Transkei, as it was called back in those days. This was the region of the country in which President Nelson Mandela was born and raised. (I had the privilege of meeting with him shortly before his election as president of the new South Africa.) There among the Xhosa people was the most spectacular stretch of wild coastline, stretching from East London, across Port St. Johns, to the edges of the Umgazana and Umngeni rivers of the south coast of Kwa-Zulu, Natal.

We loaded up our four-wheel-drive Land Rover with supplies, mostly in cans to protect them from wild animals, and headed out toward the "Hole-in-the-Wall," a magnificent fishing spot near Qoga (pronounced with a "click" that none of my friends can ever do). It was not long before we were in the middle of nowhere. Nothing but bush surrounded us, and the track we were driving on was hard to find at the best of times. The inevitable rains came, and torrents of water flooded everything with vengeance. Then it happened! Despite the four-wheel drive, we got stuck!

It was like we had nowhere to turn. We couldn't go forward or backward because the wheels were buried in the mud. Turning to the right or to the left was not even an option because the bush was so thick that not even our *pangas* (large African cutting knives) proved useful. And, to make matters worse, the wench on the front of the Land Rover was broken! There was nowhere to go, no place to turn, and no one to help us. We were totally and completely stuck!

The only thing to do was to hunker down and go to work, which we did out of sheer desperation. We all had assignments. Tony had to cut down some of the trees and design four platforms that would eventually be placed under the front of each wheel. Howard and I had to start digging what looked like bucket loads of raw mud away from the wheels, and Joe had to do much the same from about twenty yards ahead of where we were stuck. The problem was exacerbated by the fact that the mud hole extended for at least one hundred yards ahead of where we found ourselves.

Well, after hours of hard labor, the Land Rover roared out of, and then on through, the entire mess. We finally pierced the impenetrable. We were set free!

And so it is with the giving of His body, which was pierced for our sin. Jesus knew this was how the Father had designed the cross. There was nowhere else for us to turn. We were stuck. We were totally dead in our trespasses and sins.

Added to this, the giving of the body of the Lord Jesus meant He was "crushed because of our iniquities" (Isa. 53:5). Sin had a vise grip on the life of man and had to be crushed. This crushing literally meant that sin was "squeezed" to death with a force that totally destroys. Jesus' sacrifice made possible for the wages of sin to be pounded into small particles to the point at which it was obliterated. This is why believers can never suffer "the second death" as we find it recorded in the final book of the Bible.

> Then the sea gave up its dead, and Death and Hades gave up their dead; all were judged according to their works. Death and Hades were thrown into the lake of fire. This is the second death, the lake of fire. And anyone not found written in the book of life was thrown into the lake of fire. (Rev. 20:13–15)

The design of the cross had the total release of the sinner from the "second death" in mind.

The giving of Jesus' body meant He was chastened for our well-being. The word *chastened* here carries with it the notion of having suffered affliction for our benefit.

Picture yourself purchasing a number of delicious chicken breasts. Your intention is to put them on the grill and eat them. The experts tell us that a little pounding of the raw meat will, in effect, produce a better product to eat. The giving of Jesus' body was even more graphic than this picture. His body was pounded into a pulp. And the suffering inflicted on His body was designed to provide the means by which we are made "delicious" in the presence of our Father. His body was literally scourged for our healing!

To Do the Will of the Father

A fourth feature of the design of the cross will take us to an even deeper level of understanding as to the significance of the essential meaning of all that was taking place as the Lord Jesus addressed the Father. It had to do with the single most important issue in Christian discipleship—obedience!

This issue continues to be the driving motive for which my wife and I strive to serve the Lord. As I look back on my years of Christian life and ministry, I recall numerous times when I was truly blessing the name of the Lord on one hand, while on the other hand I was doing anything but that which was pleasing to the Lord. Identifying these highs and lows corresponds with one central issue—obedience! I have failed my Lord so many times.

Just reflect on the words our Savior uttered shortly after this prayer we are studying together:

> He went out and made His way as usual to the Mount of Olives, and the disciples followed Him. When He reached the place, He told them, "Pray that you may not enter into temptation."
>
> Then He withdrew from them about a stone's throw, knelt down, and began to pray, "Father, if You are willing, take this cup away from Me—nevertheless, not My will, but Yours, be done."
>
> Then an angel from heaven appeared to Him, strengthening Him. Being in anguish, He prayed more fervently, and His sweat became like drops of blood falling to the ground. (Luke 22:39–44)

And we might note, the Lord Jesus would soon be tested in the garden of His betrayal. A group of salivating thugs, escorted by Judas, would approach Him. The unfolding drama of His arrest established the determination of the Son to follow through on His willing obedience to do the Father's will.

> Then He asked them again, "Who is it you're looking for?"
>
> "Jesus the Nazarene," they said.
>
> "I told you I am He," Jesus replied. "So if you're looking for Me, let these men go." This was to fulfill the words He had said: "I have not lost one of those You have given Me."
>
> Then Simon Peter, who had a sword, drew it, struck the high priest's slave, and cut off his right ear. (The slave's name was Malchus.)
>
> At that, Jesus said to Peter, "Sheathe your sword! Am I not to drink the cup the Father has given Me?" (John 18:7–11)

Here we find the original "incredible hulk," ready to do battle for his Master. Peter, undoubtedly, aimed his sword at the slave's head. *Yes, sir,* thought Peter, *I'll show them what we are made of! I'll just lop this fellow's head off!*

But Peter's defense of the Son of Man was made up of an ignorant love born out of a warrior's heart. His impetuous bravery was a practical demonstration of his failure to understand fully the central truth of the death of Jesus. This cup had to be consumed in its entirety because it was associated not only with His suffering but with the judgment of God.

The cup of God's judgment is even portrayed in the Old Testament. This was seen in Judah's experience of the cup of God's judgment as Samaria had experienced in 722 BC and was symbolic of receiving God's wrath for disobedience.

> "You have followed the path of your sister, so I will put her cup in your hand."
> This is what the Lord GOD says:
> "You will drink your sister's cup,
> which is deep and wide.
> You will be an object of ridicule and scorn,
> for it holds so much.
> You will be filled with drunkenness and grief,
> with a cup of devastation and desolation,
> the cup of your sister Samaria.
> You will drink it and drain it;
> then you will gnaw its broken pieces,
> and tear your breasts.
> For I have spoken."
> This is the declaration of the Lord GOD. (Ezek. 23:31–34)

I well remember the moment the Lord called my young wife and me into full-time Christian ministry. The call was instant and dramatic for us. I knew God had spoken to me. Karyn knew the Lord had spoken to her. Both of us understood that the only thing the Lord required of us was absolute obedience. We realized the Lord was calling us to leave our "all" and follow Him. Without knowing where, when, or how! Perhaps this is why I still include my life verse when signing copies of my books for people:

> The Lord said to Abram:
> "Go out from your land,
> your relatives,
> and your father's house
> to the land I will show you.
> I will make you into a great nation,
> I will bless you,
> I will make your name great,
> and you will be a blessing.
> I will bless those who bless you,
> I will curse those who treat you with contempt,
> and all the peoples on earth
> will be blessed through you."
> So Abram went. (Gen. 12:1–4)

The last statement, "So Abram went," is so abrupt! It is clear-cut and to the point. God spoke and Abram acted! This is why I have tried to make this my life verse. I am no Abraham, but I take this as the clarion call of Christian discipleship. I cannot say that I truly understood this back in my earlier days, but I think I do understand it more clearly today. When the Lord first called my wife and me, we did act immediately—perhaps out of ignorance. But ours was a blind faith—a simple, childlike trust—that, fortunately, was greatly assisted by our parents on both sides, who gave us their wholehearted love and support every step of the way.

I called my father, who lived some five hundred miles away.

"Dad," I said, "God has called me into the ministry. I know He has. And Karyn knows it too. He has told us to sell it all and lay it all down. Dad," I continued, "this will mean we are going to be leaving South Africa and going to the United States. We are told there are seminaries where I can study for a PhD that is fully accredited."

My father replied, "My son, your mother and I will be sad to see you go so far away. If we never see you again in this life, knowing you are in the center of God's will, our joy will have been made complete!"

My mom and dad had done the same thing when the Lord called them. And so had my parents-in-law when the Lord had called them to serve.

I am certain there have been many others, but my wife is still the only brand-new wife I know who was willing to sell her wedding gifts, pack up her new home, leave her family, and go to a land far away with a young-buck husband!

I have often heard my father teach his three principles of discipleship. I have heard him teach others that the one thing the Lord God requires of His children is absolute obedience. This is how Dad would teach on the subject:

1. There can be no *rivalry* as far as God is concerned
2. There can be no *refusal* as far as God is concerned
3. There can be no *resignation* as far as God is concerned

Jesus put it like this when He confronted the disciples: "If anyone wants to come with Me, he must deny himself, take up his cross, and follow Me. For whoever wants to save his life will lose it, but whoever loses his life because of Me will find it. What will it benefit a man if he gains the whole world yet loses his life? Or what will a man give in exchange for his life?" (Matt. 16:24–26).

When the Son of Man spoke to the Father of the completion of "the work You gave Me to do" (John 17:4), He was not merely tying a finished assignment to the restoration of the Father's glory; He was aligning theoretical with practical discipleship. Jesus "completed" His work on earth by being practically obedient to the Father—all the way, even to His death on the cross. It was an all-or-nothing deal that encompassed three significant mandates:

1. The Mandate of the Father. One can go all the way back to the Ten Commandments to see the mandate of God concerning the extent to which He demands total obedience and servitude. The law He gave to Moses was inclusive of "do not have other gods besides Me!" (Exod. 20:3). As one of my friends has often said, "What part of 'no other' do you not seem to understand?" God is a jealous God and will not tolerate anything less than 100 percent allegiance to Himself.

2. The Example of the Son. This is the essence of all we are dealing with at this point as we hear God praying. It would have been one thing for the Son to have followed the Father's will all the way up to the point of the cross. But it would have been another thing entirely had He put the brakes on just moments before the cross. Everything Jesus did was a supreme example to us of the clarion call of discipleship. He went all the way to the cross, thus completing the work He was sent to do. Just as we hear Him say, "I have done what has needed to be done." Now you (the believer) need to do what needs to be done!

3. The Call of the Believer. I had a dramatic experience in Africa some years ago that reduced me to a radical understanding of the call of every believer. I think this illustration will help in our understanding of the Son's all-encompassing hour of decision.

I found myself in the African nation of Mozambique. The country, at that time, was still emerging from many years of bitter civil war that bore witness to every kind of atrocity known to man. Terrorist factions had sought vengeance on one another, and thousands of innocent civilians had been caught in the crossfire. My host in the capital city of Maputo was a fine Christian man. His home was a fortress, guarded around the clock by armed men. Throughout the nights we could hear and see perverse men screaming in the streets for his daughters to come out. It made me think of Sodom and Gomorrah!

One day a group of the most wonderful African pastors came to me and requested I travel with them to a remote place to share the love of Jesus with their people.

In an internal and private way I thought, *Surely these men would croak if they knew who I am!* My puffed up and arrogant self-righteousness reared its ugly head right there and then. *Goodness me,* I thought, *if only these men could understand they are talking to a man (me) who had a whole list of degrees! Besides, I have an earned doctorate with a major in New Testament evangelism. Can you just imagine asking someone like me to go into the bush and tell a bunch of uneducated people about the love of God?*

Nonetheless, I boarded a "combi" Volkswagen minibus and headed deep into the African bush with several precious African pastors. After many hours of hazardous travel, we came to an area where we were met by another group of tribesmen led by one of the dearest old preachers I have ever been around.

"I greet you, Ubaba," I said courteously, trying hard to draw on my upbringing in Zululand as a boy. The language spoken in this part of Mozambique was Shangaan, a derivative language of Zulu. Back in the 1870s, thousands of Zulus had fled the tyrannical rule of the great Zulu chiefs Dingane and Shaka. They had settled in the area in which I found myself.

"I greet you back, American preacher," Pastor Malungu said in turn as he held out both of his gnarled hands in a wonderful gesture of courtesy and peace.

"What happened to your body?" I asked politely. I couldn't help but notice he had several fingernails missing and also had various other major signs of trauma on his body.

"Of little consequence," he said as he brushed the question aside. "I have just been released from prison!"

"And what had you done, Ubaba, that they would have put you in prison?"

"Mina thanda i'Jesu," he told me. "I love Jesus!"

One of the other men came over and clarified the issue by telling me Pastor Malungu had been jailed and tortured for his faith and trust in the Lord Jesus Christ.

Over the next few hours literally thousands of tribesmen began to arrive in this amphitheater out in the bush. They came and they came. Many had no clothes on at all. Some just wore a loincloth, of sorts. All seemed to be emaciated. Babies hung desperately to their mother's breasts, clawing away in a desperate measure in the hopes of finding, perhaps, just one more drop of their mother's milk. Many of the babies themselves had bloated stomachs with a severely pronounced belly button sticking out like a tumorous lump of cancer.

I stood on an anthill, which had been crushed down into a makeshift pulpit, and began to explain, as best as I could, the love of God from John 3:16. Of course, I knew the verse by heart! I was seminary trained and educated! For more than three hours I preached, saying a sentence and then waiting as both the Portuguese and Shangaan interpreters had their turn to relay my words to the masses. No one moved. No one went to the bathroom! They just sat there in lines and listened!

The time of the invitation arrived. I told them that if they wanted to trust this God of whom I had spoken they could simply stand up where they were as an indication of their decision. And with that I stood back and waited for the expected masses to respond. Deep in my heart I wished I had brought a camera to record the whole thing. *Perhaps,* I began to think in my proud arrogance, *I can take these dramatic pictures of me in the wilds of Africa preaching to the heathens with a massive show of response and go on tour across America raising funds for orphans or something else!* But no one moved. Not even a flinch!

I panicked a little and thought, perhaps, that I had not been clear in my American way of explaining these deep truths to a simple people. And so I preached just a little more and then asked the people to do the same thing by standing as an indication of their willingness to give their hearts and lives to this great and wonderful King of whom I had spoken. But no one moved! Not even a flinch!

With my heart almost in a state of panic, and now truly grateful no cameras were there to record my big flop for all to see, I suddenly noticed a diminutive man walking toward me.

"American preacher," Pastor Malungu said in his soft and gentle voice.

"Yebo, Ubaba," I said. "Yes, father," I said with the traditional highest mark of respect for his age and office.

"Do you see all those men sitting out there with dirty white shirts on?"

"Yebo, Ubaba Umfudisi, mena bona yena," I replied as I looked out and saw them. "Yes, father preacher, I see them."

He continued without taking his eyes off mine, "Well, they are government stooges. And every time people in Mozambique give their lives to Jesus, they write their names down. And then they may be arrested and taken to jail where many will be tortured and some will never see their families again."

My heart began to break! Right there in the middle of nowhere!

Malungu, however, was not through with me yet. And neither was God!

"Did not the Lord Jesus say that if any man was to follow Him he had to deny himself and take up the cross and follow Him?" he asked while looking as though he was peering into my soul. "Well, American preacher, when you invite someone to give their hearts and lives to Jesus in my country, you don't ask them just to stand up where they are. You tell them to step out and 'go public.' In Mozambique, when someone 'goes public' for Jesus, he could lose his life. But that's the only way, is it not, American preacher?"

I was devastated to think I could be the cause of some unfortunate person losing her life. I wished, for just a short while, I could hurry up and find myself back in the comfort of my beloved America. At least there I had a microphone when I spoke. At least the people had a decent pew to sit on. After all they had to sit, sometimes for an entire hour! And sometimes the air conditioner was turned too low or too high. At least there were a few restaurants to choose from after the ordeal of church was over. At least, back home the only real agitation was to come to church and then be unable to find a parking space close enough to the sanctuary! At least I lived in a civilized world where an altar call was accepted but not really demanded, especially if it upset some of the longtime members who really considered it a bit unnecessary! At least I preached in churches where most sanctuaries had the decency to have several restrooms located at each entrance and exit so that people in church could get up and go at regular intervals during the worship service, and then take any of the kids who suddenly needed to go as well whenever they suddenly needed to go, especially just as the invitation was being extended for people to give their hearts and lives to the Lord Jesus!

That was the day God took hold of my sorry, prideful life and gave me a graphic picture of exactly what Jesus meant when He turned to the Father and said, "I have glorified You on the earth by completing the work You gave Me to do" (John 17:4).

Jesus was getting ready to go all the way! He was getting ready to do the will of God.

As I watched literally hundreds of impoverished Africans walk in silence down to where I was standing with Pastor Malungu, I thought of how the Lord Jesus Christ led the way. All the way!

The Lord "Jesus spoke these things, looked up to heaven, and said, 'Father'"
I am ready now to prove My absolute obedience to You (see John 17:1).

We have now considered four features of the Father's design for the completion of Jesus' work on the cross. The fifth feature establishes the cross as the only
means by which man can come to God.

To Establish the Only Way to God

This feature of God's design or master plan of the cross is crucial to any
understanding of the singular nature and supreme significance of the Christian
faith. In the truest sense of the word, this is the feature that sets Christianity
apart from all other religions. This is not because it is the only feature of God's
design but because it eliminates any and all other options as solution to the
problem caused by the curse and consequence of sin. Ever since the ignition
switch of sin was turned on in the garden of Eden, man has tried to invent,
discover, present, design, and offer every known brand of religion as a means
for sinful man to be reconciled to a holy and righteous God. The design of the
cross establishes, once and for all, the sacrifice of the Lord Jesus Christ as the
only way to God.

Let's be reminded of one of the most phenomenal verses of Scripture in
which the all-sufficiency of Jesus Christ is established: "By this will, we have
been sanctified through the offering of the body of Jesus Christ once and for
all" (Heb. 10:10).

The matter of our being sanctified will be covered in the next major section
when Jesus moves from this inner prayer to His exclusive prayer, directing His
attention exclusively to those people who have already come to believe in Him.
At this point, we are still focused on the one-time offering of the one and only
person who established once and for all the means by which all who believe in
His name are declared reconciled to the Father.

The Lord Jesus had, on a number of occasions, established Himself as the
only way to the Father. Early in His life and ministry the Lord preached His
sermon on the mount. In it He firmly established not only the narrowness of
the Father's design for the completion of the Son's work but also the extreme
difficulty this "only way" would present to the religions of the world.

Enter through the narrow gate. For the gate is wide and the road is broad that leads to destruction, and there are many who go through it. How narrow is the gate and difficult the road that leads to life, and few find it. (Matt. 7:13–14)

Here we find our Savior surrounded by the religious zealots of His day, each claiming his own brand of legal entry into God's kingdom. The two ways offered here set a clear road to Calvary. The narrow gate is by faith, only through the Lord Jesus Christ. It is both constricted and concise. It represents salvation God's way and leads to eternal life—this explains why the Lord Jesus claimed in His conversation with the Father, "You gave Him authority over all flesh; so He may give eternal life to all You have given Him. This is eternal life: that they may know You, the only true God, and the One You have sent—Jesus Christ" (John 17:2–3).

The wide gate and broad road include all religions of works and self-righteousness that can only lead to death and eternal hell.

What Jesus was claiming when He established the completion of His work was not an insipid form of "easy believism." Salvation is by grace alone and is not easy in any shape or form. The call of Jesus' completed work on the cross is the call to a full commitment to the believer's full identification with the suffering of the Savior.

God has always required absolute obedience from all who follow Him. His way of providing for salvation has never been the subject of negotiation. I believe this pattern of behavioral expectation was established as far back as the Old Testament. Consider the call of Moses as just one example of this expectation. This extraordinary man was called from a life of comfort (literally in Pharaoh's court) to a life of harsh struggle and dogged determination. He continually had to comply with God's way of carrying out His divine purpose for the children of Israel. And this was regardless of the opinions of the masses who constantly and continually came up with better solutions to their problems and predicaments as they journeyed through the wilderness.

Jonah provides another good example. The Lord came to him and called him to go to the city of Nineveh and preach "against it." If we accept the essential meaning of the word *preach* to mean "to cry out" or "to herald," then Jonah was instructed to "cry out" against the people of that city because God's way was the only way. There were no alternatives: "The word of the LORD came to Jonah son of Amittai: 'Get up! Go to the great city of Nineveh and preach against it, because their wickedness has confronted Me'" (Jon. 1:1–2).

Perhaps the most significant statement made concerning man's allegiance to Jesus Christ and His death on the cross is seen in Paul's instruction to Timothy. While the writer applauds and encourages Timothy's willingness to align himself with Paul's testimony, he was unapologetic about the fusion that needed to take place between redeemed sinners and the sufferings of the Savior who made their redemption possible.

> Instead, share in suffering for the gospel, relying on the power of God, who has saved us and called us with a holy calling, not according to our works, but according to His own purpose and grace, which was given to us in Christ Jesus before time began. This has now been made evident through the appearing of our Savior Christ Jesus, who has abolished death and has brought life and immortality to light through the gospel. (2 Tim. 1:8–10)

At the foundational level, the offering of the body of the Lord Jesus firmly established "the only way" in three fundamental areas.

1. The Cross Is the Only Way by Which We Are Offered Salvation. "Therefore, brothers, since we have boldness to enter the sanctuary through the blood of Jesus, by the new and living way that He has inaugurated for us, through the curtain (that is, His flesh); and since we have a great high priest over the house of God, let us draw near with a true heart in full assurance of faith, our hearts sprinkled clean from an evil conscience and our bodies washed in pure water. Let us hold on to the confession of our hope without wavering, for He who promised is faithful" (Heb. 10:19–23).

This was a particularly significant issue of monumental proportion for the Jews. Let's not lose sight of the fact that the Lord Jesus was a Jew and was called Rabbi by many of His day! As the Son stood and "looked up to heaven" and into the face of the Father, He understood clearly the far-reaching significance of His hour of completion in terms of the narrowness with which His impending death would define access to God the Father. The Jews, in this passage in Hebrews, were being invited to leave behind a levitical system that was saturated in legalism and to accept the full benefits of a new covenant in the Lord Jesus Christ.

They were exhorted to do this with "boldness." This exhortation to boldness was not only because of the confidence they would acquire through their belief and faith in the new covenant, but it was a boldness that would be needed to withstand the unmitigated persecution that was certain to come their way when they trusted and accepted the new covenant. This was not the popular thing to do! The salvation being offered was new to them, recently made possible "by the new and living way" (Heb. 10:20) when the Lord Jesus took the place of the high priest "over the house of God" (v. 21). It followed that all Jews were being invited to draw near and embark on the "living way," which is characterized by the eternal life made possible through the One who gave Himself for them.

When Jesus' flesh was torn at His crucifixion, so was the temple curtain that symbolically separated men from the presence of God. When the day of atonement was celebrated, the people waited outside for the high priest to enter and then return from within the holy of holies. This moment was so sacred and the presence of God so impregnable that the high priest even had to have a rope tied around him just in case he died inside the holy of holies. If he died, the people would have to drag him out of the holy of holies because no man other than the high priest could enter the presence of God.

Jesus knew this was all about to change forever at the cross. When we overhear God praying, we are invited into the moments of final preparation for the ultimate offering of salvation to all who believe on His name. When Jesus entered the holy of holies, He did not come back. Instead, He opened the curtain and exposed the holy of holies so that "to all who did receive Him, He gave them the right to be children of God, to those who believe in His name, who were born, not of blood, or of the will of the flesh, or of the will of man, but of God" (John 1:12–13).

This was the only way by which they could come into the presence of God. For the Jew this was a radical departure from their religious enslavement. The full restoration of Israel to the heart of God was about to become solely dependant on Jesus' sacrifice and their acceptance of Him by faith.

The only means by which salvation is made possible carries with it two incredibly important outgrowths for the Christian. First, it is the means by which man is "positionally" guaranteed a place with God. Read carefully this exposition to the Galatian Christians concerning the matter of becoming children and heirs of God through the Lord Jesus Christ.

> For as many of you as have been baptized into Christ have put on Christ. There is no Jew or Greek, slave or free, male or female; for you are all one in Christ Jesus. And if you are Christ's, then you are Abraham's seed, heirs according to the promise. Now I say that as long as the heir is a child, he differs in no way from a slave, though he is the owner of everything. Instead, he is under the guardians and stewards until the time set by his father. In the same way we also, when we were children, were in slavery under the elemental forces of the world. But when the completion of the time came, God sent His Son, born of a woman, born under the law, to redeem those under the law, so that we might receive adoption as sons. And because you are sons, God has sent the spirit of His Son into our hearts, crying, "Abba, Father!" So you are no longer a slave, but a son, and if a son, then an heir through God. (Gal. 3:27–4:7)

The writer of this profound segment of Scripture was not referring to water baptism in this regard because water baptism cannot provide salvation for anyone. Baptism by immersion, rather, was the point at which the repentant believer identified with the death, burial, and resurrection of the Lord Jesus Christ and was regarded as fully compliant with the expressly public demonstration of Jesus when He was baptized. Here, the phrase "have been baptized into Christ" (Gal. 3:27) was used in a more metaphorical sense. It indicated the special union that existed between the one who had repented of sin and the one who had the power to forgive that sin.

Hence new Christians are placed in the right "position" in their relationship before God because they have "put on" Christ. Read what Paul had to say to the church at Philippi.

More than that, I also consider everything to be a loss in view of the surpassing value of knowing Christ Jesus my Lord. Because of Him I have suffered the loss of all things and consider them filth, so that I may gain Christ and be found in Him, not having a righteousness of my own from the law, but one that is through faith in Christ—the righteousness from God based on faith. My goal is to know Him and the power of His resurrection and the fellowship of His sufferings, being conformed to His death, assuming that I will somehow reach the resurrection from among the dead. (Phil. 3:8–11)

It is the only means by which man is practically changed because of his relationship with God. And this carries with it the demand to conduct ourselves in a manner that is well pleasing to the Lord because we have "put on" Jesus Christ. It is one thing to be positionally guaranteed one's place with God, but it is entirely another to be practically changed because of our position with God. The former points to the wonderful hope we have in knowing that our eternal destiny with Christ has been sealed by the Holy Spirit forever. The latter points to the immediacy of the change that takes place when we come to know our Savior while still alive on this earth.

I will never forget a man who came to our church one Sunday and sat on the back pew while I preached the Word of God. At the invitation time he left his seat immediately and walked all the way down to the front to declare his desire to trust the Lord as His own personal Savior. During a later conversation he remarked, "I have given my life to Jesus, and my whole life has changed." I was able to affirm that this was exactly what happens when we are positionally guaranteed our place with God. We are practically changed. The apostle Paul put it like this: "Therefore if anyone is in Christ, there is a new creation; old things have passed away, and look, new things have come" (2 Cor. 5:17). This expression touches the heart by the immediate benefit of the new birth. A new level of behavior is created when Jesus Christ enters the heart and life of the new convert. This is truly what regeneration is all about.

Jesus referred to this practical change as "fruit" in His admonition to "beware of false prophets who come to you in sheep's clothing but inwardly are ravaging wolves" (Matt. 7:15). He left no misunderstanding in this regard when He taught His disciples to discern such people by the fruit of their lives.

2. *The Cross Is the Only Way by Which We Are Eternally Forgiven.* As the Lord Jesus contemplated the cross as the only means by which His work would be complete, He was presenting the Father with the only means by which we could be forgiven of our sin. This was the essence of the new covenant spoken of by the prophet Jeremiah.

> "Look, the days are coming"—this is the LORD's declaration—
> "when I will make a new covenant with the house of Israel and with the
> house of Judah. This one will not be like the covenant I made with their
> ancestors when I took them by the hand to bring them out of the land
> of Egypt—a covenant they broke even though I had married them"—
> the LORD's declaration. "Instead, this is the covenant I will make with
> the house of Israel after those days"—the LORD's declaration. "I will
> place My law within them and write it on their hearts. I will be their
> God, and they will be My people. No longer will one teach his neighbor
> or his brother, saying: Know the LORD, for they will all know Me, from
> the least to the greatest of them"—the LORD's declaration. "For
> I will forgive their wrongdoing and never again remember their sin."
> (Jer. 31:31–34)

This new covenant is seen in contrast to the old covenant under which Israel failed miserably. God's new covenant was about to be inaugurated in the person of the Lord Jesus Christ by whose sacrifice the forgiveness of sin was made possible. Jeremiah's report of God's promised new covenant was, in itself, the guarantee to all participants that they would receive all the blessings that accompanied salvation in the coming Messiah. The absolute forgiveness of sin and the unimaginable concept (to the Jews of Jeremiah's time) that this sin would never again be remembered were presented as an integral part of God's only way.

This feature of God's design for the cross lies at the heart of redemption. Redemption brings with it the limitless grace of God, and this includes the forgiveness of sin. "In Him we have redemption through His blood, the forgiveness of our trespasses, according to the riches of His grace that He lavished on us with all wisdom and understanding" (Eph. 1:7–8).

3. The Cross Is the Only Way by Which We Are Eternally Sanctified. This important matter of sanctification will be dealt with in the second part of this book. The Lord Jesus' death on the cross was the only way by which the redeemed sinner could be set apart to the righteousness of God. The law could not accomplish this, neither could the futile efforts of man alone. Only the sacrifice of the Lord Jesus could make the impossible possible.

Summarizing the main points of this section before we consider the next element may prove somewhat helpful. The five elements of the cross we have considered thus far involve a specific reason, a specific event, a specific purpose, and a specific design. For the purpose of this study we have considered six features of God's specific design for the cross. We have considered the evidence that Jesus went to the cross to make perfect, to remove the burden of sin, to give His body, to do God's will, and to establish the only way to God. The sixth element connects this pre-cross conversation between the Father and the Son with the post-ascension fulfillment of the Son's request.

To Sit Down at the Right Hand of the Father

Remember who Jesus is. He is God in the flesh! The fusion between His eternal character as God and His fleshly nature as man is clearly portrayed in this wonderful prayer. On the one hand we hear Jesus Christ, the Son of Man, presenting Himself to the Father from within the context of His earthly realm of responsibility. On the other hand we hear Jesus Christ, the Son of God, conversing with Himself as "the only true God" (John 17:3). His plea to the Father to "glorify Me in Your presence" (v. 5) is the eternal bridge that spans the time that elapsed in human terms between His departure from the Father to His reunion with the Father. This human period of time that spanned some thirty years was defined in terms of the work the Father had given the Son to do. It was His earthly mission. And this mission was now about to be consummated at Calvary.

The end result would be the throne on which the Son would be seated at the right hand of the Father. The occasion would be the restoration of His glory. This was something the repeated sacrifices offered by the priests could never accomplish: "Now every priest stands day after day ministering and offering time after time the same sacrifices, which can never take away sins. But this man, after offering one sacrifice for sins forever, sat down at the right hand of God" (Heb. 10:11–12).

The contrast provided here is clear. In the Old Testament literally thousands of priests served and sacrificed. The new covenant has but one! The old way of seeking forgiveness was based on repeated sacrifices being offered over and over again. The new sacrifice was offered but once! Even Solomon sat down on the throne of Israel but stood up "before the altar of the LORD in front of the entire congregation of Israel and spread out his hands" (2 Chron. 6:12). This is what the old priests did when serving at the altar of sacrifice. The new high priest sat down, having served once and for all at the altar of sacrifice for our sin. The repeated sacrifices for sin merely served to cover sin, whereas the effective sacrifice for sin offered by our Savior completely removes all sin!

The picture we have here is one of God's sovereign power as Ruler and King of the universe. As Jesus is seated at the right hand of God, He waits "until His enemies are made His footstool" (Heb. 10:13).

I was born in Zululand, in Kwa-Zulu, Natal, in South Africa. The Zulu people are a proud and fine people who have a rich heritage and tradition marked by periods of greatness and scarred by periods of great suffering. During the 1800s the Zulu people were ruled by some of the most notorious kings who subjected their people to unbelievable atrocities and yet formed them into some of the most formidable fighting forces the world has ever known. One of these mighty kings was Shaka.

A mighty man of great valor himself, Shaka ruled his people with an iron fist and thought little of killing a few of his men or young women just for the fun of it! Obedience to the king was absolute. It is widely accepted that when Shaka chose to sit down, he simply began to take a seat anywhere and at any time. No announcement was deemed necessary. Slaves were always on hand to see to his every wish and fancy. Being seated was the prerogative of the king only, and everyone else was obliged to stand. When any man came into the king's presence, he literally had to crawl on his belly with his face to the ground. If he so much as looked up, let alone gazed at the face of Shaka, he faced certain execution. And the king never sat on the ground. At the moment he so much as flinched in an effort to be seated, one of his slaves would immediately drop on all fours so that the king could be comfortably seated on his back. Historians have recorded some times when Shaka would be seated on the back of some unfortunate slave for long periods of time while he conducted the affairs of his army and his kingdom.

How much some people have had to suffer at the hands of tyrants whose seat of power was designed to produce suffering and death!

But not so with the One who said, "Father, the hour has come" (John 17:1).

It was time to take His rightful seat. It was the same seat He had stood up from and laid aside in order to be the fulfillment of God's eternal plan for the redemption of humankind. These wonderful words, penned by Emily Elliott, capture the full significance of Jesus' journey from the time He stood up and vacated His seat at the right hand of God, through the completion of the work the Father gave Him to do, until the glorious moment of His exaltation back, once again, at the right hand of God.

Thou didst leave Thy throne and Thy kingly crown,
When Thou camest to earth for me;
But in Bethlehem's home was there found no room
For Thy holy nativity.

Heaven's arches rang when the angels sang,
Proclaiming Thy royal decree;
But of lowly birth didst Thou come to earth, and in great humility.

The foxes found rest, and the birds their nest
In the shade of the forest tree;
But Thy couch was the sod, O Thou Son of God,
In the deserts of Galilee.

Thou camest, O Lord, with the living word,
That should set Thy people free;
But with mocking scorn, and with crown of thorn,
They bore Thee to Calvary.

When the heavens shall ring, and the angels sing,
At Thy coming to victory,

Let Thy voice call me home, saying "Yet there is room,
There is room at My side for thee."

O come to my heart, Lord Jesus, There is room in my heart for Thee.
My heart shall rejoice, Lord Jesus, When Thou comest and callest
for me.

This prayer marks the beginning of the defining moment of the completion of the work assigned to the Son. The seat He would occupy at the right hand of God would mark the crowning moment of the full and complete restoration of His glory.

And the significance of His "sitting down" cannot be ignored. Jesus would sit down because it was a sign of the honor placed on Him by the Father. He would sit down because it was a sign of the authority the Father had vested in Him. He would sit down because it was a sign of the rest He had earned through the work He had completed. He would sit down because it was a sign of His intercession on our behalf. He would sit down because it was a sign that "no condemnation now exists for those in Christ Jesus" (Rom. 8:1).

The fact that the Lord Jesus was about to be seated at the right hand of God, however, finds its greatest significance in the matter of His royalty. Whereas His preexistence established His royalty, His birth in a lowly manger in Bethlehem announced His royalty. Whereas His death on a cruel Roman cross distinguished His royalty, His glorious resurrection by the power of God confirmed His royalty. And, whereas His ascension into heaven magnified His royalty, His seat at the right hand of God declared His royalty!

This, then, was how God designed the cross. It was specific and purpose-driven in the heart of a sovereign God. God's plan for our redemption was intentional at its core. Paul put this in the proper perspective when he penned these words to the church at Corinth:

> Now everything is from God, who reconciled us to Himself
> through Christ and gave us the ministry of reconciliation: that is, in
> Christ, God was reconciling the world to Himself, not counting their
> trespasses against them, and He has committed the message of recon-
> ciliation to us. Therefore, we are ambassadors for Christ; certain that

God is appealing through us, we plead on Christ's behalf, "Be reconciled to God." He made the One who did not know sin to be sin for us, so that we might become the righteousness of God in Him. (2 Cor. 5:18–21)

We have considered four elements that help us understand better the significance of the Son's request to be restored to the glory He once enjoyed with the Father from before the world began. These included a specific reason, a specific event, a specific purpose, and a specific design. We now consider the important issue of authority. Jesus claimed to have all the authority necessary from the Father to grant eternal life to the ones who would believe in the one true God!

Chapter 4

The Authority

As Jesus spoke to the Father, He said, "You gave Him authority over all flesh" (John 17:2). What a statement and what a claim!

Webster's defines *authority* as "the power to determine, adjudicate, or otherwise settle issues" and as "the right to command or control" based on that which is "rightfully delegated to or given by" (the one who has the right to grant that authority).

The issue of His divine authority was at the forefront of everything Jesus did and presented a particular affront to the authority of the religious leaders of His day.

One classic confrontation happened when Jesus made a secret trip up to Jerusalem for the Feast of Tabernacles. Hostile Jewish authorities were lying in wait for Jesus, but the Lord used His eternal intuition to make certain they could not find Him before His time had fully come (see John 7:8). Evidently Jesus' claim to be the Messiah, coupled with His dramatic demonstrations of that power, was the cause of major discussion and deep consternation. "What audacity," they muttered among themselves. "Who does He think He is?" When He cleaned out the temple, they were so affronted by what He did that they demanded He show them a sign to prove His authority. When He spoke of His pending death and resurrection, they just didn't get it because they thought He was referring to the actual temple building that had taken them forty-six years to construct. Their blindness prevented them from understanding the source of His authority, thus preventing them from knowing the only true God. And listen to what He told them about life and judgment:

> "I assure you: Anyone who hears My word and believes Him who sent Me has eternal life and will not come under judgment but has passed from death to life.
>
> "I assure you: An hour is coming, and is now here, when the dead will hear the voice of the Son of God, and those who hear will live. For just as the Father has life in Himself, so also He has granted to the Son to have life in Himself. And He has granted to Him the right to pass judgment, because He is the Son of Man. Do not be amazed at this, because a time is coming when all who are in the graves will hear His voice and come out—those who have done good things, to the resurrection of life, but those who have done wicked things, to the resurrection of judgment.
>
> "I can do nothing on My own. I judge only as I hear, and My judgment is righteous, because I do not seek My own will, but the will of Him who sent Me." (John 5:24–30)

This claim of divine authority inflamed the Jews. But Jesus kept on doing the will of the Father as One who preached, taught, and healed with the authority of God. The Pharisees' increasing hostility toward Him was by no means a deterrent to the completion of the work God had assigned Him to do. His response to their mutterings was to teach with authority in word and deed. And as He did so, He gave five reasons in John 7 to justify His rightful claim:

1. His spiritual insights came from the Father (v. 16)
2. His teaching could be tested (v. 17)
3. His actions proved His motives (v. 18)
4. His impact outweighed even Moses (v. 19)
5. His work demonstrated His identity (vv. 20–24)

The bottom line is the matter of His divine authority. This authority gave Jesus the right to say, "I have many things to say and to judge about you, but the One who sent Me is true, and what I have heard from Him—these things I tell the world" (John 8:26).

The question is, what exactly constituted the authority given to Him? What about the nature and character of the Son qualified Him to have "authority over all flesh" (John 17:2)? The Lord Jesus tried, without success, to convince the Jews of His divine origin because this matter remained the key issue with regard to the authority He claimed to have with the Father. This was such a critical component that Jesus cried out when teaching in the temple and said, "You know Me and you know where I am from. Yet I have not come on My own, but the One who sent Me is true. You don't know Him; I know Him because I am from Him, and He sent Me" (John 7:28–29).

In a sense the Lord Jesus was using satire here because He played with their unbelief. They knew Him in the flesh as a human being, but they did not know Him as the Son of the living God. And this was why they just could not accept the authority with which He spoke and taught. And because they did not know Him as God, they certainly could not receive the eternal life that only He had the authority to grant. This eternal life was based on the acknowledgment of God as the only true God. Their disbelief and failure to recognize Jesus as the Messiah would have eternal consequences for them: "You will look for Me and you will not find Me; and where I am, you cannot come" (John 7:36).

The writer of Hebrews raises the issue of the Son's credentials when he attributes all authority to Him during the "last days" (Heb. 1:2). Whatever one's opinion concerning the timing of these last days, Peter assures us they will be turbulent days during which time "scoffers will come in the last days to scoff, following their own lusts, saying, 'Where is the promise of His coming?'" (2 Pet. 3:3–4). The Jews, of course, understood the last days to be a reference to the time when the Messiah would come. And it followed that any and all fulfillment of prophecy would be associated with the still-to-come Messiah. He would be the one who carried ultimate authority on all matters pertaining to life and death. He would authenticate the veracity of the nature of God who had remained untouchable to them from the days of Sinai. Sadly, they (the Jews) remained blinded by their own legalism.

Hence the vital importance of what we read about in Hebrews concerning the origin of the Son's authority: "In these last days, He has spoken to us by His Son, whom He has appointed heir of all things and through whom He made the universe. He is the radiance of His glory, the exact expression of His nature, and He sustains all things by His powerful word. After making purification for sins, He sat down at the right hand of the Majesty on high" (Heb. 1:2–3).

At the outset we must settle the issue of divine initiative as it pertains to this conversation between the Son and His Father. Jesus, Himself, settled this when He said, "For I have not spoken on My own, but the Father Himself who sent Me has given Me a command as to what I should say and what I should speak" (John 12:49). According to the passage in Hebrews, this founding principle of operation by which the Lord Jesus did His work finds its root in six fundamental facts that all trace back to "the glory I had with You from before the world existed."

Jesus Is the Heir of All Things

One can only imagine what it must be like to be the heir of all that God is. This defines the Lord's ultimate authority in that everything that exists will ultimately come under the control of the Messiah. Paul burst out in a doxology of praise after reminding his readers of the majesty and grandeur of God's plan for the redemption of man.

> Oh, the depth of the riches
> both of the wisdom and the knowledge of God!
> How unsearchable His judgments
> and untraceable His ways!
> For who has known the mind of the Lord?
> Or who has been His counselor?
> Or who has first given to Him,
> and has to be repaid?
> For from Him and through Him and to Him are all things.
> To Him be the glory forever. Amen. (Rom. 11:33–36)

Jesus' authority as heir essentially appointed Him to be the sole recipient of God's glory by virtue of His demonstration of grace and mercy to disobedient sinners. His heirship signified Jesus' right of inheritance and gave Him the divine authority and right of Almighty God to inherit God's rank, title, and position.

The fact of His divine appointment as heir means the Son operated on this earth according to His divine mandate. And this divine mandate, which emanated from His divine heirship, was based on four absolute truths:

1. Jesus was claimed by God. This claim was affirmed at the outset of Jesus' earthly ministry when He was baptized by John.

> "After Jesus was baptized, He went up immediately from the water. The heavens suddenly opened for Him, and He saw the Spirit of God descending like a dove and coming down on Him. And there came a voice from heaven: This is My beloved Son. I take delight in Him!" (Matt. 3:16–17).

2. Jesus was unique to God. God affirmed the absolute authority of His Son by the expression of His love. So great, in fact, was this love that God gave His "One and Only" who, by virtue of His position as God, became the only acceptable sacrifice for sin. And, as the only One unique in holiness with God, Jesus became the full reflection of the Father's "grace and truth" (John 1:14). His uniqueness with God was the means by which we were able to observe the glory of God despite His human flesh.

3. Jesus was the firstborn of God. This absolute truth lies at the heart of the preeminence of the Lord Jesus Christ, which is so much connected to His divine authority.

Paul's pastoral instruction to the church at Colossae accentuates a number of critical facts related to the divine right of the Son to carry the full authority of the Father in the work He was assigned to do. The matter of His being God's firstborn Son is particularly noteworthy because it places Jesus in the right position to "have first place in everything" (Col. 1:18).

> He is the image of the invisible God,
> the firstborn over all creation;
> because by Him everything was created,
> in heaven and on earth, the visible and the invisible,
> whether thrones or dominions or rulers or authorities—
> all things have been created through Him and for Him.
> He is before all things, and by Him all things hold together.

He is also the head of the body, the church;
He is the beginning, the firstborn from the dead,
so that He might come to have first place in everything.
For God was pleased to have all His fullness dwell in Him,
and through Him to reconcile everything to Himself
by making peace through the blood of His cross—
whether things on earth or things in heaven. (Col. 1:15–20)

This is a major statement concerning the divine authority of our Savior. Our understanding of the word *firstborn* usually is associated with the arrival of a firstborn child. In the strict sense of that understanding, Jesus was God's firstborn in the flesh. This was the means by which He became the firstfruits of those who have died in Christ. He was born first to die first, to be raised first, so that all who believe in His name would be raised up to walk in newness of life with (because of) Him.

But in this passage Paul is referring more specifically to Christ's preeminence in position and rank. Both the Jews and the Greeks had little difficulty understanding the ranking of the firstborn son who, by virtue of his position in the family, had the legal right and full authority to inherit all of his father's estate.

No wonder Jesus spoke to the Father and said: "You gave Him authority over all flesh" (John 17:2) because, as Creator of all flesh, God owned everything He had made. And He gave the Son full and complete authority over His human creation with the exclusive right to grant eternal life to all who would believe on His name.

4. Jesus was installed by God. The coronation of the King is clearly forecast in the book of Psalms. As we read the second Psalm, we can sense the journey from the installation of the lesser King David, through the Davidic line, to the coronation of the One who was of the line and lineage of David, the Lord Jesus Christ.

Why do the nations rebel
and the peoples plot in vain?
The kings of the earth take their stand

and the rulers conspire together
against the LORD and His anointed One.
"Let us tear off their chains
and free ourselves from their restraints."
The One enthroned in heaven laughs;
the Lord ridicules them.
Then He speaks to them in His anger
and terrifies them in His wrath:
"I have consecrated My King
on Zion, My holy mountain."
I will declare the LORD's decree:
He said to Me, "You are My Son;
today I have become Your Father.
Ask of Me,
and I will make the nations Your inheritance
and the ends of the earth Your possession.
You will break them with a rod of iron;
You will shatter them like pottery."
So now, kings, be wise;
receive instruction, you judges of the earth.
Serve the LORD with reverential awe,
and rejoice with trembling.
Pay homage to the Son, or He will be angry,
and you will perish in your rebellion,
for His anger may ignite at any moment.
All those who take refuge in Him are happy. (Ps. 2)

Having been installed as King of kings and Lord of lords by the Father, Jesus ruled this mighty universe with complete authority.

The Lord Jesus Christ was the heir of all things by virtue of His relationship with the Father, His establishment as King, His accomplishments as Savior, His resurrection as Conqueror, and His ascension as Lord! His heirship constituted His absolute authority.

Jesus Is the Maker of All Things

The second fundamental fact on which the Son's authority was based pertains to His functional essence as Maker of the universe. When the Lord Jesus stated, "You gave [Me] authority" (John 17:2) to the Father in this prayer, He was basing His assertion on an absolute, not a probability or even on a possibility. As the Son of Man, Jesus was set apart as unique because of His sinlessness, His righteousness, His holiness, and His ability to create.

The ability to create belongs to God alone. And the fact that Jesus creates indicates that the Son of Man, in His functional role as man, was as much the Son of God as He was God. As the One who made the worlds, Jesus had every divine right to thank the Father for the authority to make eternal life an absolute fact for all who would believe in His name. This offering of eternal life comes by virtue of His rightful authority to give eternal life because He is the only One who could have made eternal life possible. His authority moves the attainment of eternal life from probability and possibility to assurance and absolute certainty. Therein lies the heart of total security for the believer! Consider the threefold meaning behind Jesus' authority to be the Maker of all things.

JESUS IS THE DESIGNATED AGENT

An agent is authorized to act on another person's behalf. In the context of this prayer, Jesus makes the point clear. God appointed Him as the designated agent of eternal life, the One through whom the gift of eternal life would pass on to humankind.

Our understanding of the role of an ambassador sheds further light on the authority Jesus had in the giving of eternal life to all who would believe in Him. Most of the international embassies of the world are headed by a man or woman who carries the title of ambassador. This top governmental official is a representative of his own leader and is usually authorized to speak and act on behalf of his leader. Jesus certainly carried God's full and complete authority to act on man's behalf as the full sacrifice for sin, but He did not have to consult with the Father to gain permission to keep on offering the gift of eternal life. The hour of His obedience on the cross and His subsequent resurrection and ascension established the moment of His completed work. It was finished completely through

God's designated agent. The deed was about to be done, and the One who was designated to carry out the deed carried God's full and complete authority to "make" the offer of eternal life as the guarantee because of His blood!

JESUS IS THE DEFINITIVE CREATOR

The fact of Jesus' being the only means through which the universe is created further underscores His divine authority. As we hear the Son pray about the authority He had from the Father, we find ourselves listening in on the essential reiteration of the method God ordained to reconcile people to Himself. And this method of redemption was channeled through the Lord Jesus Christ, who is the definitive Creator.

Three qualifications were necessary for this to take place. First, Jesus had all the *authority* needed to create. Second, Jesus had all the *power* necessary to create. And third, Jesus had all the *praise* due because of the product of His creation! In modern-day terminology God said: "You are My Son. I am well pleased with You. I have chosen You to be the channel through whom I am going to do all that is necessary to redeem fallen man. I not only give You all the responsibility to carry out the work I assign to You, but I give You all the authority necessary to carry this work out and to grant eternal life to all who will believe that I am the one true God!"

Herein lies the heart of one of the most important elements of divine leadership. It was one thing for the Lord Jesus to be given to the world because of the love of the Father. It was one thing for the Son to be given God's work to do. It was one thing to carry out His work with obedient responsibility. But it was another thing to be given the authority so vital to the accomplishment of this redemptive responsibility. And this authority found its root in His creatorship!

JESUS IS THE DISTINCTIVE RULER

Note the extent of Jesus' authority. We are told He is the one through whom "the universe" is made. While the word *universe* captures the massive vastness of an endless sphere, it can also be translated as "worlds" and perhaps even more significantly translated by the word *ages*.

This is what John was referring to when he referenced the preincarnate work of Christ in his Gospel prologue: "All things were created through Him, and apart from Him not one thing was created that has been created" (John 1:3). The Word who became flesh continued to rule over all things even during the time He "became flesh and took up residence among us" (v. 14). This rulership, which was a manifest sign of His authority, extended not only to the universe but also to time, space, energy, and matter. In other words, Jesus Christ, the Son of Man, ruled over the entire universe and everything that makes the universe function.

Jesus Is the Radiance of God's Glory

We have previously established the connection between the glory of the Father and the glory of the Son. The Lord Jesus spoke these words, "Glorify Your Son so that the Son may glorify You," as a statement of fact as His hour rapidly approached. In so doing, the interconnectedness of glory as it related to both the Father and the Son is set.

The concept of radiance captures a major theme concerning the mission of the Lord Jesus. Jesus was repeatedly presented to the skeptics as well as to the disciples as light. John's prologue announced the eternal Word as the essence of life, "and that life was the light of men. The light shines in the darkness, yet the darkness did not overcome it" (John 1:4–5). John the Baptist bore witness to the coming light; and Jesus, Himself, claimed to be "the light of the world" (John 8:12). In short, Jesus showed forth the light of God to a lost and dying world. This divine ability as the radiator of God's glory carries two distinct meanings. First, it means that the Lord Jesus Christ as the Son of God displayed the glory of God because He was God. And second, it means that the Lord Jesus Christ as the Son of Man displayed the glory of God because He was commissioned by God to radiate His glory in a dark world.

An even closer reflection sheds even more light on why the ability to radiate God's glory enforced Jesus' authority over all flesh. This was the primary means by which blind (lost) people could see. The sweet sound of God's amazing grace that saves a "wretch" like you and me is the sound of the most powerful beam of living light that shines forth from the throne of God in heaven, illuminating an otherwise undetectable pathway back to the presence of a holy and righteous God.

This "sound of light" is the active ingredient of the radiance of God's glory. It shines forth and lights up the dark hopelessness of wicked man. It can be both heard and seen, but it is always sensed and known. And when it happened, there was never any doubt as to the authority that backed the light. This is exactly what happened to Saul of Tarsus as he journeyed on the road to Damascus.

> As he traveled and was nearing Damascus, a light from heaven
> suddenly flashed around him. Falling to the ground, he heard a voice
> saying to him, "Saul, Saul, why are you persecuting Me?"
> "Who are You, Lord?" he said.
> "I am Jesus, whom you are persecuting," He replied. "But get up
> and go into the city, and you will be told what you must do."
> The men who were traveling with him stood speechless, hearing
> the sound but seeing no one. Then Saul got up from the ground, and
> though his eyes were open, he could see nothing. So they took him by
> the hand and led him into Damascus. (Acts 9:3–8)

As the radiance of God's glory, Jesus Christ is able to accomplish three things:

1. Jesus is the transmitter of God's glory. The word here literally means He is the One who "sends forth light." In other words He is the only means by which God's light is made known to man. Jesus carries it from God to man and acts as a conductor of that light.

God's servant Moses understood what it meant to radiate God's glory. In Exodus 33, Moses said, "Please, let me see Your glory" (v. 18). But Moses was in for a shock!

> He said, "I will cause all My goodness to pass in front of you,
> and I will proclaim the name Yahweh before you. I will be gracious to
> whom I will be gracious, and I will have compassion on whom I will
> have compassion." But He answered, "You cannot see My face, for no
> one can see Me and live." The LORD said, "Here is a place near Me.
> You are to stand on the rock, and when My glory passes by, I will
> put you in the crevice of the rock and cover you with My hand until

I have passed by. Then I will take My hand away, and you will see My back, but My face will not be seen." (Exod. 33:19–23)

When Moses came down from the mountain, his face shone with the glory of the Lord even though he had not been allowed to see the face of God. No wonder the Lord Jesus had God's authority to give eternal life. He was the One authorized to transmit the glory of God to the hearts of man. And He didn't even have to hide His face from the presence of God to accomplish it!

2. Jesus is the mediator of God's glory. The matter of Jesus' divine ability to mediate is God's stamp of authority on His Son. Paul stressed this point to Timothy like this: "For there is one God and one mediator between God and man, a man, Christ Jesus, who gave Himself—a ransom for all, a testimony at the proper time" (1 Tim. 2:5–6).

The authority given to the Son by the Father is further accentuated through the means by which eternal life is attained. This life comes through the one true God. As mediator, Jesus is placed in the position of go-between, in that a holy God and an unrighteous man are placed on two opposite sides in conflict with each other. Jesus' willing obedience to be sacrificed on the cross put Him in the role as the intervening agent through whom reconciliation was made possible. As mediator He carried God's full and complete authority to ratify God's covenant of grace, the merciful extending of His love to all who would believe on His name. As such, the Lord Jesus Christ had the full right to claim the authority "You gave Me" because He was the only one who was capable of restoring peace between God and sinful man. And the absence of the article before "man" in the original Greek language suggests "Christ Jesus, Himself a man." Once again we find God's authority being conferred on the only perfect God-man who was the only man who could bring God and man together!

If Jesus' authority as the transmitter of God's glory was the means by which God's glory is brought to man, then His authority as the mediator of God's glory was the means by which man is brought to God's glory! Otherwise people remain blinded by the gods of this world. They cannot see without Jesus' ability to radiate and show forth the light of God. The believers in Corinth struggled with this warfare between the darkness of the gods of this world and the light of the one true God. "But if, in fact, our gospel is veiled, it is veiled to those who are perishing. Regarding them: the god of this age has blinded the minds of the unbelievers so they cannot see the light of the gospel of the glory of Christ, who is the image of God. For we are not proclaiming ourselves but Jesus Christ as Lord, and ourselves as your slaves because of Jesus. For God, who said, 'Light shall shine out of darkness'—He has shone in our hearts to give the light of the knowledge of God's glory in the face of Jesus Christ" (2 Cor. 4:3–6).

Paul went on to say that we have "this treasure in clay jars" (v. 7). The authority of Jesus, which is to radiate God's glory, is an extraordinary power that can only come from God. This power transcends human frailty, which is no better than a garbage bag to be thrown away when full of junk! The fact that God uses such clay pots to house the testimony of this transforming light is, within itself, the greatest testimony to the total authority with which the Son reflected the light of the Father's grace and truth. Without the mediation of the Lord Jesus Christ, man would be left at the mercy of the world's opinions, hopes, views, and goals. And the world's opinion is blinded by the lies of Satan. The same God who commanded light to shine out of darkness when He created the world is the same God who created supernatural light in the soul, which ushers the believer from the kingdom of darkness to His kingdom of light.

3. Jesus is the One who expresses God's glory. We have been reminded of two means by which the Lord Jesus is able to accomplish the radiance of God's glory. He accomplishes this by transmitting God's glory and by mediating God's glory. He also exemplifies God's glory in that the Son is the fullest expression of God.

In our previous discussion concerning the ambassadorial role of the Savior, we uncovered the meaning of representation. Jesus was given the authority to act and speak on behalf of the Father. He did not share His (the Son's) opinion concerning the Father's demand for holiness; He shared the Father's demand, period! In so doing, His expression of God the Father carried at least five understandings. First, it meant the Son revealed God exactly. Second, He expressed God exactly. Third, He communicated God exactly. Fourth, He emitted God exactly. And fifth, He sent out something unique from God exactly!

Jesus Is the Image of God's Glory

The authority vested in Jesus Christ was no less due to this fundamental fact of His unique relationship with God.

The term we translate as "exact expression" is better translated "express image" and is the only time it is used in the New Testament. Perhaps this would add further to the uniqueness of the Son who, by the express authority of the Father, carried out His work as the exact image of God.

In much of the extrabiblical literature, this term carried with it the idea of engraving on a piece of wood, an etching in metal, a brand on a hide, an impression made on a piece of clay, or even the stamp on a coin. Many of the emperors ordered their images stamped on the coinage of the day, thus ensuring their legacy beyond their lifetime and demanding obedience during their lifetime.

The writer of Hebrews qualifies the image of the Son when he states that Jesus is "the exact expression of His [the Father's] nature" (Heb. 1:3). This reference to God's nature is a direct reference to His character or, even better, to His person. We are faced once again with a justification for the Son's claim to the authority of God the Father in all things by virtue of the fact He was the perfect imprint of the Father.

In reality this conjures up an understanding of a direct duplication of the Father in that He (the Son) is not just reflecting God's glory; He is God Himself. And, as God, His image bears His own essential glory! The word *person,* furthermore, means that the Lord Jesus Christ, as the Son of Man, expresses the very nature, being, and essence of the Father in everything God assigned Him to do. Paul stated this fact like this: "He is the image of the invisible God, the firstborn over all creation" (Col. 1:15).

The picture portrayed of Jesus as the image of God conjures up two important presuppositions:

1. Jesus Is the Exact Portrait of God. From time to time churches request their members make appointments to have their pictures taken for the church directory. I have always regarded this as "the funny book," largely because of the numbers of people, including me, who constantly complain that the pictures taken do not "look like me." Hello!

Not so in the case of the One who became flesh for us! He certainly did not need His picture to be taken; and had He done so, He most certainly would not have complained about the exactness of His likeness to the Father. With or without a photograph, Jesus was the exact portrait of the Father in every way.

As such, the Lord Jesus Christ was affirming this when He claimed the full authority of the Father to grant eternal life to all flesh. As He stood there and spoke to the Father in heaven, He was the exact physical likeness of God. He was the exact optical exactness of God. He was the exact counterpart of the exactness of God. And He was the exact description of God's exactness!

2. Jesus Is the Exact Reproduction of God. The truth here is simple yet most profound. When one looks at the Lord Jesus, one looks at God. When one listens to the Lord Jesus speak, one hears the voice of God. When one sees the Lord Jesus love so unconditionally, one sees the unconditional love of God. When one observes the Lord Jesus minister to the poor, the lonely, and the desperate, one is impacted by the ministry of God. When one is touched in so many ways by the Lord Jesus Christ, one is touched by the hand of God. Such is the One called the Savior of the world!

Jesus Is the Sustainer of All Things

The central role and function of the Lord Jesus as the sole authority of God the Father is seen further in His capacity to sustain all things. "He is before all things, and by Him all things hold together" (Col. 1:17). Here again we are given a clearer understanding of total sovereignty with which the Father delegated authority to the Son. The universe and everything in it is constantly and continually sustained by the word of the Lord Jesus Christ.

This ability to sustain continually conveys the idea of movement toward a goal. This is tied to the progressive, sustaining power of Jesus by which the world is moved in the direction of God's plan for the ages. Jesus, as the Son of God, is engaged continuously in the action of directing the affairs of the universe (including the affairs of man) toward the final consummation of God's sovereign plan and purpose. God is continually involved in the affairs of mankind and "apart from Him not one thing was created that has been created" (John 1:3).

As the sustainer of all things, the Lord Jesus carries the full authority of the Father to sustain and consummate the same creation God spoke into existence. And just as He has power over the earth, so He has God's full and complete authority over all the flesh of the earth in the giving of eternal life to all who would believe on His name.

His superiority and preeminence not only means that His power sustains the earth but His grace monitors the earth. He is the principal of cohesion. He is the power of suspension. He is the full and complete partner with God in all of life's dimensions! The whole earth hangs on the arms of the Lord Jesus Christ! Two major guarantees accompany His sustaining power.

1. Jesus alone guarantees the *continuance* of all things.
2. Jesus alone guarantees the *constancy* of all things.

This means the Lord Jesus Christ will not disrupt God's plan for the ages. It also means the Lord Jesus will not relinquish His power over the universe. And it also means the Lord Jesus Christ will not suspend the laws of God concerning His creation. When all is said and done, the same power by which all things are upheld by the mere word of His mouth will be the power by which the nations that rise against Him will be trampled into oblivion:

> Then I saw heaven opened, and there was a white horse! Its rider is called Faithful and True, and in righteousness He judges and makes war. His eyes were like a fiery flame, and on His head were many crowns. He had a name written that no one knows except Himself. He wore a robe stained with blood, and His name is called the Word of God. The armies that were in heaven followed Him on white horses, wearing pure white linen. From His mouth came a sharp sword, so that with it He might strike the nations. He will shepherd them with an iron scepter. He will also trample the winepress of the fierce anger of God, the Almighty. And on His robe and on His thigh He has written:

> KING OF KINGS
> AND LORD OF LORDS.
> (Rev. 19:11–16)

The One who had the authority to sustain all things has the authority to conclude all things, all to the glory of God the Father!

Jesus Is the Sole Purger of Our Sins

Jesus was about to walk across the Kidron Valley and enter the garden of His betrayal. The hour of completion signaled that sin could be purged once and for all. And, after He had died on the cross and rose again, then He would take His seat at the right hand of the Father. His work would be finished at that point. All the requirements for the reconciliation of man to God would have been fulfilled. And so the ability to purge or purify our sin was an ultimate sign of His authority.

The removing or purgation of sin has been an active part of our search for God throughout the generations. In its purest sense it carried the idea of cleansing the bowels from the obvious presence of accumulated filth. Medical experts have promoted many forms of cathartic methods all designed to purify the physical body of ailments, and modern efforts to rid the body of varying poisons have all suggested techniques that have the same objective in mind.

Spiritually speaking, some religions have even espoused erroneous forms of purgatory that can best be described as a place or state following death in which penitent souls are purified of venial sins or undergo the temporal punishment still remaining at the time of death. This incorrect and most unbiblical doctrine is an effort by man to manipulate the inevitability of eternal punishment for unforgiven sin. The idea is ultimately to render the dead sinner cleansed and purified of all sin with the subsequent deliverance of the now saint into heaven. This desperate man-made effort to appease his need for total dependency on the Lord Jesus Christ serves to elevate the role of the priest who has the authority to forgive, especially when present just moments before the sinner slips away into eternity. A belief in purgatory also eliminates the horrors of hell because of the ultimate assurance that all people will ultimately end up in heaven.

This is not taught in the Bible. Furthermore, if it were taught, then the Lord Jesus would not have had the authority to grant eternal life to all who would believe on His name.

What the Lord Jesus Christ was about to do on the cross was designed to free the sinner from any and all contaminants or pollutants—past, present, or future—because His blood had the power to cancel all sin. The condition was simple: "Therefore, repent and turn back, that your sins may be wiped out so that seasons of refreshing may come from the presence of the Lord" (Acts 3:19).

Chapter 5

The Life

The final issue is the most critical of all. The matter of eternal life has been roundly discussed and debated since time began. What exactly is eternal life? Where is it? Who is eligible to receive eternal life, and what are the requirements for entrance into eternal life?

This entire prayer is an affirmation of God's sovereign decision to grant eternal life to all who believe in His name. As we hear Jesus speaking to the Father, we hear the Son expressing agreement as to the nature of eternal life and the means by which that life is granted. God's love is the producing agent while the Son's sacrifice is the supplying agent. The producer and the supplier are one because they are God, but in terms of function, they both need each other to accomplish God's sovereign plan of redemption.

The giving of eternal life is the foundation of the Christian faith. Jesus Christ is the cornerstone. Mark put this in the context of Jesus' rejection by the Jews when he said: "The stone that the builders rejected—this has become the cornerstone" (Mark 12:10). Of course he was using the illustration of the stones that builders typically reject until they find one that perfectly fits the building they are erecting. The stone they looked for had to be exactly symmetrical so that it could stabilize the whole building. Ironically, the stone they rejected and crucified was none other than the Lord Jesus Christ, the only one who can stabilize the world's free fall into a Christless eternity.

In the book of Acts, Peter placed the rejected cornerstone squarely on the shoulders of our Savior as the only means by which salvation is made possible:

> Let it be known to all of you and to all the people of Israel, that by the name of Jesus Christ the Nazarene—whom you crucified and whom God raised from the dead—by Him this man [who was healed] is standing here before you healthy. This Jesus is the stone despised by you builders, who has become the cornerstone. There is salvation in no one else, for there is no other name under heaven given to people by which we must be saved. (Acts 4:10–12)

We have all heard the phrase "God said it and that settles it!" This is a good time to invoke the same statement in question form: "Do you have any further questions?" Everything Jesus talks about in this prayer hinges on the authority He received from the Father to "give eternal life to all You have given Him" (John 17:2). The bottom line: Jesus Christ is the only way by which all can inherit eternal life.

Let's take a closer look at this magnificent subject. In John's Gospel alone there are ten references to eternal life. The word can also be translated "everlasting" life, which literally means the Lord Jesus has God's authority to enable us to live forever. There are two essential understandings of the rewards of eternal life. The first refers to length of time, and the second refers to the quality of time. Jesus not only gives eternal life as a guarantee of everlasting existence, but He reminds us, "I have come that they may have life and have it in abundance" (John 10:10). The blessing of knowing the only true God carries both quantity and quality of life.

As such, the Lord Jesus is solidifying the essential meaning of eternal life. Three essential meanings are implicit in His prayer:

Jesus Affirms the Nature of Eternal Life

As He looks up to heaven and prays, we hear the Son's confirmation of the nature and character of His divine commission. His ability to give eternal life is commissioned by the Father, sustained by the Father, enabled by the Father, and entrusted to Him by the Father. The Son's mission is bound up in the supreme love of God for an evil and sinful world, a love so intense that the Father gave His only Son to die on behalf of the same people who had rejected God.

Jesus Affirms the Extent of Eternal Life

Within a few short statements the Lord Jesus affirms the extent of eternal life. This is seen in the power given the Son by the Father. Despite the efforts of many religious groups over the generations to claim direct authority from God, and despite the claims by some that God had appointed them to be the right hand of God on earth, Jesus Christ left no room for divine alternatives.

The "room at the cross for you" is offering of the grace of God to all who believe on His name, not the offering to some who want to share in the authority given only to the Son. No one but Jesus can save others from their sins, and no one but Jesus has the power or capacity to forgive others for their sins. Just before the Savior ascended to be seated at the right hand of God the Father in heaven, He gave His disciples their Great Commission. Listen to what He said: "All authority has been given to Me in heaven and on earth. Go, therefore, and make disciples of all nations, baptizing them in the name of the Father and of the Son and of the Holy Spirit, teaching them to observe everything I have commanded you. And remember, I am with you always, to the end of the age" (Matt. 28:18–20).

Such is the extent of His power over eternal life. It covers everything and excludes nothing. There is no one else to turn to, no one else who has the capacity or the authority to forgive sin, and no one else who can write the believers name in God's book in heaven. Besides, there is no one else who can raise you from the dead. All Adams have failed—no matter what name they go by, no matter what visions they have received, no matter which group they belong to, no matter what historical traditions they are part of, and no matter how big the crowds are that come and listen to them. Only in Christ can we be made alive! Jesus' power is granted "over all flesh" (John 17:2).

Jesus Affirms the Ability of Eternal Life

In his discourse on the certainty of God's witness, the apostle John puts his finger on the ability of eternal life: "And we know that the Son of God has come and has given us understanding so that we may know the true One. We are in the true One—that is, in His Son Jesus Christ. He is the true God and eternal life" (1 John 5:20).

What could be more plain and down the line! Jesus Christ came to give it. We can know it! Because He is the true God and the only One who can grant eternal life!

The writer of Hebrews puts the ability of eternal salvation in the right perspective when he asks a most searching question: "How will we escape if we neglect such a great salvation?" (Heb. 2:3). Bearing in mind the ability of salvation to cancel the penalty of sin, to recreate fallen men, and to restore fellowship with God, what is man to do unless he accepts God's gift of eternal life.

> We must therefore pay even more attention to what we have heard, so that we will not drift away. For if the message spoken through angels was legally binding, and every transgression and disobedience received a just punishment, how will we escape if we neglect such a great salvation? (Heb. 2:1–3).

The issue of drifting away was borrowed from the picture of a ship passing by or drifting by the safety of a harbor. The warning implicit in this is the imperative to take hold of the only means by which safe harbor can be attained. Jesus is the only harbor of our salvation. If you believe that the wages of sin is death and that a righteous God cannot have anything to do with unrighteousness, then you must put your faith and trust in Jesus' ability to give eternal life. Salvation has an exclusive threefold ability: It has the exclusive ability to forgive sin, it has the exclusive ability to make a person brand-new, and it has the exclusive ability to guarantee life after death.

It Has the Exclusive Ability to Forgive Sin

This eternal life in the Lord Jesus Christ has the ability to do what no other can do. It has the ability to forgive sin, for "without the shedding of blood there is no forgiveness" (Heb. 9:22). Throughout the ages people have done everything they know to do in order to gain the forgiveness of sin. Brilliant minds certainly have achieved great and wonderful things. They have sent people to the moon, invented the computer, and designed every kind of gadget imaginable. But there is one thing no man can do for himself—he cannot forgive his own sin! Only Jesus Christ has God's authority to accomplish the forgiveness of sin.

IT HAS THE EXCLUSIVE ABILITY TO MAKE A PERSON BRAND-NEW

Most people spend half their lives trying to turn over a new leaf. One resolution follows another. One promise follows another. Just recently I heard a man say he would never treat his wife in such a manner again. Don Imus apologized to the members of the Rutgers University women's basketball team for his unkind and thoughtless remarks on public radio, and they accepted his apologies. But only the Lord can effect real change in people's hearts. When the Lord Jesus told Nicodemus that he must be "born again," He was pointing to the only means by which he could ever be forgiven of his sin and the only means by which he could ever be re-created as a human being. The ability of this salvation certainly changes our eternal destination from hell to heaven, but it also changes our personal disposition from an attitude governed by self to an attitude controlled by the Spirit.

> But the fruit of the Spirit is love, joy, peace, patience, kindness, goodness, faith, gentleness, self-control. . . . Now those who belong to Christ have crucified the flesh with its passions and desires. If [because] we live by the Spirit, we must also follow the Spirit. (Gal. 5:22–25).

IT HAS THE EXCLUSIVE ABILITY TO GUARANTEE LIFE AFTER DEATH

Most people wonder about life after death. Death is, after all, all around us. I remember Dr. Billy Graham being interviewed on *Larry King Live* some years ago. "Billy," Larry asked politely, "do you ever think about life after death? Do you ever truly wonder exactly what is going to happen to all of us after we die?"

"Oh, indeed, yes!" the evangelist replied. "Of course I think about it all the time. In fact, Larry, I'm looking forward to it because I know that I'm going to heaven to be with the Lord Jesus forever!"

Herein lies the ultimate ability of eternal life in the Lord Jesus Christ:

> Brothers, I tell you this: flesh and blood cannot inherit the king-
> dom of God, and corruption cannot inherit corruption. Listen! I am
> telling you a mystery:
> We will not all fall asleep, but we will all be changed,
> in a moment, in the twinkling of an eye, at the last trumpet.
> For the trumpet will sound, and the dead will be raised
>   incorruptible, and we will be changed.
> Because this incorruptible must be clothed with incorruptibility,
> and this mortal must be clothed with immortality.
> Now when this corruptible is clothed with incorruptibility,
> and this mortal is clothed with immortality,
> then the saying that is written will take place:
> Death has been swallowed up in victory.
> O Death, where is your victory?
> O Death, where is your sting?
> Now the sting of death is sin, and the power of sin is the law.
> But thanks be to God, who gives us the victory through our Lord
>   Jesus Christ! (1 Cor. 15:50–57)

Conclusion

As we move out of this inner prayer and move into the exclusive prayer of
the Lord Jesus in the next part, let's conclude with an important aspect of the
meaning of salvation. There are two reasons for this. First, because the granting
of eternal life is a continuous action for the One who gives. The act of giving
"eternal life to all You have given Him" (John 17:2) continues until the return
of our Savior and the creation of the "new heaven and a new earth" (Rev. 21:1).
Second, the opportunity to receive the gift of eternal life continues until death.
But having believed in His name, salvation is not stagnant. It becomes an active
ingredient as the life of Christ working in and through the believer from the
moment of salvation until the moment of the believer's glorification in the presence of the King of kings and the Lord of lords!

The fact of God's love is a continuous action that can be described in three phases, all of which are one continuous action. He has always loved us (past tense); He does love us (present tense); and He always will love us (eternal future tense). The same truth is applicable to those who believe on His name. Believers were saved (past tense, when Jesus died on the cross), are saved (present tense, when they believe in Jesus Christ), and shall be saved (eternal future tense).

Now this is important when considering the words of Jesus "so He may give eternal life" (John 17:2) in the inner prayer. It is even more significant for the next part of this book. Because the Son focuses all His attention on those who "have believed that You sent Me," I have entitled the next part of the book The Exclusive Prayer. Everything Jesus speaks to the Father about in verses 16–19 is centered on an exclusive group of people who are clearly defined as disciples of the Lord Jesus Christ.

The New Testament clearly teaches that evangelism is an all-encompassing, life-changing, growing concept. It is divided into three equally important components in the New Testament.

THE THREE COMPONENTS OF EVANGELISM

Salvation Evangelism

Salvation evangelism is the beginning point of the spiritual journey of every believer because it defines the moment at which Christ enters the sinner's life.

This is exactly what Jesus was doing when He told Nicodemus, "You must be born again." Eligibility for salvation evangelism comes at the time of water birth. In other words, all of God's created human beings are eligible to be saved from their sin at the moment of their arrival in the world. This must not be confused with the erroneous tradition of infant baptism that is never taught in the Word of God and can never make a person eligible for the kingdom of heaven. Water birth speaks to the issue of eligibility for salvation and not an automatic justification for salvation. A person has to be born first (of mom) in order to be born again (of the Holy Spirit).

Salvation evangelism is the imperative of the Great Commission and is the essential arm of the New Testament church. No church can survive without an active, ongoing engagement in salvation evangelism. And the responsibility for this activity has been entrusted to those who have received Christ as their Savior. Jesus makes this point clear in verse 20 when He establishes the means by which future believers come to believe in Him "through their message" (John 17:20).

The point made concerns the mandate to share the message and not the act of salvation itself. No person has ever, and could ever, be given authority to give eternal life because that authority belongs to God alone. Jesus Christ alone is the author and finisher of salvation. But the witnessing of the message of the gospel is an indispensable mandate of the essence of salvation evangelism and cannot be ignored or simply overlooked by any believer.

Perhaps one of the most intriguing illustrations of man's role and responsibility in salvation evangelism is seen in Jesus' account of the rich man and Lazarus in Luke 16. The rich man's plea on behalf of his (still alive) brothers to give their lives to Christ is directed to the Word of God (Law of Moses) and the men of God (the prophets). Surely the Lord Jesus would not have fabricated a role for the believer in introducing the sinner to the Lord Jesus if he had no role to play?

Discipleship Evangelism

Discipleship evangelism is the next vital ingredient of New Testament evangelism. One cannot over stress the significance of this dynamic in the actions and activities of the local church. Its application and relevance in the life of all believers is vital to an understanding of how God has put the church together as a living organism.

Implicit in our understanding of the word *disciple* is the concept of a follower. Even *Webster's* defines such a person as "a pupil or an adherent of another." Jesus made the point clear when He called on the Twelve to "follow Me." Any disciple of the Lord Jesus Christ is one who follows Him in every way. Such a person becomes an imitator of Christ and strives to become more like Him in every way throughout the journey of life.

In practice, it is biblically impossible to be a Christian and not be a disciple in the truest sense of the word. All believers are disciples because Jesus cannot be made or invited to become Lord; He is Lord! No action on the part of any person and no tradition on the part of any church can alter or affect who Jesus is as God. His place is signed, sealed, and delivered by virtue of who He is and not by virtue of the court of public opinion.

But an examination of the character and behavior of the disciples of Jesus' day leaves little doubt as to the dire need for maturational growth. Even the disciples were a bunch of men whose actions and activities must have left the Lord Jesus shaking His head in disbelief. A study of their general behavior quickly shows an ugly picture. They grumbled constantly. They complained bitterly. They fought with one another. They jostled for position. They doubted. They even denied the Savior at His most vulnerable point of need!

This is a picture of the church today. And this is why discipleship evangelism is so important. Churches are filled with people of every description who have taken the first step: salvation evangelism. They have put their faith and trust in the Lord Jesus. They are "born again." They are going to heaven one day! But they have so much growing to do. They are still babes in Christ. They need to be fed the meat of the Word of God. They need to be cuddled and rocked. They need to be loved and nurtured. They need guidance and counsel. They even need to be corrected and disciplined. They need to be led by spiritual leaders.

Disciple-Making Evangelism

This ought to be the goal of every action and activity of the church. To "make disciples" means to bring every lost person to a saving knowledge of Jesus Christ, then to do whatever is necessary to help them grow in the grace of God to the point at which they, themselves, are facilitating others' growth.

The mandate of the New Testament church can be stated in one phrase: evangelism is incomplete until the evangelized become the evangelists!

Every ministry and every endeavor of the local church ought to be directed toward the fulfillment of New Testament evangelism. But the proper balance in terms of the whole counsel of God is essential for the proper functioning and total health of the church. Here are the reasons:

1. A church that majors exclusively on salvation evangelism (to the exclusion of the other two components) will eventually become a weak church.

2. A church that majors exclusively on discipleship evangelism (to the exclusion of the other two components) will eventually become a plateaued church.

3. A church that majors exclusively on disciple-making evangelism (to the exclusion of the other two components) will eventually become a dead church!

Why is this important? Because I see the three components of New Testament evangelism in this wonderful prayer of our Savior. In the inner prayer (John 17:1–5) Jesus' theme is essentially salvation evangelism. In the exclusive prayer (vv. 6–19) Jesus' theme is essentially discipleship evangelism. And in the inclusive prayer (vv. 20–26) Jesus' theme is essentially disciple-making evangelism.

As we transition from the inner prayer to the exclusive prayer, this thematic emphasis will become apparent. As Jesus turns His attention from the giving of eternal life and the means by which He accomplished the giving of eternal life, He establishes the progressive movement of God's gracious love in and through the fabric of man's earthly existence.

An understanding of the components of New Testament evangelism provides an important foundation upon which to lay the words of the Son of God as He prays for an exclusive group of people known as His disciples.

Part II

The Exclusive Prayer

Introduction

There is a noticeable shift in the content of Jesus' prayer immediately after the Son asks the Father to "glorify Me in Your presence with that glory I had with You before the world existed" (John 17:5). As we have seen in the first part of *When God Prayed,* He converses exclusively from His heart to the heart of the Father. In one sense there is a single blood flow between the Father and the Son. This singular inner prayer is divinely private and takes the listener to levels that defy human explanation or understanding. No human being can truly uncover the mysteries of the beginning of the Godhead!

The Son of Man now directs His attention from God to man. In this sense the single blood flow now changes to a triple blood flow in that we find God the Father, Jesus Christ the Son, and an exclusive group of redeemed followers all included in this conversation. The actual conversation only takes place from the Son's mouth to the Father's ear because redeemed man is not invited to speak his opinion on the matters discussed. Man's opinion is not sought because man's opinion is not valid. It has neither voice nor credence regardless of position, history, or tradition.

This is not to suggest that God has not used thousands of incredible people to preach and teach the Word of God. Of course He has! Particularly "in times past," the prophets had high value in all they said and did, but "in these last days, He has spoken to us by His Son" (Heb. 1:2). I believe this establishes, once again, the authority of the Son. It reminds us of the way in which God established the authority of the Son on the Mount of Transfiguration.

Jesus had just finished exhorting the disciples and teaching them about the imperative of taking up the cross in order to follow the Lord Jesus (see Matt. 16:24). Peter, of course, had established the authority and total reliability of Jesus as Messiah when he exclaimed, "You are the Messiah, the Son of the living God!" (16:16). At this point the Lord Jesus took Peter, James, and John up a mountain where the Lord Jesus was transfigured before their eyes. Moses and Elijah appeared alongside the Son, talking with Him about His pending death. Here is where the story gets interesting.

Peter, who had just made his bold pronouncement concerning the pre-eminence of the Lord Jesus Christ, now gets carried away with the presence of these two famous and highly regarded prophets. Peter, in fact, is so delighted he offers to make three small booths, similar to the ones they would erect for the Feast of the Tabernacles, in honor of each of the three who stood before him. The Scriptures tell us that God interrupted Peter in midconversation.

> Then Peter said to Jesus, "Lord, it's good for us to be here! If You want, I will make three tabernacles here: one for You, one for Moses, and one for Elijah."
> While he was still speaking, suddenly a bright cloud covered them, and a voice from the cloud said:
> This is My beloved Son.
> I take delight in Him.
> Listen to Him.
> When the disciples heard it, they fell facedown and were terrified.
> (Matt. 17:4–6)

Among all the issues raised by this dramatic encounter, God established a pattern of positional authority when He admonished Peter for having the audacity to think he could place Elijah and Moses on the same level as the Son of God. In so doing, God's Word helps us to understand the nature of a cult. A cult is any religion that places any person on a level equal to or higher than the Lord Jesus Christ. Period!

And so we find the Father, the Son, and redeemed man involved in this section of Jesus' prayer. Man is the subject of the conversation but is not a participant in the conversation. But the mere fact that he is included as the subject under discussion makes him part of an exclusive group of people.

This exclusive prayer of the Lord Jesus directs the attention of the reader toward an exclusive group of people for whom the Son of Man was about to die. As Jesus prepared to go to the cross, He provided a résumé of those given to Him by the Father. They are clearly defined as the "all" who may "know You, the only true God" (John 17:3). These are the people God gave to the Son, and what follows is Jesus' definition of what a Christian ought to look like.

My senior year in high school was packed with athletics and the inevitable battle to get the right grades! But the thing I remember most clearly was the day we all received our military papers. Every able-bodied high school student was conscripted to serve, regardless! Even conscientious objection, for any reason, was unacceptable to the regime that controlled the country.

For some reason I was duly "selected" to enter The School of Armor, an elite officer's training institute for tank and armored warfare. It was the officer's division of the First Special Services Battalion. I arrived with the other 325 men in less than ceremonial fashion after a long train ride that was more like riding in a cattle truck. Six months later I was commissioned as a second lieutenant and shipped off to South West Africa, now known as Namibia. I was assigned to D-Squadron, "Desert Rats," and was based out of Rooikop just north of Walvis Bay in the heart of the Namib Desert.

When the day arrived for me to return to civilian life, I struggled, in a way, to get accustomed to the loss of my exclusive band of brothers. We had gone through a great deal together. We had come to depend on one another in a strange sort of way, perhaps united by the common pursuit of survival. We had trained together, hurt together, laughed together, and even hated together. We were an exclusive bunch of self-styled bandits, united by a common mission and a common purpose even though we were an uncommon selection of men.

Think about the disciples of Christ for a moment! An uncommon bunch of men and women, selected and chosen from every walk of life, united in a common purpose by one commanding officer!

On the human level we went through three phases in our military training. First, we began as nothing. We were, in fact, lower than the lowest! Any army recruit will understand exactly what I mean. Second, we became commissioned officers after a period of intense scrutiny. Nonetheless we were most certainly junior officers. Third, we gradually became seasoned officers. This third phase took time, discipline, hard experience, and a lot of determination. And even then I do not believe I ever arrived at the point where I fully matured into the kind of officer I was intended to be.

In a similar way, the Christian life is an exclusive life, and its membership is made up of an exclusively selected group of men, women, boys, and girls. These are the people presented in this prayer by our Savior.

As we hear God pray in this high priestly prayer of our Lord, we gain more insight into the progressive way in which people are invited to become joint heirs with the Son. The pattern of human existence from creation to eternal life is included in this section of Jesus' prayer. The cycle of eternal life is presented from the time of creation, to physical birth, to spiritual birth, and then on to eternal life.

Here is the cycle in simplistic and brief terms. All people begin as nothing outside of the Lord Jesus Christ. This is the way we are born of the flesh, lost in our trespasses and sins. Then we are recruited for service (by the Holy Spirit) and commissioned (converted) as officers (disciples) in the Lord's army. But we still begin this spiritual journey as babes in Christ or as junior officers who know little about the character and conduct expected of a follower of the Lord Jesus. Finally, we embark on a lifelong process of growth through the disciplines of the Christian faith, pushing on toward the goal of our high calling in Christ Jesus. I do not believe any of us ever arrive spiritually to the point at which we can truly say we have risen to the level where our Lord and Savior considers us complete. We will only attain perfection when we hear the Savior welcome us into the presence of our Father in heaven.

The Son of Man sets this commonality of origin, state of being, and mission purpose in eternal concrete in this prayer! Through words we discover exactly what a true disciple of Jesus Christ looks like. No one outside the Godhead is consulted. No church constitution is analyzed. No opinion polls are taken! Jesus Christ is "the way, the truth, and the life" (John 14:6) and the only true change that can possibly take place in a person's life and attitude takes place through the transforming power of the gospel!

The truth of the life-changing power of the gospel as the only agent of genuine and lasting change has never been appreciated or fully understood. It can never, nor will it ever, be understood by a pagan world. The lessons learned from the Lord Jesus Christ in His conversation with the Father continue to elude commanding officers, governments, and self-styled Napoleon Bonapartes to this day.

There are two dominant forms of paganism in the world—tribal paganism and religious paganism. Tribal paganism is best seen in Africa, and religious paganism is best seen in the Middle East. Every nation of the world, however, from the United States to Great Britain, from Australia to Europe, contains what are essentially significant elements of tribal and religious paganism. For generations governments and regimes of every description have gone to great lengths to change varying forms of governance and institutionalized rulership to suit the common good of all the people of a particular nation, all to no avail.

A good example of this is the effort to democratize Iraq. The removal of the tyrannical dictatorship of Saddam Hussein was essential and absolutely necessary, but the subsequent gallant effort to change a country from religious paganism to American-styled democracy is entirely another thing. It cannot be done outside the life-changing power of the gospel.

The only thing that can change people is that which can effect real change from the inside out, the power of the gospel! One of the greatest lessons we learn from history is that we never seem to learn any lessons from history!

Listen to this prayer carefully. Jesus is speaking to the Father about an exclusive group of people, created in the image of God, converted by the power of God, and ultimately changed by the work of God to the point at which they became new creations.

This exclusive prayer outlines for us the exclusive selection process whereby an exclusive set of people are selected by God to become sanctified and sent out to effect change in others. And this can only take place by means of "the truth" by which "they also may be sanctified" (John 17:19).

The debate over this issue has gone on for centuries. Does God, in fact, have an exclusive club of hand-chosen, pre-selected followers? And does this mean the majority of the others were selected for eternal damnation before they were even born? And what qualifies a person to become a Christian? Is there a set of rules or criteria to follow? Does a person need to prequalify somehow?

Few people have difficulty understanding the need to qualify for any given opportunity. Take the academic world, for example. Students study and apply themselves in various kinds of disciplines in order to make themselves eligible for certain types of work-related vocations. A good friend told me on one occasion that he had a "job opening" in his business. We spent a few minutes discussing the job itself, and then my friend told me the kind of person he was looking for. What was important, he said, was not simply the person's academic résumé but his or her "heart" résumé. The employer believed that the potential employee's personality and character were as much of a recommendation to him as anything else. He went on to tell me that he had built his vast business on people skills more than on academic qualifications. While academia was important, character superceded it.

As Jesus "spoke these things" (John 17:1), we hear the Son establish, once and for all, the means by which every believer becomes a disciple of the Lord, the evidence or proof of the Christian disciple, and the benefits made available to the disciple in and through the Lord Jesus Christ.

Before we begin to outline and analyze exactly what the Lord Jesus was saying about this exclusive group of believers, it will be helpful to give serious consideration to a significant part of Paul's teaching on this subject as a cross-reference. As far as Paul was concerned, the whole issue of spiritual conversion and regeneration is represented by the difference between the Spirit and the flesh. If, in fact, the Lord Jesus was given God's authority "over all flesh" (v. 2), then it followed that the end product of salvation was an absolute victory of the Spirit over the flesh. This is how Paul established this issue.

> I say then, walk by the Spirit and you will not carry out the desire
> of the flesh. For the flesh desires what is against the Spirit, and the
> Spirit desires what is against the flesh; these are opposed to each other,
> so that you don't do what you want. But if you are led by the Spirit,
> you are not under the law.
>
> Now the works of the flesh are obvious: sexual immorality,
> moral impurity, promiscuity, idolatry, sorcery, hatreds, strife,

jealousy, outbursts of anger, selfish ambitions, dissensions, factions, envy, drunkenness, carousing, and anything similar, about which I tell you in advance—as I told you before—that those who practice such things will not inherit the kingdom of God.

But the fruit of the Spirit is love, joy, peace, patience, kindness, goodness, faith, gentleness, self-control. Against such things there is no law. Now those who belong to Christ Jesus have crucified the flesh with its passions and desires. If we live by the Spirit, we must also follow the Spirit. We must not become conceited, provoking one another, envying one another. (Gal. 5:16–26)

The contrast between the flesh and the Spirit is clearly presented here. The "works of the flesh" (v. 19) reveal the reality of a life disconnected from the life of Christ. Paul puts this revealing sin into three categories: first, sexual sin including immorality and impurity; second, worship sin including idolatry, witchcraft, and heresies; and third, character sin including hate, jealousy, and strife. Then Paul points to the releasing love of the Lord Jesus Christ by which these revealing sins have been crucified to death. The fruit of the Spirit is the evidence of a life changed forever by the Lord Jesus Christ. Paul's contention here is based on the presupposition that any encounter with the living Christ will always produce reflecting results. These reflecting results form the basis of the content of the Son's exclusive prayer.

Because "all Scripture is inspired by God and is profitable for teaching, for rebuking, for correcting, for training in righteousness, so that the man of God may be complete, equipped for every good work" (2 Tim. 3:16–17), the apostle was simply expanding the fabric of Jesus' prayer in this portrait of a disciple. Paul did so in his pastoral role and capacity. This, he was saying, is what the Son meant when He spoke of "the men You gave Me" (John 17:6) in His prayer to the Father.

This exclusive prayer focuses on the essential nature and character of the disciple of Christ and begins with man's point of origin.

Chapter 6

Jesus Announces the Greatest of All Blessings

"I have revealed Your name" (John 17:6).

Have you ever been introduced to someone you had always wanted to meet? Perhaps that "someone" was unapproachable or too important to be bothered with you? Perhaps you spent hours on end begging someone else to act as a go-between and make the necessary introductions. Perhaps this is exactly how you met the love of your life!

A number of years ago my telephone rang. On the line was one of the dearest and most precious men I have ever had the pleasure of knowing in all my life. It was George Beverly Shea! This humble servant of the Lord Jesus Christ asked me a simple question: "Don, do you remember that incredible time you had with Dr. Billy Graham in Scotland?"

"Yes, sir," I replied.

"I was wondering if you would mind if I included it in my latest book, *How Sweet the Sound*?" Bev asked me.

And so I was honored and humbled to think that an event in my life would find its way into a book written by a man used so mightily of the Lord across the world.

Little did I realize back then the significance of the life lesson God would teach me. It all began when my good friend, Johnny, longtime Billy Graham radio producer for Dr. Graham and Cliff Barrows, invited me to accompany him to the Billy Graham Scotland crusades. It turned into a major learning experience for me in more ways than I could ever recount.

On one special occasion I found myself at the dinner table in Edinburgh in the company of many of the team members. Sitting opposite from me was none other than Sir David McNee, retired commissioner of police of the Metropolis (London) based at Scotland Yard. Sir David was serving as the chairman of the Billy Graham Scotland Crusades and was one of the most respected men in the United Kingdom. We struck up a wonderful conversation that centered around my Scottish heritage and New Orleans jazz music. I told him all about my grandparents and also about the French Quarter in the Crescent City and that one can walk around in certain places and hear jazz musicians playing their instruments, even on the sidewalks around Café Du Monde. Little did I realize just how important that meeting would be to me the next day.

Later that evening Johnny came to me with the exciting news that Dr. Graham had been invited to address the Scottish Parliament, an honor few foreign dignitaries are ever afforded. Johnny pointed out to me that only a few tickets had been issued to members of the Billy Graham team to accompany the evangelist up the hill. "You are not one of them!" he told me with a smile on his face.

Johnny followed up my letdown with a suggestion that I go to the castle and simply position myself to see all the dignitaries who would arrive to hear Dr. Graham speak. They would be coming from all over the world, he said. It would be worth my while just to stand outside the gates and watch the procession.

And so I went!

While standing there, awestruck by the occasion, I was suddenly approached by one of Dr. Graham's top men who was, himself, on the way into Parliament. Around his neck hung one of those prized tickets of entry! He had access! He had the right connections! He had permission to enter the Scottish holy of holies!

Well, I thought, *if he can go in there, so can I—permission or no permission!*

One can only imagine the picture of this relatively short preacher from New Orleans walking (nervously) alongside that tall Texan as together we passed through one security gate after another. One can only imagine just how tight the security was in a place like that and on an occasion like the one about to take place. Fortunately, one security guard after another looked in our direction and saw not this diminutive little American preacher with a strange sounding Southern accent but a tall, strong, and determined man with a straight jaw and the absolute blessing of the highest authority in the land hanging around his neck! I even tried to look the part and am certain my best American accent came to the fore with phrases like, "How ya'll doin'!"

By the time I had successfully passed through all the checkpoints without being arrested and hauled off to the Tower for public execution, I was a nervous wreck. I found myself on the upper deck of the parliament, not unlike the upper balcony in the United States House of Representatives. I stepped down a stair or two and summarily seated myself in the absolute most comfortable seat I believe I have ever sat in.

When I looked up, I stared in disbelief as I observed what seemed like every television camera in the world pointed in my direction from the opposite side of the upper balcony where I sat. The next minute I heard a commotion and looked around to see none other than Dr. Billy Graham being escorted to the seat immediately in front of mine. As he sat down, he looked around at Larry to greet him, and, of course, most courteously greeted me.

When he did so, I knew immediately that he knew that I knew that I was not supposed to be there! I felt like a little boy with his hand caught in the cookie jar! I smiled sheepishly and even tried to look like I was a secret service agent, there to protect and to serve. Beads of sweat began to break out on my brow!

Then I heard another commotion behind me. I turned and saw a line of officials being seated in the row behind me. At the end of the row sat none other than Sir David McNee, the top cop in all of the British Empire!

Standing next to him with his hands behind his back was the captain of the security guard for the Scottish Parliament. To this day I will never understand myself, but I just could not stop turning my head and looking at this captain as if I was begging for him to come and allow me to join the ranks of Braveheart and the many other heroes who had died for the cause!

Finally the captain of the guard turned to Sir David while pointing directly at me and said at the top of his voice, "Sir David, who is that man?"

Sir David looked at me. My whole life began to flash before my eyes in a desperate final act. I knew that he knew that I was not supposed to be there. After all, Sir David was most likely the one who had issued the tickets!

While still staring expressionless at me, Sir David said at the top of his voice, "It's all right, Captain. He's with me!"

I cannot tell you the relief I experienced at that moment. A calm came over me, and my whole being seemed to unravel back into its proper perspective. I was free at last!

The captain of security left his station and came up behind me. He leaned over my left shoulder and whispered very politely, "Excuse me, sir. I wonder if you would be so kind as to move into that section over there. The seat you're sitting in is the Royal Box!"

Have mercy on my soul! I was sitting in the Queen's chair!

Needless to say I moved. And then was privileged to hear Billy Graham deliver one of the most remarkable addresses on the gospel of the Lord Jesus Christ I have ever heard.

This is what I learned that day in Scotland. God showed me that, in a sense of human understanding, this is what it is going to be like when I arrive at the gates of heaven. There is a sense in which God the Father is going to look at me from the throne of God and say at the top of His voice, "Son, who is that man with You?"

And the Son is going to say to the Father: "It's OK, Father, he's with Me!"

George Beverly Shea even wrote a song about this experience:

"He's with Me"

Oh, wonder of wonders
The worlds cannot equal;
Nothing can compare
When I hear
My Savior say,
"He's with me!"

Jesus says, "He's with me!"
Leave him alone.
The world is calling,
And Jesus says,
"He's with me!"

The folly of sin,
The foolishness of man
Is only redeemed by our Savior's hand.
"I am not worthy,"
We all want to say:
But Jesus reaches out and says,
"He's with Me!"
—from *How Sweet the Sound* (page 256)

Just as Sir David was the only man who had the authority to give me permission to be in that place, so we hear the Son make an announcement concerning the greatest of all blessings: "I have revealed Your name" (John 17:6).

Let's understand the significance of this statement. Because the Lord Jesus Christ is the Son of God, because Jesus Christ was completely obedient to the Father and came down to this earth; because Jesus Christ laid aside His essential glory so that He could become the substitute for the sin of man, He thereby gained the Father's permission to reveal God. Only the Son of God could have done this.

Remember that the Old Testament way of gaining access to God had failed because man was unable to touch the untouchable One. Only the high priest could enter the holy of holies. Jesus was now the means by which God would be revealed during "these last days."

Two important questions must be asked at this point. Both of them will help us to understand more clearly the nature and character of God's revelation. These two questions are: How does Jesus reveal the name of God, and what is revealed through the revelation of the name of God? What could be a greater blessing than to know that we can know God?

How Does Jesus Reveal the Name of God?

Jesus reveals God in two ways. These two important statements of biblical fact will assist a greater understanding of the means by which the Son makes the Father's name known.

HE DOES SO AS THE MANIFESTATION OF THE FATHER'S NAME

This is a magnificent fact to contemplate. As the manifestation of God, the Lord Jesus is the absolute clearest evidence of all that God is. If the word *manifest* means "to make clear or evident to the eye," then Jesus reveals God because He is "the exact expression [image] of His [the Father's] nature" (Heb. 1:3). We have already seen this in the inner prayer.

Most parents fill up with pride and gratitude when other people comment on how much "Poofykins looks just like her daddy," even though we all know the good comes with the bad. I don't know how many times Karyn and I have commented on all the good things our children have inherited from us in their genetic makeup and how many not-so-good things they have inherited too.

Not so when it comes to the Lord Jesus. When He claimed to have "revealed Your name to the men You gave Me from the world" (John 17:6), He was referring to the way He talked, the way He worked, the way He loved, the way He disciplined, the way He became angry without sinning—the way He was in every way. In every circumstance He manifested God's nature and character exactly!

In the flesh Jesus became the outward and humanly perceptible indicator of the exactness of God the Father, without error! And as the manifestation of the Father, He was the full and complete revelation of God in His person—just as He was, even without doing anything.

I remember times when various people found themselves hurting for whatever reason. One dear woman, in particular, called me one day and just cried over the phone. "What's wrong?" I asked her. "Pastor, ever since my husband of sixty years went to be with the Lord, I feel so lonely!"

I went to visit her, and after a few hugs and comforting words, I confess I ran out of things to say. So we just sat there. She took my hands in hers after a while and said something important to me. "Pastor," she said, "what means more to me than any words you may share or anything you may do is just to have someone like you here in person. You don't even have to say anything. Your presence says it all!"

As the manifestation of God, the Lord Jesus made God known solely by virtue of who He was in person. His presence was an exact display of the person of God.

HE DOES SO AS THE MANIFESTOR OF THE FATHER'S NAME

By virtue of His essential glory, Jesus is the manifestation of all that God is because He is God! But He is also the manifestor of all that God is by virtue of His acquired glory. His acquired glory is the glory He put on when He became sin for us, even though He knew no sin. In His acquired glory in the flesh, He passes along and reveals the name of God by doing the work of the One that sent Him. As manifestor He is our access to God, passing to us four major attributes of God:

1. The holiness of God
2. The faithfulness of God
3. The fullness of God
4. The love of God

The Son is the perfect and exact picture of the Father. A close friend shared with me the story of a rather well-known author and speaker who was traveling through an airport in the United States. Because of his extensive travel schedule, he had developed the habit of carrying all of his personal effects, including his identification pictures and such, around his neck in a traveler's pouch. On this particular occasion he made the mistake of leaving this pouch at home. The person at the ticket check-in counter asked him for his identification, which, of course, he had left at home. The official informed the author that he would not be able to give him permission to pass through the gate and to board his plane. After thinking for just a moment, this famous man told the official he would be right back. With that he ran quickly to the airport bookstore and purchased one of his books that had his picture and biography printed clearly on the cover. The official looked at the picture on the cover of the book and, after comparing the cover picture with the real picture of the face standing before him, he graciously allowed the man to continue his journey. Evidently the official was totally satisfied that they were, indeed, the same person!

During His earthly ministry, the Son of Man revealed in John 17 the true identity of the only true God in three major ways:

1. Through His person: "I have glorified You" (v. 4).
2. Through His works: "The work You gave Me to do" (v. 4).
3. Through His words: "They have received them" (v. 8).

The true nature and character of God the Father was blazoned on the cover of the life, work, and testimony of the Lord Jesus Christ. Every time anyone looked at the Son in every capacity of His ministry on earth, they looked at the face of God and saw Him as He really is.

In summary then, the Son reveals the name of God as the manifestation of God as well as the manifestor of God. Both His person and His work are active agents involved in making God known to man. What a blessing, indeed!

What Does the Name of God Reveal?

We have tried to understand the first of two important questions related to Jesus' revelation of the name of God. He does so as the manifestation and the manifestor of God's name. The revelation of God's name is the unveiling of the character of God.

Some people in the United States will remember the Duke University lacrosse rape case. Following a party one night, a young woman who had been invited to strip for the players accused three of them of rape and assault. The district attorney brought an indictment against the three men, and for more than a year their case was put on public display across the country. Eventually the three were declared to be innocent of all charges. At their press conference, one of the young men correctly asked, "How can we regain our lost character?" Character is the most valuable asset a person can have.

The nature and character of God is a window to the heart of a God who loves us despite ourselves. The Son's claim, to have "revealed Your name to the men You gave Me" (John 17:6) is a direct reference to the role He played in giving eternal life. By His definition, eternal life is knowing You, "the only true God" (v. 3). It follows that the revelation of the name of God is nothing short of the presentation of the facts related to the character of God. Jesus did exactly this through His person and by means of His work.

The names of God in the Bible serve as a road map for the character of God. They reveal His true nature to us. Every time the Lord Jesus revealed the Father's name, a number of spiritual things were taking place. For one, they were being introduced to who He is as God. They were also being presented with what He does as God. Every name carried with it a description of His ability as God.

The psalmist says, "The LORD is a refuge for the oppressed, a refuge in times of trouble" (Ps. 9:9). Anyone who places their faith and trust in such a God finds refuge and a stronghold in times of trouble. In another example we find Gideon cowering in fear when "the Lord said to him, 'Peace to you. Don't be afraid, for you will not die.' So Gideon built an altar to the LORD there and called it Yahweh Shalom" (Judg. 6:23–24). It follows again that revealing God to the people meant they had solid evidence in a shaky world to find peace.

The very name of God was a revelation of His magnificence as God. The Hebrews understood this as well as anyone because the Hebrew names of God are powerful indicators of His character and nature.

Adonai-Jehovah means "the Lord our Sovereign."

El-Elyon means "the Lord Most High."

El-Olam means "the everlasting God."

El-Shaddai means "the God who is sufficient for the needs of His people."

Jehovah-Elohim means "the eternal Creator."

Jehovah-Jireh means "the Lord our provider."

Jehovah-Nissi means "the Lord our banner."

Jehovah-Ropheka means "the Lord our healer."

Jehovah-Shalom means "the Lord our peace."

Jehovah-Tsidkenu means "the Lord our righteousness."

Jehovah-Mekaddishkem means "the Lord our sanctifier."

Jehovah-Sabaoth means "the Lord of hosts."

Jehovah-Shammah means "the Lord is present."

Jehovah-Rohi means "the Lord our shepherd."

Jehovah-Hoseenu means "the Lord our maker."

Jehovah-Eloheenu means "the Lord our God."

A large religious organization found itself dealing with the issue of having to find a replacement for the chief executive officer. For months they conducted an intense search. Many people waited anxiously because they had stock in the company. Opinions were shared, and advice was given as to who the person ought to be to replace the retiring executive. The futures of many people rested on the decision. Without proper leadership at the top, the company could quickly find itself in bad shape.

The day of the big announcement arrived. All the stockholders gathered in a hotel conference room. The chairman of the search committee stood to his feet and began to extol the virtues of the man they had found. He spent at least thirty minutes delving into his character, his abilities, and his potential. Everything was almost too good to be true. They had found the perfect person! Then the chairman announced the man's name. He stepped out from behind a curtain. The people saw him. They knew him by reputation. They immediately matched his name and his character. They knew they had been presented with the right man, the only man who could save the company and carry out the work necessary to take them all to new heights. They were willing to follow him and act on his every command. They were in the best hands. They stood as one and applauded!

The revelation of God by the Son is not unlike the presentation of the chief by the chairman. If you will forgive me for trying to "modernize" the words of the Lord Jesus as He looked up into the heavens and poured His heart out to the Father, this is what He said: "My Father, in these few moments just before I bring to a conclusion the work You have given Me to do while on this earth, I want to talk with You about our children. They are an exclusive group of people because they have believed on Your name. In a few days I will be coming back to heaven to be with You. I cannot wait to be restored to the same glorious position I had with You from before the world began. But we must talk about these precious followers of Mine who have tried their best to honor Me. They have failed so many times, but I do not condemn them. Using the authority You gave Me to give them eternal life, I am pleased to tell You that they have put their faith and trust in You, believing that You are, indeed, the one true God. The way I accomplished this was by revealing Your name to them. They could not do this on their own. Thank You for giving them to Me!"

Jesus then shifts the focus of this exclusive prayer from the One who is revealed to the people to whom He is revealed!

Chapter 7

Jesus Reveals the Point When It All Began

In the opening part of His prayer, it is important for us to note that the Lord Jesus uses the phrase "from the world" to describe the point of origination for all of "the men You gave Me."

The Lord Jesus breaks down God's human creation into three components in this high priestly prayer. These three components are "states of being" for every living person. All people ever born find themselves in one of these three states of being. And the supreme goal of evangelism is to "go . . . and make disciples of all nations" (Matt. 28:19). In other words the work assigned to all believers is to take the message of the gospel to all people so that all people may move from the initial state of being to the final state of being. The Great Commission of Matthew 28 is the command for all believers to engage in sharing the gospel so that "all nations" will move from the created state of being to the converted state of being to the sanctified state of being. In terms of the evangelism formula, this encompasses a movement from salvation evangelism to discipleship evangelism and ultimately to disciple-making evangelism.

At the conclusion of this exclusive prayer, Jesus connects His life of sacrifice and sanctification to that of every believer. He prayed, "As You sent Me into the world, I also have sent them into the world" (John 17:18).

I want to take you through these states of being. I propose to describe each state briefly from the perspective of Jesus' exclusive prayer. In verse 6 He speaks of created man; in verse 8 He speaks of believing man, and in verse 19 He concludes by sending out sanctified man.

Created Man (Who Is a Candidate for Salvation Evangelism)

Every human being, created in God's image, begins at this point. This is the point of origin and the essence of human existence. This is the logical beginning point in life's journey and encompasses the reason man was created in the first place.

According to the evangelism formula previously outlined in chapter 4, man is eligible for the salvation offered in and through the sacrifice of the Lord Jesus Christ. As simplistic as it may sound, man has to be born in the flesh in order to be born of the Spirit. But while water birth is not the choice of the one being born, Spirit birth is the choice of the one who has been born.

Admittedly, a great theological tension exists at this point between our free will and God's divine choice. This tension lies at the heart of election and predestination. God, undoubtedly, "gave them to Me" (v. 6) because they were His to give. They were God's by virtue of His created ownership over them, not because of His predestined offering of grace to certain ones of them. They came from the heart of God who made them in His image with the express purpose of having fellowship through worship with Him. As man hides in the garden of his sinfulness, he chooses whether or not to respond to the voice of God who actively seeks him out. If he responds to that voice of grace and mercy, he finds a Savior who laid down His life for the redemption of that man. If he rejects and turns away from the voice of God, he becomes guilty of the unpardonable sin, which is the sin of rejecting the Holy Spirit, the only means by which a person can come to know the Lord Jesus Christ as personal Savior and Lord.

While it is not the object of this book to write a defense of either the choice of God or the free will of man, only the Lord Jesus knows what lies beneath. During His third appearance to the disciples after His resurrection, Jesus found a few of them busy doing what they had done before they accepted His call to follow Him. They were fishing, but this time as their profession! Peter, of course, was still smarting from his denial of the Savior. Perhaps he was sulking in his guiltiness. Perhaps he was overcome by his self-condemnation over the fact that he had forsaken his calling into the ministry and went back to what he had done before he met the Lord Jesus and answered the call.

Observe what these men were doing and focus on the fish:

> "I'm going fishing," Simon Peter said to them.
>
> "We're coming with you," they told him. They went out and got into the boat, but that night they caught nothing.
>
> When daybreak came, Jesus stood on the shore. However, the disciples did not know it was Jesus.
>
> "Men," Jesus called to them, "you don't have any fish, do you?"
>
> "No," they answered.
>
> "Cast the net on the right side of the boat," He told them, "and you'll find some." So they did, and they were unable to haul it in because of the large number of fish. (John 21:3–6)

What happened here lies at the heart of evangelism. First, the men were fishing. They were doing everything they knew to catch fish. Jesus has told us to become fishers of men! They accepted the fact that there were fish present, and they were prepared to do whatever it took to catch them. This lies at the heart of the commission of the Lord to go into the world and fish! But only Jesus knew what lay beneath the water. He told them where to cast the net, and all He required of them was absolute obedience to His command. This is what lies at the heart of the sovereign choice and command of God who created us and knows us from before we were even born.

I have always seen the correlation between predestination and election as a picture of two parallel railroad tracks. They run together forever and are both vital to the train that must stay on track. I have also pictured in my mind a motor speedway, which symbolizes the track of life. Here I am, in my car, driving down the highway of life. In the distance I notice a large sign that reads most clearly, "Whosoever believes in Him." As I drive under the sign and pass on through it, I turn back in my seat and continue pressing toward the finish line. Then I notice that there is writing on the other side of the same sign. As I look back, I read "You are My elect." And with that I cross the finish line and hear a wonderful and most familiar voice say to me, "Well done, good and faithful slave!" Come and "share your Master's joy!" (Matt. 25:21).

And all of this began at the beginning when man and woman were created by the hand of God.

> Then God said, "Let Us make man in Our image, according to
> Our likeness. They will rule the fish of the sea, the birds of the sky,
> the animals, all the earth, and the creatures that crawl on the earth.
>
> So God created man in His own image;
> He created him in the image of God;
> He created them male and female.
>
> God blessed them, and God said to them, "Be fruitful, multiply,
> fill the earth, and subdue it. Rule the fish of the sea, the birds of
> the sky, and every creature that crawls on the earth." God also said,
> "Look, I have given you every seed-bearing plant on the surface of the
> entire earth, and every tree whose fruit contains seed. This food will
> be for you, for all the wildlife of the earth, for every bird of the sky,
> and for every creature that crawls on the earth—everything having the
> breath of life in it. I have given every green plant for food." And it was
> so. God saw all that He had made, and it was very good."
> (Gen. 1:26–31)

These are the men Jesus referred to when He referenced them by saying, "You gave [them] to Me from the world" (John 17:6). In this context Jesus was placing man at his point of origin, in the hands of Creator God.

Earlier in His life and ministry, the Lord Jesus went to great lengths to explain the significance of man's created state of being to Nicodemus as it (water birth) related to the issue of salvation. Here was this most learned man who came to Jesus at night and asked how He could do the things He did—signs, miracles and wonders—that defied human explanation. Jesus seized the opportunity to remind this ruler of the Jews that water birth was the first but insufficient step to being born again.

Jesus replied, "I assure you: Unless someone is born again, he cannot see the kingdom of God."

"But how can anyone be born when he is old?" Nicodemus asked Him. "Can he enter his mother's womb a second time and be born?"

Jesus answered, "I assure you: Unless someone is born of water and the Spirit, he cannot enter the kingdom of God. Whatever is born of the flesh is flesh, and whatever is born of the Spirit is spirit. Do not be amazed that I told you that you must be born again." (John 3:3–7)

Later on, when Jesus was predicting His imminent departure, the Jews challenged Him and questioned His assertion that He would be going to a place where none of them (the Jews) could follow: "'You are from below,'" He told them, "I am from above. You are of this world; I am not of this world. Therefore I told you that you will die in your sins. For if you do not believe that I am He, you will die in your sins" (John 8:23–24).

Just prior to this conversation between the Son and the Father, the Lord Jesus reminded His disciples that they would face persecution because He had "chosen you out of [the world]" (John 15:19). The Lord Jesus even made a disclaimer to Pontius Pilate who challenged Jesus on His claim to be the King of the Jews.

Then Pilate went back into the headquarters, summoned Jesus, and said to Him, "Are You the King of the Jews?"

Jesus answered, "Are you asking this on your own, or have others told you about Me?"

"I'm not a Jew, am I?" Pilate replied. "Your own nation and the chief priests handed You over to me. What have You done?"

"My kingdom is not of this world," said Jesus. "If My kingdom were of this world, My servants would fight, so that I wouldn't be handed over to the Jews. As it is, My kingdom does not have its origin here." (John 18:33–36)

Paul used this logic to help the Corinthian Christians understand the complexities associated with life after death. In his long and definitive discourse in his first letter to the church at Corinth, he announced, "But now Christ has been raised from the dead, the firstfruits of those who have fallen asleep.

For since death came through a man, the resurrection of the dead also comes through a man. For just as in Adam all die, so also in Christ all will be made alive" (1 Cor. 15:20–22). They, of course, struggled to understand this fully in light of their own human limitations.

And so Paul turns the discussion to the nature of the resurrected body.

> So it is with the resurrection of the dead: Sown in corruption, raised in incorruption; sown in dishonor, raised in glory; sown in weakness, raised in power; sown a natural body, raised a spiritual body. If there is a natural body, there is also a spiritual body. So it is written: The first man Adam became a living being; the last Adam became a life-giving Spirit. However, the spiritual is not first, but the natural; then the spiritual. (1 Cor. 15:42–46)

This is clear. Water birth comes first, then spiritual birth. Jesus came to this earth to die for people! And every living person is eligible to receive God's gift of eternal life through His Son, the Lord Jesus Christ. People are the focus of all Jesus has done, which explains why Paul reminded his readers that all will die physically only once, after which we will face the judgment of God.

Believing Man (Who Is a Candidate for Discipleship Evangelism)

If created man is the point of origin and the initial state of being, then believing man is the second. The first state of being renders us eligible for salvation; the second renders us eligible for discipleship. All believers are disciples of the Lord Jesus Christ. But the journey of the disciple from spiritual infancy to spiritual adulthood is called discipleship. Discipleship is the growth arm of the process whereby the born-again believer graduates from the class for beginners to the class of senior graduates.

Three words spoken by the Lord Jesus define this person: "They have believed" (John 17:8). The great Protestant reformer Martin Luther came to a radical realization of this fact when he understood Paul's admonition to the church at Rome: "For I am not ashamed of the gospel, because it is God's power for salvation to everyone who believes, first to the Jew, and also to the Greek.

For in it God's righteousness is revealed from faith to faith, just as it is written: The righteous will live by faith" (Rom. 1:16–17).

Note the meaning of *salvation* at this point. The key word at its basic understanding means "deliverance." This conjures up our understanding of the power of the gospel of Jesus Christ to deliver sinful man from the anger of a righteous God. Salvation results in eternal deliverance to an eternal heaven and removes condemnation to an eternal hell. The emphasis on the word *believe* points to the active ingredient necessary to maybe initiate the reality of this eternal rescue operation called "salvation."

The word *believe* points to the second state of being that is vitally connected to the ongoing activity of salvation. To *believe* means "to trust or rely completely on or have faith in (the Lord Jesus Christ)." It is nearly always used in the present tense that is an indicator of the ongoing nature of salvation. The ongoing nature of salvation emphasizes God's continuing action related to salvation. Here's how this works.

God has always been active in providing the means for people to be reconciled to Him. When the Lord Jesus came to this earth and died for our sin, this event occurred as a historical fact in time past. When people confess that Jesus is Lord and believe that God raised Jesus from the dead, they are saved at that moment in time present. But they continue to be saved through the process of sanctification until they are ultimately saved eternally through glorification. So there are three stages of believing that all signify the movement of the salvation process from death to life: I am saved because of what Jesus did—past tense. I am saved because of what I have believed—present tense. I am being saved because of what I am becoming—future tense. In doctrinal terms salvation is led by justification, followed by sanctification, and rewarded with glorification!

With these principles providing the background of our understanding of a belief that produces salvation, it is important to analyze the substance of that belief. What exactly did the members of this exclusive fraternity believe? In this exclusive prayer Jesus defined the basis of their belief in three ways.

First, they believed that every person given to the Son was given by God. Second, they believed that everything ("all things") Jesus did was given by God. And third, they believed that every word that came out of the mouth of the Son of Man was spoken by God.

THE THREE THINGS THEY BELIEVED

Every Person Given to the Son Was Given by God

"I have revealed Your name to the men You gave Me from the world" (John 17:6).

As we have already seen in the section on created man, this exclusive group of people who qualified as believers had a simple faith and trust in God's ability to create man. In short, man had his origin in the heart of a sovereign God.

Everything Done by the Son Was Done by God

"Now they know that all things You have given to Me are from You" (John 17:7).

The question is, What "things" did the Father give the Son as a means to accomplish His earthly work? Jesus did things as part of His work in accomplishing God's purpose for redemption. What follows is just a sample selection of some of these things.

The Authority to Give Eternal Life. The apostle John wrote about this authority when he addressed the issue of the sureness of God's testimony.

> If we accept the testimony of men, God's testimony is greater, because it is God's testimony that He has given us about His Son. (The one who believes in the Son of God has the testimony in himself. The one who does not believe God has made Him a liar, because he has not believed in the testimony that God has given about His Son.) And this is the testimony: God has given us eternal life, and this life is in His Son. The one who has the Son has life. The one who doesn't have the Son of God does not have life. (1 John 5:9–12)

This was exactly what the Son claimed when He stated, "You gave Him authority over all flesh" (John 17:2).

The Ability to Perform Signs and Wonders. This is a repeated theme throughout the life and ministry of the Lord Jesus. Following the second prediction of His death, the Messiah appointed seventy others to go out ahead of Him in pairs to every town and place where He was about to go. The narrative description of their actions and activities was accompanied by the Savior's promise and assurance that "all things have been entrusted to Me by My Father" (Luke 10:22).

Shortly after the Lord Jesus had been rejected at Chorazin, Bethsaida, and Capernaum, He uttered a deliberate prayer to the Father.

> At that time Jesus said, "I praise You, Father, Lord of heaven and earth, because You have hidden these things from the wise and learned and revealed them to infants. Yes, Father, because this was Your good pleasure. All things have been entrusted to Me by My Father. No one knows the Son except the Father, and no one knows the Father except the Son and anyone to whom the Son desires to reveal Him."
> (Matt. 11:25–27)

Here the Jewish leaders are ironically identified as wise and prudent while the disciples and followers of the Lord Jesus are identified as babies. The irony lies in the fact that God had revealed Himself to mere infants, and the way He had done so was through the things He had entrusted to the Son. This is not only a powerful affirmation of the sovereignty of God over all the affairs of man, but it is a powerful statement of the divine will of the Father. It had been given to Him alone and was accomplished through His God-given ability to perform signs and wonders. This, of course, amounted to nothing short of utter blasphemy in the eyes and opinion of the Jewish leaders. It would not be long before His healings on the Sabbath and His claims to be God would lead the Pharisees to plot "against Him, how they might destroy Him" (12:14).

The Power to Forgive Sin. We have discussed the issue of Jesus' right to claim the authority of the Father to "give eternal life to all You have given Him" (John 17:2). The central issue related to the forgiveness of sin was the cause of much consternation among His critics who rallied together, believing He had provided them with an excuse to cry "blasphemy." In one particular instance Jesus was responding to the faith (belief) expressed by a group of friends who brought their paralytic friend to Him for healing. They simply believed He was the one who could do the impossible and heal their friend.

Just then some men brought to Him a paralytic lying on a stretcher. Seeing their faith, Jesus told the paralytic, "Have courage, son, your sins are forgiven."

At this, some of the scribes said among themselves, "He's blaspheming!"

But perceiving their thoughts, Jesus said, "Why are you thinking evil things in your hearts? For which is easier: to say, 'Your sins are forgiven,' or to say, 'Get up and walk'? But so you may know that the Son of Man has authority on earth to forgive sins"—then He told the paralytic, "Get up, pick up your stretcher and go home." (Matt. 9:2–6)

The Right to Be Called Messiah. If the basis of their belief was an acceptance of the things Jesus did by virtue of His authority to give eternal life, His ability to perform signs and wonders, His power to forgive sin, and an acknowledgment that these things came from God, then His claim to be the Messiah bore equal, if not more, weight. When the leaders turned against Him, He responded by healing all who came to Him because it showed His power as Messiah. Physical healings were rare in the Old Testament; and so Jesus' public display of healings, the raising of the dead, and the casting out of demons were designed to put His deity on display. These activities were coupled with gentleness and meekness, which proved the truthfulness and validity of Isaiah's assertion that the Messiah would not come with a political agenda but would declare the message of salvation—even to the Gentiles!

When Jesus became aware of this, He withdrew from there. Huge crowds followed Him, and He healed them all. He warned them not to make Him known, so that what was spoken through the prophet Isaiah might be fulfilled:

Here is My Servant, whom I have chosen,
My beloved in whom My soul delights;
I will put My Spirit on Him,
and He will proclaim justice to the nations.
He will not argue or shout,
and no one will hear His voice in the streets.

He will not break a bruised reed, and He will not put out a
  smoldering wick,
until He has led justice to victory.
The nations will put their hope in His name. (Matt. 12:15–21)

The question of His messianic identity infuriated the Jews at the best of times. Look at what happened to Him and the questions that were asked of Him in Jerusalem.

Some of the people of Jerusalem were saying, "Isn't this the man they want to kill? Yet, look! He's speaking publicly and they're saying nothing to Him. Can it be true that the authorities know He is the Messiah? But we know where this man is from. When the Messiah comes, nobody will know where He is from."

As He was teaching in the temple complex, Jesus cried out, "You know Me and you know where I am from. Yet I have not come on My own, but the One who sent Me is true. You don't know Him; I know Him because I am from Him, and He sent Me."

Then they tried to seize Him. Yet no one laid a hand on Him because His hour had not yet come. However, many from the crowd believed in Him and said, "When the Messiah comes, He won't perform more signs than this man has done, will He?" (John 7:25–31)

The Promise of an Imminent Return. Perhaps the most comforting thing the Lord Jesus told His disciples concerned the assuring words of His return. His departure had been firmly established even though they struggled to accept it and even believe it. In a similar fashion this group of men had become so bound together as brothers in the heart of the Lord Jesus that any suggestion of a rapid return of their Master was hard to understand but most welcome. This is what Jesus said to them: "Your heart must not be troubled. Believe in God; believe also in Me. In My Father's house are many dwelling places; if not, I would have told you. I am going away to prepare a place for you. If I go away and prepare a place for you, I will come back and receive you to Myself, so that where I am you may be also. You know the way where I am going" (John 14:1–4).

Admittedly, doubting Thomas needed a little help and explanation to convince him of all of these things, but the disciples accepted what Jesus said by faith. They believed Him.

Every Word Spoken by the Son Was Spoken by God

"Because the words that You gave Me, I have given them. They have received them" (John 17:8).

As obvious as it may seem, the way the disciples accepted the words spoken by the Lord Jesus was a great testimony to the depth of their faith in Him. We hear the Son of Man sharing the words of life with those who gathered around Him. Some believed and some did not.

In His exclusive prayer the Lord Jesus established the three steps taken by every believer who has come to the point of a full and unapologetic acceptance of the words of our Savior.

First, "they have received them." A believer is one who has allowed the words of God to be received. This speaks to the openness of a receptive heart. You may recall the wonderful parable of the seed and the sower in Matthew 13. Of the four kinds of soil described, Jesus highlighted the good soil where the seed fell and took root. The first step toward becoming a believer in Christ is to have a receptive and fertile heart, open and available to the Word of God.

In today's world too many people sit and even listen to the preaching and teaching of the Word of God, but their hearts are not open to receive the Word. People's minds are all too often cluttered with all the business of their lives, many are distracted continually, and the challenges presented by modern-day technology see many individuals sending e-mails, text messaging, and generally being distracted when the Word of God is being presented. The soil is not fertile. The first step is never taken!

Second, they "have known for certain that I came from You" (John 17:8). A believer is one who has not only received the Word of God but has accepted the source of the Word. This acceptance is the essence of believing faith—that it originated in the heart of the only true God. This second step leads logically to the third and final step.

Third, "they have believed that You sent Me." Bottom line—salvation! A person who believes that God sent His Son, the Lord Jesus Christ, to this earth has placed their faith and trust in God's plan for our redemption. Only the Spirit of God can accomplish this point of acceptance because it places ultimate faith in the righteousness of a holy God. The act of knowing for certain that Jesus Christ came from God is the distinguishing feature of Christianity. This is what separates God from all the other gods of this world!

There are many features of the words spoken by the Son. Here is a selection of some of these features:

- His words endure forever (Luke 21:33)
- His words point to eternal life (John 12:50)
- His words provide the basis for belief (John 8:30)
- His words demand habitual obedience (John 14:23)
- His words offer sound teaching and doctrine (1 Tim. 6:3)
- His words stand as faithful and true (Rev. 21:5)

There are hundreds more of these features, each one a distinguishing fact of the Christian faith and every one part and parcel of the growing disciples' operating manual for life. When the Son speaks to the Father about this exclusive group of believers, He presents a people who have accepted by faith all the accompanying features of His word.

Sanctified Man (Who Is a Candidate for Disciplemaking Evangelism)

"I sanctify Myself for them, so they also may be sanctified by the truth" (John 17:19).

This is the final state of being for every believer. I do not believe any Christian arrives at the ultimate point of sanctification because this occurs only at the moment of glorification when the believer is rewarded in the presence of God the Father in heaven.

The Lord Jesus connects the Word, which is truth, with the sanctifying of the believer. God's Word not only brings the believer joy, love, and peace but is also the means by which power for holy living is imparted. Practical holy living is the essence of Jesus' emphasis at this point. The practical issue of being set apart for God's service comes through the ministry of the Word of God and is affected by the Spirit of God. When Jesus taught about the vine and the branches shortly before this prayer, He made the connection between the Word and sanctified man by saying, "You are already clean because of the word I have spoken to you" (John 15:3).

As the disciple gradually grows in faith and understanding, He loves sin less and loves the Lord far more!

In this context the Son readily acknowledges that He was set apart for the specific purpose of accomplishing the Father's will. In John 4:34 Jesus responded to the disciples' concern for His need to eat by saying, "My food is to do the will of Him who sent Me and to finish His work." This was why He was ready to claim the rightful restoration of His glory with the Father. He was about to complete the "will of Him who sent Me." When He claimed to be "the bread of life" (John 6:35), He invoked the meaning of His sanctification by stating, "For I have come down from heaven, not to do My will, but the will of Him who sent Me" (v. 38). When asked about the source of His knowledge of the Scriptures, Jesus answered the Jews: "My teaching isn't Mine but is from the One who sent Me. If anyone wants to do His will, he will understand whether the teaching is from God or if I am speaking on My own. The one who speaks for himself seeks his own glory. But He who seeks the glory of the One who sent Him is true, and there is no unrighteousness in Him" (7:16–18).

In the final analysis the Lord Jesus stressed the urgency of His self-sanctification when He healed the man who was born blind. Pointing to the purpose for which the man was healed, Jesus said: "This came about so that God's works might be displayed in him. We must do the works of Him who sent Me while it is day. Night is coming when no one can work. As long as I am in the world, I am the light of the world" (John 9:3–5). Once again we find the Lord Jesus Christ leading the way.

The idea of spiritual sanctification is the setting apart of someone for the purpose of spiritual service. Believers are set apart for God and His purposes alone so that the believer only does what God wants done and literally rejects all other opportunities and options. And no specific or logical reason is needed outside of the fact that God is God! There is no other reason to do God's bidding other than that God demands we do His bidding! This is the basic premise of Peter's exhortation to "be holy, because I am holy!"

Therefore, get your minds ready for action, being self-disciplined, and set your hope completely on the grace to be brought to you at the revelation of Jesus Christ. As obedient children, do not be conformed to the desires of your former ignorance but, as the One who called you is holy, you also are to be holy in all your conduct; for it is written, Be holy, because I am holy. (1 Pet. 1:13–16)

This reminds me of one of my favorite illustrations about the matter of unquestioning obedience. All parents can easily identify with the precious manner with which teenagers manipulate the system (parents) to get permission to do whatever they intend to do. The conversation usually goes like this:

"Dad, can I go and hang out with all my friends tonight?"

"This is not a good night to be away from home, Poofykins!" Dad replies in as gentle a fashion as possible.

"Please, Dad, all my other friends' parents said all my other friends could hang out!"

"I'm sure they did, my sweet Poofykins, but your Mother and I have planned our time tonight."

"That's not fair, Dad! I promise you I'll be back (in time to wake the dog up)," she pleads with an ever increasing scowl on her face.

"No!"

"You always do this to me! Why can't I go and be with my friends. We never do anything anyway!"

"You mean the friend with the bull ring through his nose and the other one, what's-his-name, the one who has the tattoo of one of Marilyn Manson's eyes just under his left ear?"

"That's your problem, Dad! You just judge people! I hate the way you do that! Please Dad. Just this once!"

"No, honey!"

"Why can't I?"

"Because I said no!"

"But why, Daddy!"

"No, no, no. You can't go!"

"Why can't I go?"

"Because *Y* is a crooked letter and you can't make it straight!"

This is the bottom line of Peter's teaching on the subject. In a sense we are hearing the Son imploring the Father continually to sanctify believers by means of who He is. The results are described in a similar fashion to the gathering up of one's robes in ancient days in order to move more quickly and more effectively. The sanctifying process is the spiritual means by which all believers are assisted by the indwelling presence of the Holy Spirit through the Word of God to focus their attention on the grace of God that is made available to all believers.

The Christian disciple maker will progressively become more and more mature and sober minded in relation to the things of God. As he is set apart, he will develop a spiritual steadfastness, accompanied by a deep sense of self-control, clear thinking, and moral decisiveness. The indwelling presence of the Holy Spirit will enable him to be in charge of all he does, and he will have a deep and abiding sense of purpose for the Lord Jesus Christ. Knowing and doing the will of God will be paramount in all of his decisions because he will know that is the best and safest place to be.

Holiness essentially defines who the believer becomes and is the goal for which the Savior strives in the heart and life of every believer. This is why He concludes this exclusive prayer with "I sanctify Myself for them, so they also may be sanctified by the truth" (John 17:19).

Chapter 8

Jesus Establishes the Portrait of a Disciple

One of my fondest memories will always be related to the time when the Lord impressed on my heart that He was calling me to serve First Baptist Church in Spartanburg, South Carolina. I remember well the day my telephone rang and a man identified himself as Neil Philips, the chairman of the pastor search committee. The committee had been elected by the church to seek out a man and his wife who, they believed, was God's man to lead their church into the future and make a difference for the Lord Jesus Christ.

I had little idea just how dear and precious this man would become to me over the years. At this point we did not know each other. In all honesty I was not interested in leaving my beloved school of providence and prayer, the New Orleans Baptist Theological Seminary, where I was happy in the role the Lord had given me to serve Him there. I told Neil, in fact, that I was not looking for a job and meant every word of it. So what were they to do?

God knew otherwise, I guess! Through many means and after many weeks of soul-searching, a group of people in a place called Spartanburg and a couple from a place called New Orleans agreed with God that He had spoken and brought us together. What a wonderful place to be. Right in the center of God's will.

I have told many people since that day that the people who comprised the congregation in Spartanburg did not call me to that church. I have also added that neither Karyn nor I made the decision to move to Spartanburg. God made the decision. God issued the call. Both sides simply agreed with God. But both sides had the manual of absolute truth to go by! My testimony of my conversion experience and call into the ministry had to match God's portrait, not the members of the search committee. The question they had to ask was whether or not my compatibility aligned itself with the Scriptures, God's manual for personal behavior and practical discipleship. I, in turn, needed to be vitally interested in them not as a perfect church but as a people who were decidedly willing to follow the precepts and principles of the Word of God.

Now this is important to understand in light of this word from our Savior. As I understand the sovereign work of a sovereign God, I am reminded of Paul's exhortation to the people at Rome: "We know that all things work together for the good of those who love God: those who are called according to His purpose" (Rom. 8:28). The important point to make lies at the heart of the determination of God. He made us, He convicts us by His Spirit, and He determines what we should look like as believers. Our opinion is neither sought after nor valued. And that is important. People often struggle to differentiate between the people who make decisions and the people whose opinions about decisions are valued.

Many church congregations operate in this manner. A congregational form of church government does not negate the fact that the buck has to stop somewhere. Usually that final decision is left to the elders, the deacons, or the senior pastor. But the opinion of every member of that congregation is valued, which means their input in the matter at hand is not only encouraged but also practically sought after and valued. And here's the catch. The values and opinion of any member can sometimes sway the final decision, even if the final decision does not line up with the absolute truth of God's Word. Final decisions are often determined by power plays—the oldest member or the loudest voice. It is small wonder that so many churches are in serious trouble! The truth of the matter is that the New Testament church was not a democracy but a theocracy! It is God's church, and He is the "head of the body, the church" (Col. 1:18).

Three issues lie at the heart of the church. They are the most critical issues that face the church. A church that settles these issues will most likely by God's grace become a light in this dark world.

Three Critical Issues

THE ISSUE OF ABSOLUTE TRUTH

This is the most critical issue in the church today. The debate as to whether or not there is such a thing as absolute truth has raged for centuries. As believers we know the truth! This is how we were given eternal life by the Son, by knowing the only true God. Any understanding of absolute truth begins in the beginning with God (Gen. 1:1). The Bible is filled with absolute truth because God is truth. Jesus made the connection between truth and faith when He said to the Jews who had come to believe in Him, "If you continue in My Word, you really are My disciples. You will know the truth, and the truth will set you free" (John 8:31–32).

Absolutes are the governing principles of Christian conduct. They are the beacons of light that shine in darkness. I strongly believe that this is the most important principle upon which the church is built. Without it the church is in deep trouble because it is left to the opinions of man, and that is a dangerous place to be!

In a personal way, I have often encouraged God's people in our congregation never to compromise when it comes to absolute truth. If the Word of God supports it, do it. If the Word of God demands it, do it regardless of constitutions and bylaws. These documents ought to reflect absolute truth and not vice versa.

THE ISSUE OF PERSONAL CONVICTION

The issue of personal conviction is important in society. One would certainly pray that more and more people would increase in their personal convictions. Most student ministries spend major time, money, and effort endeavoring to teach their young people to cultivate strong personal convictions. Parents invest their lives in their sons and daughters, praying they will grow up to be men and women of deep and abiding personal conviction.

Personal convictions for the believer ought to find their root in absolute truth. The strong teaching of absolute truth will always produce future leaders who take their stand on strong personal convictions.

But personal conviction can never, and must never, become a substitute for absolute truth. Many congregations are smitten with strong personalities who have strong convictions about a great number of issues and things that are important, but if they are not absolute according to the Word of God, they cannot become the foundation upon which the believer stands.

THE ISSUE OF PERSONAL PREFERENCE

Now we have a potential problem, especially for believers who make up the local New Testament body of believers, the church. Personal preferences are the modus operandus for most people. The whole world is on a search, mostly trying to find satisfaction for personal preferences. If you want to see this in its purist form, simply station yourself at a fast-food window. While many may thoroughly enjoy a good hamburger, it will only take a few customers to help you realize the essential nature and character of personal preference. Some like their hamburgers well-done while some prefer medium-well, if not rare! Some want tomatoes; others would rather have three months on death row than eat a tomato!

Just take a peek inside the average church congregation. Many choose the church of their choice based only on one issue—personal preference. Most congregations are being ripped apart as a result. Some like to sit down; others prefer to stand. Some love the old-fashioned hymns of the faith; others love to sing choruses. Some people want the sanctuary warmer on Sunday mornings, others prefer it much cooler. Some like preachers who stand behind the pulpit and deliver homilies in a calm manner; others prefer the hell, fire, and brimstone approach to preaching.

Many churches are being built not on absolute truth but on personal preference! No wonder so many churches are dead and dying! No wonder the average tenure of the average pastor in the average church is only eighteen months. He arrives with much fanfare and great expectation, but after a few months have gone by, he gets a little too close to the line of preference for some of the members. When that happens, he is soon accused of everything under the sun, and in many cases the band of merry personal preferences stir the pot and express their personal displeasure because their personal preference is being threatened. Church meetings are called to order by the leaders of the pack, and the new pastor is sent packing. Then the next one arrives! The second verse is the same as the first!

When God prays, we, the church, hear the final word on every one of the issues and subjects raised by our Savior. Not once do we hear or see the Son beckon to the disciples and say, "Gentlemen, would you come over here for just a minute. I am so sorry to disturb your nap time, but I need to make a final decision about this exclusive group of people who have come to believe in the one true God. I am about to go to the cross to finish, once and for all, the only means by which all sinners can be reconciled to My Father. If you would be so kind as to help me think through a few important matters for a minute, I would certainly appreciate it. I will be leaving this earth to go back to heaven to be with the Father. I don't want to leave you as a bunch of orphans because you are not! But I do want you to help me come up with a résumé of what a Christian disciple ought to look like. Many churches over the generations will be looking for pastors to lead them. Many churches will be electing leaders from within the congregations to serve as leaders of the churches. Many of them will be developing bylaws and constitutions of every description that will determine who can join the church, what the church is comprised of, and how the church conducts its business.

"Gentlemen, I need your help. I don't ever want to be accused of being narrow-minded or dictatorial. I know what the future holds because I am already there. Some of the members of this exclusive group are going to live in turbulent and difficult times when people will be lovers of themselves, lovers of money, boastful, proud, blasphemers, disobedient to parents, ungrateful, unholy, unloving, irreconcilable, slanderers, without self-control, brutal, without love for what is good, traitors, reckless, conceited, lovers of pleasure rather than lovers of God, holding to the form of religion but denying its power!

"This is why I need to ask your opinion. During these days without Me around in the flesh, many people will worm their way into the churches. Gentlemen, there is nothing worse to Me than a dogmatic bunch of men who won't be gentle and loving when it comes to these things so that people like this won't have their feelings hurt. I did not come down to this world to hurt feelings. I came to accommodate every feeling and every opinion and fancy of all people. I love them so much, and all I want to do is make them happy and teach them how to get along with one another in a way that won't offend anybody. So let's gather around for a few minutes and come up with the portrait of a believer in a manner that accommodates all of you."

This issue lies at the heart of all Jesus has to say to the Father. Look at some of the issues we have already considered from the inner prayer:

1. The issue of heaven
2. The issue of God's timing
3. The issue of authority
4. The issue of the flash
5. The issue of eternal life
6. The issue of knowing God
7. The issue of the one true God
8. The issue of His work
9. The issue of Jesus' work
10. The issue of God's presence
11. The issue of Jesus' preexistence
12. The issue of glorification

Every one of these issues raised by our Savior stands or falls on the issue of absolute truth. This section of Jesus' prayer, which establishes the portrait of a disciple, rises and falls on the same issue. Are we willing to place our complete and utter faith and trust in His definition of a disciple, or are we only willing to accept part of this description? Or, perhaps we want to add a few pointers here and there to suit our individual needs and preferences. Hence this prayer on the eve of His sacrifice!

This would be His final word. What He had to say about this exclusive person would be written in stone for all the world to see. It would not only provide a résumé of the character and nature of these men, but it would be the mirror into which these men would forever be able to look as they sought to measure up to the expectation of the only One who could set the expectation!

In modern-day terminology, Jesus was providing the final word on the marks of the believer. Who are these people, and is it possible to describe them? He tells us what a Christian looks like, where he comes from, and what he can expect to receive from the Lord as he tries to live in this world.

It would seem that Jesus is alluding to fourteen distinguishing features of disciple. We will take a fairly brief look at each one and then use one litmus test in application as an example to consider. Some of these characteristics have been duly covered in other sections under discussion. Here, then, are fourteen descriptions that may help us better understand Jesus, the portrait of a disciple.

The Portrait of a Disciple

A PERSON WHO IS GIVEN BY GOD

My wife and I have been blessed in many ways. God has been so kind and gracious to us. Our two sons, Rob and Greg, have grown into two fine men. They love the Lord and serve Him with such determination and courage. It's hard to keep up with them as they preach and teach God's Word around the country. And then the Lord blessed us with a precious daughter-in-law, Annabeth, who brings us much joy and fills our hearts with gratitude to the Lord. When our oldest was just ten years of age, we thought we had it all, but our Savior had kept the most wonderful gift of all until last! A little girl! I shall never forget the day my Shelley Ann was born! Today she is all grown up, and her Daddy loves her even more! But what a special delivery! What a special gift she became to us as a family!

The disciple of the Lord Jesus Christ is God's gift to His Son. Jesus put it like this: "I have revealed Your name to the men You gave Me" (John 17:6). Enough said! How incredibly special indeed! We have taken a good look at this feature of the believer. What this means is simple. Every believer is a gift from God. *Webster's* defines a *gift* as "something given voluntarily" or "something bestowed or acquired without being sought after." God gave every believer as His gift to Jesus Christ! A gift is something special to both the giver of the gift and the receiver of the gift.

It may be helpful to consider the radical change that takes place in the life of every disciple. As God's special gift, the Christian disciple must have undergone a significant change of heart and life. "If you just knew where I came from" is a phrase often heard from people whose lives have been radically altered or changed from where they first began. I remember the wonderful story of a man who, at one time, was truly down and out. He spent his days scrounging for food and trying to raise his infant son in public restrooms and less-than-desirable places for a youngster to be brought up. Then one day his fortune changed. He went from the worst of circumstances to becoming rich and famous to the point at which even a wonderfully inspirational movie was made about his life. This is similar to the story of John Newton's great hymn "Amazing Grace"—"I once was lost, but now am found!" A movie was made about this remarkable journey as well, involving the great William Wilberforce who, together with the British prime minister, William Pitt, was instrumental in the emancipation of slavery that was the curse of the British Empire.

Corinth, in the time of Paul, was a busy city bound by every strain of sin imaginable. When the church was founded in that city, new believers had great difficulty in separating themselves from the world they had left behind. In Paul's letters to the church, this coming out from the world was presenting, perhaps, their greatest challenge as Christians. Evidently not a great deal distinguished them from the world. The first epistle, in fact, is really a treatise on the essentials of Christian discipleship. Consider some of the subjects addressed: divisions (1 Cor. 1:10f), godly wisdom (1:18f), boasting (1:26f), immaturity (3:1f), humility (4:6f), immorality (5:1f), lawsuits among believers (6:1f), marriage God's way (7:1f), idolatry (10:14f), order in church meetings (14:26f), and the list goes on. Paul addressed this issue in his second letter when he spoke to the matter of the ministry of reconciliation: "From now on, then, we do not know anyone in a purely human way. Even if we have known Christ in a purely human way, yet now we no longer know Him like that. Therefore if anyone is in Christ, there is a new creation; old things have passed away, and look, new things have come" (2 Cor. 5:16–17).

The implication here is that all believers are distinguishable by a dramatic change caused by a radical difference between what they were *in* the world and what they have become *out from* the world. In Colossians we find Paul once again stressing the point that the believer, who he refers to as "the new man," is bound to seek those things that are of God. The mind of the disciple is to be set on things that are above, not on those things that are from the place the believer came out from! Because the Christian has become born again, his "old man" has "died in Christ," and so his old life is hidden with the Messiah in God. He goes on to demonstrate the logical consequence of the practical life of someone who has been crucified with Christ Jesus.

> Therefore, put to death whatever in you is worldly: sexual immorality, impurity, lust, evil desire, and greed, which is idolatry. Because of these, God's wrath comes on the disobedient, and you once walked in these things when you were living in them. But now you must put away all the following: anger, wrath, malice, slander, and filthy language from your mouth. Do not lie to one another, since you have put off the old man with his practices and have put on the new man who is being renewed in knowledge according to the image of his Creator. . . . Therefore, God's chosen ones, holy and loved, put on heartfelt compassion, kindness, humility, gentleness, and patience, accepting one another and forgiving one another if anyone has a complaint against one another. Just as the Lord has forgiven you, so also you must forgive. (Col. 3:5–13)

As the Son of Man spoke these things to the Father, the most important issue of change is set in motion. If the believer has been given from the world, then all the world has to offer has been "put to death" (v. 5). This is why the believer becomes a new creation; the old has passed away, and all things have become brand-new. Under the inspiration of the Holy Spirit, Paul stressed this issue time without number to those who were placed under his pastoral charge. One example of this clearly demonstrates the mandate to leave the behaviors of this world from which you have been delivered. He was speaking in the context of one Christian bringing a lawsuit against another Christian. Such behavior mirrored the behavior of the world. Christian behavior ought to be different because the believer has been changed.

> Do you not know that the unjust will not inherit God's kingdom? Do not be deceived: no sexually immoral people, idolaters, adulterers, male prostitutes, homosexuals, thieves, greedy people, drunkards, revilers, or swindlers will inherit God's kingdom. Some of you were like this; but you were washed, you were sanctified, you were justified

in the name of the Lord Jesus Christ and by the Spirit of our God.
(1 Cor. 6:9–11)

Believers are, once again, given a reminder of the change that must be evident in the lives of those who have been given from out of the world. Someone has said that the greatest testimony for the good news of the gospel of the Lord Jesus Christ is the testimony of a changed life. One can argue and debate about every minute detail of the Christian faith, but no one can argue with the testimony of a changed life. After many years a man in my church finally came to know the Lord Jesus as his personal Savior. His wife came up to me and said, "You know, pastor, of all the things I am grateful for these days, the best is that my husband is a different man!"

Such is another vital component of the portrait of a disciple!

A Person Who Is Created with Purpose

Rick Warren's best-selling book *The Purpose Driven Life* has not only popularized the concept of purpose, it has helped immeasurably to establish a fresh understanding of the deep significance of divine purpose in every person's life. When the Lord Jesus spoke the words "Now they know that all things You have given to Me are from You" (John 17:7), He was speaking of an exclusive group of people who have the divine capacity to interpret life's data through spiritual eyes.

If the disciple is created with purpose, he becomes fused with God's intended plan for his life. It means the believer is characterized as one who is at all times under the constant guidance and direction of God! It must be so considering the extent to which "all things" are applied.

The writer of Hebrews emphasizes this point when establishing the importance of running the race of life with endurance. The way the believer sticks to his guns and keeps on keeping on is by setting his sights on the Lord Jesus Christ: "Therefore since we also have such a large cloud of witnesses surrounding us, let us lay aside every weight and the sin that so easily ensnares us, and run with endurance the race that lies before us, keeping our eyes on Jesus, the source and perfecter of our faith, who for the joy that lay before Him endured a cross and despised the shame, and has sat down at the right hand of God's throne" (Heb. 12:1–2).

This passage brings two major issues to the surface concerning the extent to which "all things" reach in the heart of our Savior.

Jesus Is the Source of Salvation

This literally means He is the originator of salvation not only because of His finished work on the cross but because He is the preeminent example of our salvation. In other words, the disciple knows that everything (about everything) began with God!

Jesus Is the Perfecter of Salvation

He is the "finisher" of salvation not only because of His finished work on the cross but because He is the only One authorized to bring us into heaven and complete our journey of faith. In this context the term *perfecter* carries the idea of Jesus Christ having the power and authority to carry through to perfect completion. Looking at it from the perspective of thanksgiving and prayer, which is surely an imperative for every believer, Paul says, "I am sure of this, that He who started a good work in you will carry it on to completion until the day of Christ Jesus" (Phil. 1:6).

As He paints this picture of the believer, Jesus establishes the pattern of divine guidance, direction, and will in such a person's life. This is why Abram had such incredible faith when God came to him in Ur of the Chaldeans:

> The LORD said to Abram:
> "Go out from your land,
> your relatives,
> and your father's house
> to the land that I will show you.
> I will make you into a great nation,
> I will bless you,
> I will make your name great,
> and you will be a blessing.
> I will bless those who bless you,
> I will curse those who treat you with contempt,
> and all the peoples on earth

will be blessed through you."

So Abram went, as the LORD had told him. (Gen. 12:1–4)

Abram's faith was pure in the purest sense! Note all the future tenses through the use of the emphatic "I will" used repeatedly throughout this Abrahamic covenant. The pattern for Christian discipleship is firmly established right here in the story of Abram because he did what God told him to do based on the belief that God controlled all things. Christian disciples, therefore, abdicate the right to control their own destiny. They simply submit in obedience to the will of a God, who "knows all things" (1 John 3:20). Jeremiah had this to say:

> Blessed is the man who trusts in the LORD,
> whose confidence indeed is the LORD.
> He will be like a tree planted by water:
> it sends its roots out toward a stream,
> it doesn't fear when heat comes,
> and its foliage remains green.
> It will not worry in a year of drought
> or cease producing fruit. (Jer. 17:7–8)

In short, the disciple is a person who has absolute confidence in God's ability because he knows God is in control of all the affairs of man.

A PERSON WHO IMITATES CHRIST

I have always loved watching little children imitating their parents. I remember going to watch a ball game with my two sons when they were still young boys. We were standing on the sideline cheering on the favorite team with much enthusiasm. It was amazing to me the manner with which both Rob and Greg copied my every move—sadly even when I became real upset with the decision of the referee! *Webster's* tells us imitation involves impersonation. On the human level it points to mimicking another person.

The term *disciple* means "to follow after." This is exactly what Jesus meant when He asked the Twelve to follow Him. Christian followship is much more than simply putting one foot ahead of another and getting in step with the one leading the pack. The leader, after all, is none other than the Lord Jesus Christ, and He is perfect in every way. So the disciple has a tall order on his hands! Jesus is the ultimate example of selfless humility (Phil. 2) and expects His children to imitate His selfless example. Where this leaves us is made clear.

> So then, my dear friends, just as you have always obeyed, not only
> in my presence, but now even more in my absence, work out your
> own salvation with fear and trembling. For it is God who is working
> in you, enabling you both to will and to act for His good purpose.
> Do everything without grumbling and arguing, so that you may be
> blameless and pure, children of God who are faultless in a crooked
> and perverted generation, among whom you shine like stars in the
> world. Hold firmly the message of life. Then I can boast in the day of
> Christ that I didn't run in vain or labor for nothing. (Phil. 2:12–16)

This is an interesting and an extremely challenging characteristic of a believer. Jesus established the basic premise of their active faith when He said, "They have kept Your word" (John 17:6). The word *keep* here refers to an essential character trait whereby the Christian person expresses a continuing desire to be like the Lord Jesus Christ. If someone asked you to keep your word about something you said or promised, she would be asking you to hold that word in sacred trust. In essence you would be asked to imitate what you have said by carrying out what you have said. Probably one of the most sought-after character traits is to be known as a person of your word. You not only say something, but you also adhere to what you say by doing what you say. In many regards this amounts to the highest calling of the believer. This is what the Ephesian Christians heard about the subject:

> Therefore, be imitators of God, dearly loved children. And
> walk in love, as the Messiah also loved us and gave Himself for us,
> a sacrificial and fragrant offering to God. But sexual immorality and
> any impurity or greed should not even be heard of among you, as is
> proper for saints. And coarse and foolish talking or crude joking are
> not suitable, but rather giving thanks. For know and recognize this: no
> sexually immoral or impure or greedy person, who is an idolater, has an
> inheritance in the kingdom of the Messiah and of God. (Eph. 5:1–5)

As we will see later on, this is the purpose of sanctification. The genuineness of the disciple is evidenced by the fact that he or she becomes more like the Lord Jesus Christ because the Word of God is being held (kept) in the heart and manifest in actions. This is a functional part of the design of the Christian life. The end result is the gradual and progressive production of godliness in the life of every believer. Believers are to become more and more like their heavenly Father as they keep His Word and imitate what it (He) teaches.

The end product of keeping His Word is clearly stated in Ephesians 3:16–19:

> I pray that He may grant you, according to the riches of His glory,
> to be strengthened with power through His Spirit in the inner man,
> and that the Messiah may dwell in your hearts through faith. I pray
> that you, being rooted and firmly established in love, may be able to
> comprehend with all the saints what is the breadth and width, height
> and depth, and to know the Messiah's love that surpasses knowledge,
> so you may be filled with all the fullness of God.

The list is really endless when it comes to imitating God by keeping His word. Such is the portrait of the disciple. Believers keep God's Word; they obey it, long for it, learn from it, practice it. In so doing they become imitators of the Lord Jesus Christ with all the benefits pertaining thereto!

A Person Who Expresses Genuine Faith

Many of the churches in America are filled with casualties of modern-day evangelism. This most certainly does not take away from the scores of godly, precious servants of the Lord whose lives are a mirror image of the grace of God and are always front and center in their faithful service of the Lord Jesus Christ. I know because I am surrounded by people like this. But the growing numbers of deadpan looks on the faces of people who come and fill the houses of God when it suits their schedules has become alarming. The reasons are numerous and yet simple at the same time. Much of this problem has been brought on by the tactics of modern-day evangelism that has sought to make things easier for a person to accept Christ and be included in the community of faith. Many of the practices of the invitation have been reduced to the level of a game in which anybody who feels like coming forward to join the church is invited to come, with the guarantee that they will have their hands held all the way and, most certainly, will not have to be embarrassed in any way in front of all the people.

Sadly to say these methods of easy believism have produced radical reactionary movements that have scampered to the other end of the spectrum. Scores of movements have arisen out of the ashes to the point where some groups are appalled by the thought of inviting someone to step out in a public manner. This has become so serious that many wonderful Christians are walking out of their churches and forming their own churches. The new churches are usually small in number and comprised of a group of mainly deep-thinking, serious-minded people who consider themselves (without necessarily saying so) spiritually superior to all the other misguided Christians. They whisper to one another in the hallways and form more special conclaves and convocations and conference meetings than they could possibly attend. Many of these believers would think nothing of traveling across the country to gather with a group of their like-minded friends rather than walk across the street to tell a desperate man about the Lord Jesus Christ!

I believe this is a reactionary movement born out of two major considerations. First is the sheer number of pastors and churches who have labored for many years with little fruit to show for their labor and toil. Every effort to get their people excited about soul-winning, let alone to so much as bring a lost friend to church, became like pulling teeth. The majority of churches around have become status quo institutions in which maintenance and not ministry is the work of the church. This has all but destroyed the fervor of many of our pastors and faithful people. And so they have run after a theology that gives them permission not to be concerned about something God has excluded them from being concerned about. Their ministry, they believe, is simply a ministry of deep spiritual soul-searching for the believer who is fortunate enough to have been chosen by God to be one of His exclusive club members. I know this sounds a little harsh, but it sure takes the strain out of the compulsion to go into all the world and become fishers of men!

The second reason many have followed this line is serious in cause and equally serious in effect. This reaction to the apathy of man toward the gospel has served to bring to the surface the real hunger on the part of some Christians, for the deep study of the Word of God. Many of them have been left high and dry by the lack of systematic biblical exposition in many pulpits. The effort to evangelize the lost has been used by some as an excuse to preach a shallow gospel.

Many pastors hardly refer to the Bible anymore. Illustrations have become the means by which life is illustrated rather than the way in which the Word is illustrated. Rather than using illustrations to throw light on the meaning of the Word of God, the Word of God is being used to throw light on illustrations. The end result of this shallow approach has seen many defect to the other side. This has particular appeal to the academic mind, and so many of our bright and gifted young people are being drawn away from the imperative to preach the whole counsel of God.

This is so important in light of all Jesus had to say to the Father in this exclusive prayer. In light of the three components of New Testament evangelism, the whole counsel of God is the overriding imperative to follow. Evangelism is incomplete until the evangelized become the evangelists! A church that majors its entire preaching and teaching ministry on salvation evangelism will, inevitably, become a very weak church! A church that majors its entire preaching and teaching ministry on disciple-making evangelism will, inevitably, become a dead church! These two extremes are both vitally important to the church. Both are needed in order to reach our world for Christ.

And so the words of our Savior! It is more than critical to understand exactly what it means that a disciple is a believer! How do we attest to the genuineness of a person's "decision" to follow Christ?

When Paul wrote to the church at Rome, he was careful to lay down the fundamental basis by which a person comes to know the Lord Jesus Christ as personal Savior.

> This is the message of faith that we proclaim: If you confess with your mouth, "Jesus is Lord," and believe in your heart that God raised Him from the dead, you will be saved. With the heart one believes, resulting in righteousness, and with the mouth one confesses, resulting in salvation. Now the Scripture says, No one who believes on Him will be put to shame, for there is no distinction between Jew and Greek,

since the same Lord of all is rich to all who call on Him. For everyone who calls on the name of the Lord will be saved. (Rom. 10:8–13)

Listen to what the Son says to the Father about this exclusive person when He states, "They have believed that You sent Me" (John 17:8).

It is evident they are the ones to whom the Son had given eternal life because they came to the point in their lives when they accepted (by faith) the testimony of the Word of God concerning the Savior of the world. This was the essential problem with the skeptics of Jesus' time on earth. Many received Him, certainly, and those that did receive Him believed in His name. The ones who did not receive Him did not believe He was the One sent by God as the Messiah, the Savior of the world. "He was in the world, and the world was created through Him, yet the world did not recognize Him. He came to His own [His created ones], and His own people [the Jews] did not receive Him. But to all [His created ones] who did receive Him, He gave them the right to be children of God, to those who believe in His name, who were born, not of blood, or of the will of the flesh, or of the will of man, but of God" (John 1:10–13).

The receivers of the Word typified Jesus' description of the ones who believed "that You sent Me" (John 17:8) in this exclusive prayer. The act of believing or receiving the Word involves three actions.

1. The acknowledgment of Jesus' claims as Messiah
2. The literal placing of faith in His person
3. The demonstrable yielding of allegiance to Him

All three of these actions must be evident. The result is clear. Those who receive Christ, the Word, receive full authority (right) to claim the exalted title of "God's children." And because they have placed that trust specifically in His name, they receive all the accompanying resources available in and through the character of the Lord Jesus.

As Jesus spoke these things to the Father, His hour was rapidly approaching. This would be an hour of great loss for the disciples. But He comforted them with the means that would provide them with all the necessary resources to carry out their mission without Him there beside them in the flesh.

In His teaching Jesus puts the focus squarely on praying in His name, not in the simplistic way of attaching Jesus' name to the end of every prayer but rather as the key ingredient to determining Jesus' plan and purpose for their lives. "I assure you: The one who believes in Me will also do the works that I do. And he will do even greater works than these, because I am going to the Father. Whatever you ask in My name, I will do it so that the Father may be glorified in the Son. If you ask Me anything in My name, I will do it" (John 14:12–14).

Jesus was not referring to a greater power than Himself when He talked of "greater works." He was simply saying that His exclusive ones would enjoy a greater range or extent of their ministry than what they were seeing at that time. The Holy Spirit was going to come and fill them with power so that they would be enabled to "go into all the world." Jesus was pointing to the future, a future accompanied by the Holy Spirit who would enable them to do great and wonderful things in the name of the Lord. Remember, He would say to them, that after the coming of the Holy Spirit they would receive the power necessary to do all He was asking them to do.

A Person Who Has Deep and Abiding Conviction

One cannot help but notice Jesus' use of the word *know* on two occasions in His conversation concerning these believers. The first time He does so He refers to their knowing "that all things You have given to Me are from You" (John 17:7) and the second time is when He says that they "have known for certain that I came from You" (v. 8). Both of these utterances established the deep and abiding conviction of the heart of the Christian. Two considerations need to be offered in this regard.

First, salvation belief, or "saving faith," is conviction of the highest order when one thinks of the resurrection of the Lord Jesus Christ. The whole concept of someone being raised from the dead is not a concept that finds simplistic accommodation in any human being's heart and understanding. But through the Holy Spirit, conviction is effected and belief is produced. This is trust at its highest level. It is the very expression of acceptance because the believing one entrusts his acceptance of the facts to the realm of fact, not because he understands it but because he is willing to accept it!

The second consideration takes this matter of conviction to an even deeper level. It concerns the human impossibility of understanding and accepting the basic premise of the mystery of the Godhead. So much of this conversation between the Father and the Son has to do with this mystery. Just think about it. Who is God? How can Jesus be God? When was the beginning? If God created man and then gives man to Christ, how does this affect the will of man? Or does man actually have no choice? Is man simply a robot or some kind of machine? And if he is simply a machine, then why would it have been necessary for the Lord Jesus to come to this earth to finish the work God gave Him to do? And what point is there to God's plan for the redemption of man through the Lord Jesus, if, in fact, His sacrifice on the cross makes no difference to man's salvation because God has already decided who is to be saved and who is to be condemned. And is the New Testament church only intended to be a place where exclusive, handpicked members gather to congratulate one another on having been selected by God from before they were even born? Why call out the disciples and tell them they would be made into fishers of men if, in fact, He knew all along they would be wasting their time? And what is the point of Jesus' telling us that we are sought after if, indeed, He is seeking after an exclusive group who had already been sought out by the Father? If this were the case, why did not the Lord Jesus simply thank the Father for allowing Him the privilege of going through the motions of obedience and suffering without an actual purpose, because the purpose had already been taken care of? And why did Jesus share the story about the rich man and Lazarus in Luke 16? Just to give preachers something to say in case they were looking for something that might liven up their preaching? And what about Abraham's reply to the futile request of the man in hell to send someone back from the dead to persuade his living brothers concerning the absolute certainty of life after death? Jesus made it clear they had Moses and the prophets, a reference to the law (Bible) and to all the preachers of the Word of God, who evidently would not be necessary if indeed they were not even needed as a means to introduce people to the Lord Jesus.

The biblical portrait of the believer finds conviction at its heart and soul. The heart cry of spiritual conviction is demonstrated in Paul's reminder about the faith of Abraham. "He did not waver in unbelief at God's promise, but was strengthened in his faith and gave glory to God, because he was fully convinced that what He had promised He was also able to perform" (Rom. 4:20–21). And this conviction (act of faith) was the means by which Abraham was "credited . . . with righteousness" (Rom. 4:9). That is, he was justified by faith! In Romans 8:38–39 the significance of the character trait is seen in the apostle's remarkable statement, "I am persuaded that neither death nor life, nor angels nor rulers, nor things present, nor things to come, nor powers, nor height, nor depth, nor any other created thing will have the power to separate us from the love of God that is in Christ Jesus our Lord!"

The whole premise on which Paul based his unapologetic stand with the sufferings of our Savior was firmly attached to the matter of conviction. "For this gospel I was appointed a herald, apostle, and teacher, and that is why I suffer these things. But I am not ashamed, because I know whom I have believed and am persuaded that He is able to guard what has been entrusted to me until that day" (2 Tim. 1:11–12).

What extraordinary conviction! If you had any doubt about this man's salvation, just listen to what he says and then watch what he does!

A Person Who Is the Subject of Prayer

This seventh feature of the disciple of the Lord Jesus Christ is more precious than any written word can record. What an amazing thing to hear the Son say to the Father, "I pray for them!" What more could anyone ask?

Here we find the disciples at the moment of their abandonment. Their Lord and Master was about to leave them. He had been their source of strength and encouragement, and one can only wonder the numbers of times He had bailed them out. He had spoken for them, demonstrated to them, taught them, shielded and protected them. And now He was about to leave them.

I will be looking at the matter of prayer as one of the key elements of salvation in the next chapter. But I do want us to see the correlation between prayer and what the Lord Jesus was saying to the Father at this point in His prayer. Jesus followed His declaration with an immediate statement about "not praying for the world but for those You have given Me" (John 17:9).

The fact that Christians belong to God is one of the absolute certainties of knowing the Lord Jesus Christ. According to the Scriptures there are only two types of people in this world: children of God and children of Satan. In his comments about the imperative of love, the apostle John establishes the fact that all people either belong to God or belong to Satan:

> Little children, let no one deceive you! The one who does what is right is righteous, just as He is righteous. The one who commits sin is of the Devil, for the Devil has sinned from the beginning. The Son of God was revealed for this purpose: to destroy the Devil's works. Everyone who has been born of God does not sin, because His seed remains in him; he is not able to sin, because he has been born of God. This is how God's children—and the Devil's children—are made evident. (1 John 3:7–10)

Jesus, Himself, made this point in the greatest sermon ever preached. "No one can be a slave of two masters, since either he will hate one and love the other, or be devoted to one and despise the other. You cannot be slaves of God and of money [man]" (Matt. 6:24).

If I may be so forward to put what Jesus was saying in different terms, this is what He said: "Father, when I leave this earth to come back to heaven to be with You, I will not be abandoning my children and turn them into orphans. While I certainly will not be with them in person, as I now am with them, I thank You that My return to heaven is making it possible for the Comforter to come and be with them. They will need a lot of prayer because of all the things they are going to face and struggle through as they try to live lives pleasing to You. The prayer that I will pray for all those who have yet to believe on Your name is a different matter. I will be praying for My disciples continually after I have ascended into heaven."

In other words, the Son was talking about an exclusive prayer that focuses on an exclusive group of people who had placed their faith and trust in Him.

It is important to note, however, that the Son was impressed to mention "I am not praying for the world." Evidently, and at this point in His conversation with the Father, there was a world of people that Jesus did not pray for. These people of the world must be nonbelievers. They are the ones who, at this time of the Son's appointed hour, had still not come to believe in His name even though He had been about the work of revealing the Father to them. Jesus is not saying that He will never pray for these unbelievers. We know this because He will soon switch gears and focus on those "who [will yet] believe in Me through their [the believers'] message" (John 17:20). We will take a good look at this in the next part of this book that I have chosen to entitle "The Inclusive Prayer."

Jesus prays for this exclusive group of believers only because He knows who they are and where they came from. Their identity rises out of His perfect vision as God, and their need rises out of His particular desire to make certain they are not left as orphans in a cruel and unkind world. His perfect vision allowed the Son to see them as His children, while His particular desire allowed Him to care for them as His children.

There is a sense that we can hear the voice of our Savior loving on His own family first. Perhaps this illustration might help. The life of the average pastor is always interesting when it comes to the demands placed on him to love and care for his people as a shepherd cares for his flock. Picture this scene with me for a moment. I have just completed my message from God's Word for the morning. As is my custom, I try to greet as many people as possible. The conversation is uplifting, and it is so good to see everyone and to share one another's burdens. One hand after another is shaken, and one hug after another is given. All of a sudden a little girl makes her appearance. But this time she's not just another little girl. She just happens to be my daughter. And so I look into the face of the person with whom I am currently talking and say something like this: "Please excuse me for a minute. This is my daughter, and I need to talk to her for a while."

Get the picture? Despite all the other people, there is one who commands the attention of her daddy. And for a while my attention is directed exclusively toward her. After we have hugged and talked and shared, off she toddles just as happy as a lark because she knows she is special.

The Son is making a special statement about a special group of people here. His focus is on them because they are the people He has poured His life into. They are the ones who have come to believe in His name. They accepted the revelation about the one true God. They are God's elect!

These believers were a functional part of the success of Jesus' mission on earth. They had received the words of revelation, they had kept the words of the Lord, they had affirmed that Jesus came from God, and they had sealed all they believed by knowing who God is. No wonder they were special!

And it is not as though Jesus is simply ignoring the others. He is most certainly not praying against them! He is simply passing them by at this moment of special attention. Their names are not written in God's book in heaven. It was time to let His children know they would always be the focus of Jesus' special prayer. I guess this is one of the most wonderful blessings of knowing the Lord Jesus Christ as Savior.

We must remember that the Lord Jesus had been given these people by the express hand of God. This fact alone carried a sacred trust and a solemn but joyful charge. This is not unlike the trust placed in the hands of parents when God blesses them with children. It is the parents' solemn responsibility and joy to bring them up in the knowledge and admonition of the Lord. And so there are six petitions made by the Son in behalf of the believers.

The six petitions from John 17 are for:

1. Eternal security (vv. 11–12)
2. Uncommon unity (v. 11)
3. Complete joy (v. 13)
4. Absolute protection (vv. 14–15)
5. Spiritual sanctification (vv. 17, 19)
6. Distinctive commission (v. 18)

These six petitions form the basis of the next six essential elements of the disciples' portrait.

A Person Who Is Eternally Secure

The matter of eternal security is a critical component of the Christian faith. Here we see the Son, on the eve of His betrayal, petitioning the Father on behalf of those who had come to place their trust in Him. This issue is so important for the believer to understand that Jesus makes a double reference to it. He first says, "Holy Father, protect them by Your name" (John 17:11), and then follows this up by saying, "I was protecting them by Your name that You have given Me. I guarded them, and not one of them is lost, except the son of destruction, so that the Scriptures may be fulfilled" (v. 12).

This exclusive prayer makes reference to the issue of protection on two distinct occasions. The first reference, which is quoted in the previous paragraph, is a direct reference to eternal security. This is the matter we are looking into at this point. The second reference is made further on in Jesus' prayer when He says "protect them from the evil one" (v. 15). This is a reference not to eternal but to living security. The former applies to the guarantee of being absolutely certain of life after death. The latter applies to the guarantee of being certain of an abundant life in Christ during life. In both cases, dead or alive, the believer is totally guaranteed the permanent guardianship of our Savior and Lord and the absolute safety afforded by His watchful care. The means by which this is achieved is by the indwelling presence and power of the Holy Spirit.

In this first utterance Jesus was guaranteeing all believers their eternal security. He did this in three ways: by invoking the nature of God, the salvation of God, and the Word of God—both spoken and written. He contextualizes the issue with the real-life (to the disciples) illustration of Judas Iscariot. I call them the "three pillars of eternal security" because they are truly three foundations upon which the believer can base his eternal security.

Three Pillars of Eternal Security

The Nature of God

"Holy Father," Jesus prayed, "protect them by Your name" (John 17:11).

Every time the name of God is brought to bear on the life of the believer, all the attributes of God are put on display. Many courts of law require a witness to place his hand on the Bible and say, "I promise to tell the truth, the whole truth, and nothing but the truth, so help me God!" Whether one agrees with this or not, the idea here is to invoke the absoluteness of a person's testimony by guaranteeing it on the attributes of the only true God! When the Son spoke the name of God, He invoked the attributes of God. He called upon the nature of God in all His (the Father's) fullness because this is the first truth upon which the eternal security of the believer is based.

We have covered the significance of the name of God in a previous section. God has put His name down as a guarantee of eternal life because He is God. Abraham took his stand on this fact. "He did not waiver in unbelief at God's promise, but was strengthened in his faith and gave glory to God, because he was convinced that what He had promised He was also able to perform" (Rom. 4:20–21).

Most importantly, however, Jesus taught His followers that God was their heavenly Father. The word *Father* is used 53 times in John 13 through 17 and 122 times in John's Gospel as a whole! Despite the fact that the Jews refused to believe Him, Jesus continually and constantly connected Himself to the Father, the God of Abraham, Isaac, and Jacob! He made clear that His Father had sent Him. He made clear that He was equal to the Father. He made clear that His words and His works came from the Father. But they would not believe!

When Jesus spoke of His revelation of the Father's name, He was making the nature of God known to them. In this section, the Son calls God "Holy Father," and invokes the eternal safety that accompanies knowing Him. This means two very important things concerning their eternal security.

1. They could depend on Him. What He was trying to tell them was that they could depend on Him. If the disciples could have depended on the Savior in His limited capacity in the flesh, surely He (the Son) together with God (the Father) and the Holy Spirit, could guard them for all time and for all eternity!

Herein lay the ultimate comfort to the believers. Jesus Christ, the Son, has committed them into the care of a loving Father. Could they be more safe and secure than that? They could depend on God to protect them in their work and ministry as well as in their person.

Jesus was not only making the nature of God known to the disciples at this point, but He was personalizing the relationship that exists between a Father and His children. The personal nature of this relationship not only would help them as they struggled through life but would enable them to see that they were held firmly in the hands of the only One who would not let them go for any reason.

The best illustration of the fatherhood of God is the story of the prodigal son. The wonderful strength of the son's dependency on the father is clearly evident despite the son's behavior!

2. They would be protected by Him. Our heavenly Father not only wants us to know that we can depend on His divine ability but also that we will be protected by His divine name. The title Jesus gives to God enforces this truth because all of God's attributes are made available through His holiness. When God is described as holy, He is being described within the context of everything

He is. The psalmist makes this point when he states, "Once and for all I have sworn an oath by My holiness" (Ps. 89:35). In other words the guarantee of the protection of believers is automatically engaged through God's holiness. As a holy and righteous God who hates sin, He will not only make those holy who are His, but He will also protect them from the wages of sin, which is death. These wages cannot be brought back into play once they have been washed in the blood of the Lamb! As Father to His children, God will keep them teach them, and protect them because of His divine nature.

The Salvation of God

Jesus went on to say, "Protect them by Your name that You have given Me, so that they may be one as We are one" (John 17:11).

The second wonderful truth on which eternal security is based is the issue of salvation in the Lord Jesus Christ. If the Old Testament Jew knew God as the great I AM (see Exod. 3:11–14), and he certainly did, then the life and ministry of the Lord Jesus was the living example of the fact that there is a bottom line. The bottom line is that what God starts God finishes! What God began from before the foundation of the world to secure those who believe in Him, He completes in the salvation offered though His grace and mercy.

Jesus' statement that the name of God was given to Him has tremendous significance, especially when it comes to the matter of eternal security. If the Old Testament Jews found meaning in the name of Jehovah, then Jesus made His name even more meaningful to the disciples. He referred to Himself as "the bread of life" (John 6:35), "the light of the world" (John 8:12), and "the good shepherd" (John 10:11). Each of these names demonstrated not only the total adequacy of God's provision for the physical needs of the disciples but also total security for the eternal needs of every believer.

In his first letter to the temporary residents of the Dispersion, Peter grounded the matter of eternal security in the fact of our salvation in and through the Lord Jesus Christ:

> Blessed be the God and Father of our Lord Jesus Christ.
> According to His great mercy, He has given us a new birth into a
> living hope through the resurrection of Jesus Christ from the dead,
> and into an inheritance that is imperishable, uncorrupted, and unfad-

ing, kept in heaven for you, who are being protected by God's power, through faith for a salvation that is ready to be revealed in the last time. You rejoice in this, though now for a short time you have had to be distressed by various trials so that the genuineness of your faith— more valuable than gold, which perishes though refined by fire—may result in praise, glory, and honor at the revelation of Jesus Christ. You love Him, though you have not seen Him. And though not seeing Him now, you believe in Him and rejoice with inexpressible and glorious joy, because you are receiving the goal of your faith, the salvation of your souls. (1 Pet. 1:3–9)

The important matter of protection is seen clearly in this passage. It is interesting to note how the Lord Jesus makes reference to the protection He gave them "while I was with them" (John 17:12). This protection was far more than protection from harm and danger. He certainly acted as a refuge for them in many ways. He protected them by providing for them. He provided food for their hungry stomachs and the greatest lines of spoken defense when they were harassed by the many who came after them. But He was protecting them from ever being lured away from Him.

In the context of Jesus' spoken words to the Father, the protection He was referring to was twofold.

1. Believers are protected against the loss of their living hope. What good, do you suppose, is a living hope if it is not protected and guaranteed? This is why this passage is so special.

The confidence upon which all believers can base their faith is garrisoned about by the power of God to the point of ultimate protection. This military metaphor carries with it the idea of a group of men under attack from the enemy. God, who is all-powerful, guarantees not only their protection from all harm and danger but guarantees their safe delivery to total freedom from all harm and danger.

There are ten aspects to this living hope:

1. It comes from God (Ps. 43:5).
2. It is a gift of God's grace (2 Thess. 2:16).
3. It is defined by Scripture (Rom. 15:4).

4. It is an absolute reality (Rom. 15:13).

5. It is secured by the resurrection (John 11:25–26).

6. It is confirmed by the witness of the Holy Spirit (Rom. 15:13).

7. It is the means of defense against Satan (1 Thess. 5:8).

8. It is confirmed through suffering (Rom. 5:3–4).

9. It is the producer of joy (Ps. 146:5).

10. It is fulfilled in Jesus' return (Titus 2:13).

Every one of these ten aspects would take a book to write about! Just think of the power of the resurrection alone! This is the culminating crescendo of the power of God. Talk about a guarantee—here it is!

> Now if Christ is preached as raised from the dead, how can some of you say, "There is no resurrection of the dead"? But if there is no resurrection of the dead, then Christ has not been raised; and if Christ has not been raised, then our preaching is without foundation, and so is your faith. In addition, we are found to be false witnesses about God, because we have testified about God that He raised up Christ— whom He did not raise up if in fact the dead are not raised. For if the dead are not raised, Christ has not been raised. And if Christ has not been raised, your faith is worthless; you are still in your sins. Therefore those who have fallen asleep in Christ have also perished. If we have placed our hope in Christ for this life only, we should be pitied more than anyone. (1 Cor. 15:12–19)

The Corinthian Christians obviously believed in the resurrection, or else they would not have been Christians. But they struggled in their acceptance and belief of it. Paul understood their struggle. Many of these people had been influenced by the Sadducees, who did not believe that Jesus had risen from the dead. Many had come under the influence of the ancient Greek philosophy of dualism, which taught that everything physical was intrinsically evil. So they were confused and suffered in their eternal security as a result. In this passage Paul points out the disastrous results of such hopelessness. The fact of the resurrection became the cornerstone of Christian hope both in this world and in the next.

2. Believers are protected against the loss of their inheritance. Jesus was not only speaking about protection against the loss of a living hope through eternal life but about protection against the loss of inheritance. The question of the Christian's inheritance is a huge subject. When you become a Christian, you are adopted to become a joint heir with the Son in all the Father has for His only Son.

> All those led by God's Spirit are God's sons. For you did not receive a spirit of slavery to fall back into fear, but you received the Spirit of adoption, by whom we cry out, "Abba, Father!" The Spirit Himself testifies together with our spirit that we are God's children, and if children, also heirs—heirs of God and co-heirs with Christ— seeing that we suffer with Him so that we may also be glorified with Him. (Rom. 8:14–17)

Every believer is made an heir of God. We inherit eternal salvation, we will see God, and we will be glorified with Him forever! In the last days God appointed His Son to be "heir of all things" (Heb. 1:2). By divine grace every adopted child of God will receive the full inheritance Christ receives because the believer is in Christ and Christ is in him.

In His great discourse on the sheep and the goats, Jesus said, "Then the King will say to those on His right, 'Come, you who are blessed by My Father, inherit the kingdom prepared for you from the foundation of the world" (Matt. 25:34). In his classic defense before Agrippa, Paul recalled his conversion and commission by the Lord on the road to Damascus with the very words of the Lord, who said, "I will rescue you from the people and from the Gentiles, to whom I now send you, to open their eyes that they may turn from darkness to light and from the power of Satan to God, that they may receive forgiveness of sins and a share among those who are sanctified by faith in Me" (Acts 26:17–18). In Ephesians Paul put it like this: "In Him we were also made His inheritance, predestined according to the purpose of the One who works out everything in agreement with the decision of His will" (1:11). Later on the same author said, "May you be strengthened with all power, according to His glorious might, for all endurance and patience, with joy giving thanks to the Father, who has enabled you to share in the saints' inheritance in the light" (Col. 1:11–12).

Ephesians 1:14 reminds us that it is the Holy Spirit who makes this all possible and guarantees that what God had done for us will remain undefiled and will not fade away. Because the believer's inheritance is incorruptible, it is not subject to passing away and will remain unravaged, undefiled, and unpolluted by the enemy.

The Word of God

Jesus placed all He was saying to the Father in the context of "I have given them Your word" (John 17:14).

The "given word" of God involves both the spoken word and the written Word. Both are guarantors of eternal life.

The Spoken Word. I think we would all agree that another book will be required to write down all the spoken words uttered by the Son of Man as He carried out the work the Father had assigned Him to do. We know these words came from the Father because Jesus said as much in the prayer. At the Festival of Dedication, which took place in Jerusalem, Jesus found Himself walking in the temple complex in Solomon's Colonnade. The Jews surrounded Him and challenged the Savior to level with them and tell them, once and for all, whether or not He considered Himself the Messiah. We know they were trying to trap Him into what they believed was blasphemy. Jesus, of course, knew better, and immediately exposed them as false teachers and unbelievers: "'I did tell you and you don't believe,' Jesus answered them. 'The works that I do in My Father's name testify about Me. But you don't believe because you are not My sheep. My sheep hear My voice, I know them, and they follow Me. I give them eternal life, and they will never perish—ever! No one will snatch them out of My hand. My Father, who has given them to Me, is greater than all. No one is able to snatch them out of the Father's hand. The Father and I are one'" (John 10:25–30).

Needless to say, the justification for killing Him was mounting, and so they picked up stones to stone Him. Jesus' spoken word clarified at least five important facts related to eternal security.

1. It is given.
2. It is everlasting.
3. It is totally secure.

4. It is guaranteed.

5. It is sealed.

The written word. The written Word of God provides the second source of absolute certainty as far as the matter of eternal security is concerned. Consider the long list of things the apostle Paul presented as powerless to separate the believer from the love of God that is in the Lord Jesus Christ. This list includes death and life, angels, powers, rulers, height, depth, or any other created thing; none of these have the capability or the authority to deny eternal life to one who has trusted in the finished work of the Savior. As one person said, "What part of nothing do you not seem to understand?"

Jude's magnificent benediction is a powerful statement in this regard. It centers on the theme of eternal salvation and provides a tremendous source of encouragement to those who thought they would become the victims of apostasy.

He begins with an exhortation to believers to build themselves up and become fortified in their faith because of the love of God. The believer, furthermore, can expect "the mercy of our Lord Jesus Christ for eternal life" (Jude 21). And because of this expectation, "Now to Him who is able to protect you from stumbling and to make you stand in the presence of His glory, blameless and with great joy, to the only God our Savior, through Jesus Christ our Lord, be glory, majesty, power, and authority before all time, now, and forever. Amen" (Jude 24–25).

What a joy to know the Son has given us His word!

At this point the Lord Jesus uses Judas Iscariot as an example of one, who was never given eternal life even though he was such a part of the life and ministry of Jesus. How could this be that someone could have been so close to Jesus and yet not know Him as the Messiah?

This wonderful injunction on eternal security contains the remarkable disclaimer that "the son of destruction" (John 17:12) is excluded from all Jesus was saying to the Father about believers. The use of the word *except* stands in stark contrast to the inclusiveness with which the exclusive ones are included. The question is, why Judas? Did this mean he had lost his salvation? Or had he crossed over the line with his betrayal of the Lord Jesus and was now paying the consequence of his actions? It may surprise some of you but Judas was never saved!

Luke tells us something about Judas that is said of no one else in Scripture: "Then Satan entered Judas, called Iscariot, who was numbered among the Twelve" (22:3). We know it is spiritually impossible for darkness to occupy the same space as light. Satan can certainly hover about, and he certainly can tempt, but he cannot possess the child of God! The other designation used to describe Judas is the phrase "son of perdition." It is used twice in the New Testament, once where Jesus referred to him in our passage and the other where Paul refers to the him in 2 Thessalonians 2:3.

The bottom line is that perdition is the fate of all who do not repent of their sin and place their faith and trust in the Lord Jesus Christ. It is applied not only to a condition while on this earth but to eternal consequence. The writers of the Gospels used it to mean everlasting judgment and eternal separation from God. A person who falls victim to perdition has failed to respond to the act of God's grace through His Son's death on the cross.

Judas's crime was threefold. First, he was guilty of the crime of rejecting the revelation of God through Jesus. Second, he was guilty of the crime of loving man (money and materialism) over the love of God in Christ Jesus. And third, he was guilty of the crime of betraying the Son instead of obeying the Son.

Let's take a look at the upper room for a moment. Jesus was about to be betrayed, and so He took the disciples, taught them about the significance of His pending death on the cross, and then predicted that one of them would betray Him. This led to an argument as to who among them would be the greatest. Peter obviously had much to say as usual. Jesus then predicted Peter's denial of his Savior. "Simon, Simon, look out! Satan has asked to sift you like wheat. But I have prayed for you that your faith may not fail. And you, when you have turned back, strengthen your brothers" (Luke 22:31–32).

Peter, of course, vehemently denied he was capable of failing and even pledged to go all the way with his Master, even if it meant going to prison!

What a wonderful reminder of the sustaining power of Jesus' prayer!

The repetition of Simon's name enforced the somberness of Jesus' warning to him. But the issue here is the comparison offered between the "son of destruction" (John 17:12), who was always lost, and Peter, who would always be eternally secure. Peter's faith was being guaranteed despite the fact that he would be sifted as wheat. The image here is of wheat being harvested, collected, and then thrown up into the wind in order to allow the chaff to be blown away. Although he could not have realized exactly what he was going to face, Jesus told Peter he was about to be thrown up to the wind by the trials that were going to come his way. This was applicable, of course, to all the disciples who had gathered and were listening to the Lord. Jesus then personalizes Peter again when He says, "but I have prayed for you" (the pronoun *you* is singular). He was obviously praying for all of them, but the Lord Jesus wanted to assure Peter of his ultimate victory despite his pending failure. Jesus even closes the admonition by stating that Peter's faith, itself, would not fail and that he would become an encourager to others because of his experience at failure (and restoration).

So the fulfillment of Scripture concerned the eternal lostness of Judas who was never saved, as well as the eternal security of those who had been saved!

A PERSON WHO IS UNCOMMONLY UNITED

In this exclusive prayer the Lord Jesus establishes one of the most important characteristics of the believer. Unity is, evidently, so important to the life of a believer that He brings the subject up again when He focuses attention on those people who would come to accept Him as Savior through the message of the apostles. I will address this in the next part of the book under the heading of "The Inclusive Prayer." At this juncture we hear the Lord Jesus utter these words that carry such significance for the witness of the church in today's world. Jesus prayed that believers "may be one as We are one" (John 17:11).

A follower of the Lord Jesus Christ has an imperative mandate to act in unity with fellow believers, behave in unity with fellow believers, and demonstrate unity with fellow believers.

Drawing on the unity of the Godhead, the Son attaches the believer's eternal security and protection with the demand to be one in the Spirit of Christ. Needless to say, the manner with which so many congregations conduct themselves is one of the major reasons fewer people are being drawn into the evangelical church. Much of the witness of the church has been seriously marred because of the behavior of church members who claim to know Christ but act with no regard for the unity of the body of Christ. The sad truth is that many of our children watch these kinds of behavior and become adversely affected by it.

The significance of Christian love cannot be underestimated in this matter of unity. Love is the defining factor. It is both the producer of unity and the product of unity.

In this regard the Savior gave His new commandment to love one another. In direct response to the love of Christ, all disciples are commanded to love one another, thereby proving to the world the genuineness of their discipleship (see John 13:34).

The importance of unity is clearly spelled out by Paul when he exhorted believers to be unified: "I therefore, the prisoner in the Lord, urge you to walk worthy of the calling you have received, with all humility and gentleness, with patience, accepting one another in love, diligently keeping the unity of the Spirit with the peace that binds us. There is one body and one Spirit, just as you were called to one hope at your calling; one Lord, one faith, one baptism, one God and Father of all, who is above all and through all and in all" (Eph. 4:1–6).

This passage on unity continues in a major way. Paul points out that unity is only made possible through the grace of God that was given to every believer "according to the measure of the Messiah's gift" (v. 7). The gift he was referring to must be none other than the gift of the triune God who is one!

And continuing on, Paul maintains that the giftedness the Lord gives to His children in the body is designed to bring believers to a point of spiritual maturity that is marked by the attainment of "unity in the faith." The result is significant. "Then we will no longer be little children, tossed by the waves and blown around by every wind of teaching, by human cunning with cleverness in the techniques of deceit. But speaking the truth in love, let us grow in every way into Him who is the head—Christ. From Him the whole body, fitted and knit together by every supporting ligament, promotes the growth of the body for building up itself in love by the proper working of each individual part" (vv. 14–16).

The bottom line of Jesus' prayer for unity is that oneness and harmony among believers are possible only when they are built on the solid foundation of doctrine. The Spirit-bestowed oneness creates a bond of spiritual accord that binds God's people together. The focus Jesus places on the Trinity ("as We are one") is not designed to distinguish between the persons of the Godhead but rather to emphasize that they are completely unified in every aspect of divine nature and purpose, despite their unique roles as Father, Son, and Holy Spirit. The oneness of the Father, as He works in conjunction with the Son, gives one hope though the Spirit that is eternal life. While every disciple is uniquely made and uniquely gifted, his portrait must be characterized by a determination to be unified with fellow believers.

A Person Who Is Complete in Joy

It is wonderful to hear the Savior say that He has spoken these things in the world "so that they may have My joy completed in them" (John 17:13). The issue of joy and happiness in Christ has always been the subject of much discussion and even debate.

I have a rather jaundiced view of ministers who stand up in worship services in our churches and say something like this to the congregation: "Welcome to the house of God today! Is it not the most wonderful thing to be here like this? Now let's all put a smile on our faces while we all stand and sing "Let's just praise the Lord!" The reason I have a problem with this is not because Jesus has come to give us the abundant life. It is not because the thought of total forgiveness of sin is not the most wonderful blessing in all the world. It is simply the fact that many true believers suffer in many ways. A mother who has recently lost her son in a tragic accident surely does not feel like smiling, let alone someone telling her she must do so! And so the joy of which the Savior speaks in this exclusive prayer carries deep significance when properly understood as a hallmark of the Christian disciple.

I do not believe the Lord was suggesting confusion between faith and feelings at this point. Salvation is based squarely on many facts, all of which are rooted in the person and work of the Lord Jesus Christ. Listen to Peter's magnificent proclamation of the facts to the Gentiles.

> Then Peter began to speak: "In truth, I understand that God
> doesn't show favoritism, but in every nation the person who fears
> Him and does righteousness is acceptable to Him. He sent the mes-
> sage to the sons of Israel, proclaiming the good news of peace through

Jesus Christ—He is Lord of all. You know the events that took place throughout all Judea, beginning from Galilee after the baptism that John preached: how God anointed Jesus of Nazareth with the Holy Spirit and with power, and how He went about doing good and curing all who were under the tyranny of the Devil, because God was with Him. We ourselves are witnesses of everything He did in both the Judean country and in Jerusalem; yet they killed Him by hanging Him on a tree. God raised up this man on the third day and permitted Him to be seen, not by all the people, but by us, witnesses appointed beforehand by God, who ate and drank with Him after He rose from the dead. He commanded us to preach to the people, and to solemnly testify that He is the One appointed by God to be the Judge of the living and the dead. All the prophets testify about Him that through His name everyone who believes in Him will receive forgiveness of sins." (Acts 10:34–43)

These are the facts of the good news of the gospel. When the Lord Jesus spoke about the completeness of His joy in them, He was establishing doctrinal truth at its highest outcome. The joy of Christ is made evident in two areas:

1. The giving of eternal life—which was achieved in the lives of everyone who believed in His name. These exclusive people, of whom the Son was speaking, had already attained that same joy.
2. The completion of eternal life—which signified the Savior's ability to complete the work He had begun in the granting of salvation. Simply stated, coming to know Christ as Savior and Lord is one thing; going to be with Him in heaven for all time and eternity is entirely another.

Even in prison the apostle Paul responded to his critics with joyful contentment. He knew they were jealous of his apostolic power and authority. They were jealous of his unique giftedness and success in ministry and were only interested in their personal self-advancement. They wanted to promote their own agendas and prestige by accusing Paul of being so sinful that the Lord was punishing him by putting him in prison. But Paul's joy was not linked to his torturous circumstances or to his critics. He was not in the least concerned about who received the credit. His joy remained inextricably intertwined with the proclamation of the gospel resulting in the salvation of many who believed in the name of the Savior. And so both the giving of eternal life and the completion of eternal life are brought together in Paul's own life and result in joy. His words contain some of the most powerful statements ever made on the subject of the disciples' joy.

> Now I want you to know, brothers, that what has happened to me has actually resulted in the advancement of the gospel, so that it has become known throughout the whole imperial guard, and to everyone else, that my imprisonment is for Christ. . . . What does it matter? Just that in every way, whether out of false motives or true, Christ is proclaimed. And in this I rejoice. Yes, and I will rejoice because I know this will lead to my deliverance through your prayers and help from the Spirit of Jesus Christ. My eager expectation and hope is that I will not be ashamed about anything, but that now as always, with all boldness, Christ will be highly honored in my body, whether by life or by death.
>
> For me, living is Christ and dying is gain. Now if I live on in the flesh, this means fruitful work for me; and I don't know which one I should choose. I am pressured by both. I have the desire to depart and be with Christ—which is far better—but to remain in the flesh is more necessary for you. Since I am persuaded of this, I know that I will remain and continue with all of you for your advancement and joy in the faith, so that, because of me, your confidence may grow in Christ Jesus when I come to you again. (Phil. 1:12–26)

What a fundamental basis of joy is presented here! Paul brings both of these actions together in the context of the believer's joy. "I give thanks to my God for every remembrance of you, always praying with joy for all of you in my every prayer, because of your partnership in the gospel from the first day until now. I am sure of this, that He who started a good work in you will carry it on to completion until the day of Jesus Christ" (Phil. 1:3–6). Joy is the badge of honor worn by every believer!

A PERSON WHO IS ABSOLUTELY PROTECTED

One of the greatest characteristics of those who believe on the name of the Lord is the matter of divine protection. Let's consider this for a moment because the shelter of the Lord's care is the umbrella under which the believer is able to stand against the devil and serve the Savior.

I love this hymn so much because it tells me of the firm foundation of Christ's secure and steadfast love.

How firm a foundation, ye saints of the Lord,
Is laid for your faith in His excellent Word!
What more can He say than to you He hath said,
To you who for refuge to Jesus have fled?

"Fear not, I am with thee; O be not dismayed,
For I am thy God, and will still give thee aid,
I'll strengthen thee, help thee, and cause thee to stand,
Upheld by My righteous, omnipotent hand.

"When thro' fiery trials thy pathway may lie,
My grace, all sufficient, shall be thy supply;
The flame shall not hurt thee; I only design
Thy dross to consume, and thy gold to refine.

"The soul that on Jesus hath leaned for repose
I will not, I will not, desert to his foes;
That soul, tho' all hell should endeavor to shake,
I'll never, no, never, no, never forsake!"
—John Rippon, 1787

The Old Testament book of Kings tells us about the rise and fall of King Solomon (1 Kings 3–9). Few would doubt his greatness in the eyes of man. His achievements were vast, and his wisdom the envy of many. God appeared to this man on many occasions, and he soon came to realize that without the protection of Almighty God he was nothing. Among the many lessons we learn from Solomon were the four things he could not live without:

1. The guarantee of the presence of God
2. The placing of the name of God
3. The conferring of the grace of God
4. The gaze of the eyes of God

All of these blessings are brought to bear on the believer through the finished work of the Savior on the cross. In essence, the Son is announcing the fact of the believer's preservation at this point. In this prayer the Lord speaks to the Father about the means by which protection is guaranteed and the person from whom the believer is protected.

The Means by Which the Believer Is Protected

Simply stated, the means by which the disciple is preserved and protected is the name of the Lord. The greatest treasure a person has is his name. As we discussed earlier, the blessings that accompany the name of the Lord is far-reaching for the believer.

I remember when the Byrnes High School football team was ranked in the top five teams in the United States. Their coach, Bobby Bentley, is one of the most talented and godly men I have ever known. My respect for him is profound! When the team was invited to play on a nationally televised game, Coach Bentley invited me to speak to the crowds that had gathered for the game. Security was extremely tight, as one can imagine, and the game was sold out! I still remember being ushered through all the crowds and gateways for one reason: I had the right name hanging around my neck!

Blessed be the name of the Lord! The great hymn writer Charles Wesley put it like this: "O for a thousand tongues to sing, Blessed be the name of the Lord!" Jesus understood this when He said, "I was protecting them by Your name that You have given Me."

The Person from Whom the Believer Is Protected

The disciples would have had little problem recalling the time the Lord Jesus taught them how to pray. We know, of course, that the Lord's Prayer is as much a doctrinal statement as it is a lesson on prayer. The Messiah was teaching the Twelve so many things about God, His kingdom, His provision for our daily needs, forgiveness, and so much more. But He also gave the believer permission to call on His name and ask for deliverance from the evil one. The authority for deliverance is the power and glory that all belong to Him alone.

The reality of Satan as the ruler of this world is clearly established in the Word of God. Paul makes this point without hesitation.

> And you were dead in your trespasses and sins in which you previously walked according to this worldly age, according to the ruler of the atmospheric domain, the spirit now working in the disobedient. We too all previously lived among them in our fleshly desires, carrying out the inclinations of our flesh and thoughts, and by nature we were children under wrath, as others were also. But God, who s abundant in mercy, because of His great love that He had for us, made us alive with the Messiah even though we were dead in trespasses. By grace you are saved!" (Eph. 2:1–5)

This sober statement to the believers in Ephesus is a reminder of their total lostness and sinfulness outside the finished work of the Savior. The use of the preposition *in* takes them back into the realm or sphere out of which all believers have come. This leaves all unbelievers trapped in an atmospheric domain under the express command of Satan. Satan's world order is dominated by humanity's values and standards that are in diametric opposition to the standards and values of God. In 2 Corinthians 10:4–5, Paul refers to these ideologies that are like a fortress where people are imprisoned by "arguments and every high-minded thing that is raised up against the knowledge of God." The only way to be set free is by being brought under the captivity of God's amazing grace. "The god of this age has blinded the minds of unbelievers so they cannot see the light of the gospel of the glory of Christ, who is the image of God" (2 Cor. 4:4).

Satan's power over this world and his ability to wreak havoc on all he can lay his hands on is the reason Jesus turns to the Father and asks that believers not be taken out of the world but rather that they be protected from the one who desires to destroy them in the world.

This magnificent part of this exclusive prayer is such a word of encouragement to every believer. It is one of the most powerful words of assurance for all who face the giants of this world. It serves as a constant reminder that the

Lord will never leave or forsake those who have believed on His name. No wonder we are able to cast "all your care upon Him, because He cares about you" (1 Pet. 5:7).

Peter goes on to issue a stark warning to all believers: "Be sober! Be on the alert! Your adversary the Devil is prowling around like a roaring lion, looking for anyone he can devour. Resist him, firm in the faith, knowing that the same sufferings are being experienced by your brothers in the world" (1 Pet. 5:8–9).

I was fortunate enough to grow up in Africa, the home of many of the world's most famous felines. The picture given by Peter here is clear. Picture with me the beautiful and vast plains of Africa. Thornbushes decorate the landscape, and the tall grasses wave to and fro in the wind like masses of submissive servants bending and bowing before their king. To the right of the picture we see a whole group of the cutest deer ever seen by man. They are grazing quietly. It would seem that nothing could be more tranquil. These deer are minding their own business. They are not disturbing anyone or anything. No harm could possibly befall such magnificently innocent creatures.

Every now and then one of them thinks he hears something. Heads pop up like pop-up tarts popping up out of the toaster for breakfast. Their big ears shift and seem to take turns. One lies down while the other one lifts up and vice versa. After a little conversation, perhaps, maybe a little consultation with some of the more experienced deer, they all lower their heads and continue their munching!

Meanwhile, not too far away in the thicket, a lion waits! Yes, he's quiet now, but he's a master tactician. He even knows which way the wind is blowing. The meal that awaits him is worth every effort of the highest order. Nothing is too much trouble for him. Not with the goal in sight.

And so he begins to stalk. He carefully lifts one paw at a time. As he lifts the one, the other is suspended in the air, dangling delicately, with the padded foot bent slightly from the ankle as though he was about to sip from a cup of hot tea. Not one twig is snapped. Not one sound is made. Not one breath is heard.

And meanwhile the little deer continue to mind their own business. After all, who would want to hurt such tender loving creatures?

Suddenly the lion pounces! Within seconds he lands on the back of one of the unsuspecting deer and sinks his long fangs into the small of the deer's neck where the jugular pumps his very life into him. The deer begins to bleat and cry but cannot. He wants to kick wildly but he cannot move. And so he kicks and kicks and kicks and kicks until all that is left is a bloodied carcass in the wilderness for the vultures to come and feed on. Every believer is that deer. Satan is that lion. And Jesus says He will protect us from him!

We must allow the Word of God to have the final say: "We know that everyone who has been born of God does not sin, but the One who is born of God keeps him, and the evil one does not touch him. We know that we are of God, and that the whole world is under the sway of the evil one. And we know that the Son of God has come and has given us understanding so that we may know the true One. We are in the true One—that is, in His Son Jesus Christ. He is the true God and eternal life" (1 John 5:18–20).

A Person Who Is Spiritually Sanctified

The word *sanctify* literally means "to make holy or to be set apart from sin" to a life in Christ. In His prayer the Lord Jesus points to Himself as the One who made sanctification possible and the believers who are sanctified by virtue of their having believed in Him.

The verb *sanctify*, which is used here and in John 10:36, is the setting apart of something for a particular use. In other words, believers are not simply set apart for their own benefit but for the purpose of relating to man as well as to God. Believers are, accordingly, singled out for the purpose of accomplishing all that God wants accomplished while, at the same time, rejecting all God does not want accomplished. The process of sanctification comes by means of the truth, which is the full revelation that the Son gave regarding all the Father had assigned Him to do, which we now can read in the Word of God.

When the Son of Man fulfilled the will of God by going to the cross, He provided for the believer a continuing, permanent condition of holiness. All believers, as Paul noted, have put off the conduct and habits of "the old man" and are "renewed in the spirit of [their] minds," and "you put on the new man, the one created according to God's likeness in righteousness and purity of the truth" (Eph. 4:22–24). In other words, becoming like the Lord Jesus is not possible apart from the One who has made it all possible. The renewal of the mind in and through salvation does not simply result in a renovated mind and character, but it brings forth a total transformation of the old to the new! The two by-products of sanctification are indispensable components of the character of the Christian disciple. Here they are:

Righteousness

Because of the righteousness of the Lord Jesus Christ, all believers are covered with this same righteousness as they live out their lives in the world. We have talked about the imputed righteousness of God in Christ Jesus in the inner prayer. One of the functions of the Holy Spirit is to convict lost people of God's righteousness. Without that conviction, salvation would be impossible because in it (the gospel) God's righteousness is revealed. This righteousness, which is a mark of the believer, relates to the Christian's moral responsibility to his fellowman. It is the means by which his behavior is determined and will be reflected in the manner with which he conducts himself in the world. This is why God has not called the believer "to impurity, but to sanctification" (1 Thess. 4:7).

Holiness

Whereas righteousness relates to the believer's behavior toward others, holiness refers to the believer's responsibility toward God. We are to be holy because God is holy! Paul summarized this process of sanctification when he instructed the Romans to "put on the Lord Jesus Christ, and make no plans to satisfy the fleshly desires" (Rom. 13:14).

Every believer, then, is characterized by the continuing process in which those who have been saved through faith are transformed into His image and likeness. When the Lord spoke these words to the Father just prior to His betrayal in the garden, He knew He was about to make this process possible. His words are words of assurance and comfort. They are words of empowerment. They serve to embolden every believer because they help to give clarity to the process of salvation. Every believer is first justified through the forgiveness of sin. He is then sanctified through the work of the Holy Spirit. And then he is glorified by the power of the resurrection to walk in the presence of God for all time and eternity.

The writer of Hebrews urged his readers to hold fast to the confession of their faith. The finished work of our Savior on the cross enabled every believer to enter the holy of holies because of the "new and living way." He shed His blood and became our high priest; "let us draw near with a true heart in full assurance of faith, our hearts sprinkled clean from an evil conscience and our bodies washed in pure water" (Heb. 10:19–22).

In a sense we hear the Son saying, "Father, please hold the hands of these, our children, as they journey through the ups and downs of life. I have already asked You to protect them from the evil one, but I also ask that You sanctify them by the truth of Your Word so that they can live lives pleasing to You as I send them out into the world."

A Person Who Is Distinctively Commissioned

God sends His children out into the world in the same way He sent His only Son to the world. Jesus put it like this: "As You sent Me into the world, I also have sent them into the world" (John 17:18).

All believers are commissioned to go into all the world (Matt. 28:20). There are no exceptions! Not one person is saved by God's grace for the purpose of sitting idly by and watching as the world continues to reject the Savior. Jesus made it clear to His disciples when He commanded them to follow Him with the accompanying promise to make them "fishers of men." Surely the Lord Jesus was not playing some kind of mind game with them at this point? Rather He was sending them out into the world with a specific purpose, to share the good news of the gospel of the Lord Jesus Christ.

When Jesus spoke these words, He was focusing on this exclusive group of people and giving them a specific set of marching orders. Needless to say, Jesus understood exactly what was about to happen to Him. What He said in this prayer is reflected, more directly and with far greater explanation, in what He said to the disciples when He appeared to them after the resurrection.

> While He was together with them, He commanded them not to leave Jerusalem, but to wait for the Father's promise. "This," He said, "is what you heard from Me; for John baptized with water, but you will be baptized with the Holy Spirit not many days from now."
>
> So when they had come together, they asked Him, "Lord, at this time are You restoring the kingdom to Israel?"

He said to them, "It is not for you to know times or periods that the Father has set by His own authority. But you will receive power when the Holy Spirit is come upon you, and you will be My witnesses in Jerusalem, in all Judea and Samaria, and to the ends of the earth." (Acts 1:4–8)

Implicit in this account, and in particular the words of Jesus Himself, are six foundations upon which the sending out of every believer is laid.

The Wait

Jesus told them to wait. And this was after He had risen from the grave. We know Jesus was referring to the Day of Pentecost that would occur ten days from the time of His instruction to them (Acts 2). The bottom line was Jesus' demand that they simply follow His instructions and do what He was telling them to do. Needless to say, willing and complete submission to God's commands provides one of the essential characteristics of the Christian disciple and is also one of the ways the genuineness of salvation can be tested. John put it like this: "This is how we are sure that we have come to know Him: by keeping His commands" (1 John 2:3).

The Issue

When the Lord spoke about sending believers out, He was raising a number of important issues. To begin with, He had spoken! He expected that His spoken word would be obeyed. Second, a change was about to happen. The Holy Spirit was set to arrive in power and glory. Whereas Old Testament followers of God had needed to be baptized with water as a sign of their "salvation," the New Testament believers would be baptized into salvation through the Holy Spirit. And third, it was no business of the disciples to be concerned with the timing of Jesus' return to the earth or the restoration of His kingdom; their business would always be to go out into the world because they were the sent ones.

So, there are three issues all related to the sending out of the believer:

1. Mind God
2. Mind the Holy Spirit
3. Mind your own business

The Power

The apostles's mission of spreading the gospel was the major reason the Holy Spirit empowered them. The time between the promise of the Holy Spirit and the inauguration of the Holy Spirit at Pentecost was the most powerless period of time in all the Scriptures. When Jesus spoke of sending them out, He was looking ahead to the most dramatic change in world history. The disciples had already witnessed the Holy Spirit's saving, guiding, teaching, and miracle-working power. But ten days after this announcement, they would experience the wonder-working power of the presence of God!

Almost immediately after Pentecost, Peter "stood up with the Eleven, raised his voice, and proclaimed to them: 'Jewish men and all you residents of Jerusalem, let this be known to you and pay attention to my words'" (Acts 2:14). Sounds different from the wimp who sneaked off and ran away from the Savior after having denied even knowing Him.

The power of God was about to be made available to all who believed in His name. Jesus knew it! That's why He spoke of it in His prayer. He was not going to send them out unequipped. He would make them ready for battle.

The Scope

Jesus clearly defined the scope of His assignment. It was to be divided into four zones:

1. Jerusalem—This was where they were! Witnessing begins in the backyard!
2. Judea—This was where they were from! Witnessing goes back to our roots and to places where we might have been before!
3. Samaria—This was where *they* come from! Witnessing extends to the people we most certainly would prefer not to have to be around!
4. Ends of the earth—This was where they had never been! Witnessing defies the furthermost borders of the world!

Jesus said: "I also have sent them into the world" (John 17:18). This was not simply to roam around at loose ends, looking for something to do and somewhere to be. The scope of His commission was clear.

The Joy

The joy of being one of the Lord's sent ones is unsurpassed. This has certainly been my experience. Little did my wife and I know when we first realized our Savior had determined to send us out to serve Him. All those years ago in Africa seem just like yesterday in some ways. I think it is because of the sustained sense of joy we have experienced. There is nothing like the joy of knowing you are in the center of the will of God.

I realize the Lord does not call every one of His children to serve Him in a full-time capacity. When Jesus spoke of sending us out, He included all believers. Some of the most wonderful servants of the Lord are friends I know who serve Him as Christian physicians, teachers, homemakers, engineers, lawyers, and, yes, even politicians! I know the Son of Man had this joy in mind as He contemplated the agony of the cross!

I must share my favorite story with you because it represents the joy of which I speak. It was my very first day of ministry in Spartanburg, South Carolina. There I was, all brand-new, standing in my office with boxes of books piled up to the ceiling. Into my office walked one of the dearest men I have ever known, Bill Adams. What a soul-winner he is!

"Pastor," he said most politely as he put out his hand to give me a warm welcome, "would you help all of us pray for Sam Rhodes?"

"Of course I will," I replied. "Who is he and where is he?" I asked Bill.

"Well, he's a pretty rough fellow who really needs the Lord. Our church has been praying for Sam for years and years! In fact, if you look out of your office window, you will see his restaurant at the bottom end of the parking lot on St. John Street. It's called Papa Sam's! You see it, Pastor?"

"Suppose he's there right now?" I asked Bill, not knowing what I was about to let my big mouth get me into!

"Well, let's go visit him!"

And with that, Bill and I marched out and down the stairs, through the glass doors, across the parking lot, and into the smoke-filled Papa Sam's.

Just as we entered the place, Bill turned to me and said, "Oh, by the way, Pastor, Sam really doesn't like preachers too well!"

Thanks a lot!

And was Bill right or what?

I walked up to this big man who looked like he could have eaten everything in the restaurant by himself and stuck my hand out to him.

"This is the new preacher," Bill introduced me and made me feel as though I had just stepped into a Roman arena dressed as a genuine Christian martyr!

"That right, huh?"

I do want you to know that what happened next will always be the proof to me that the power and presence of the Holy Spirit are real.

"Mr. Rhodes," I said in a somewhat timid voice, "I have just arrived in Spartanburg today, and I have something important to ask you."

"Start talking!" he growled.

"No, sir, what I have to ask you is too important. Is there a place where we can sit down in private?"

And with that I walked straight into his office, sat down in his chair, and offered him a seat!

"Sam, I came here to ask if you would give your heart and life to the Lord Jesus Christ."

Sam Rhodes looked at me, then at Bill, and then at me again. I thought I detected some moisture in his eyes when he said, "Yea, preacher, I sure will!"

I looked at Bill and Bill looked at me. Despite all our training, both of us were dumbfounded. Not Sam Rhodes! Not the man who had been prayed for so many years!

When I gained my composure, I nearly made the biggest mistake I have ever made in my Christian life.

"OK, then, Sam, why don't we get down on our knees, and you just talk to the Lord Jesus. Tell him all about yourself. Confess your sin to Him and invite Him to come into your heart and life."

With that we all went crashing to our knees. Right there in Sam's smoke-filled office. Just across the way from my new office, the same place where I would prepare all those sermons to tell all those people that Jesus had sent them into all the world to be His witnesses.

I do not believe I have ever heard a worse prayer in all of my life. Sam cussed at least four times! He didn't know how to pray or what to say or what was proper and what was not! No, sir, he was just this sorry old sinner on his knees before a loving Savior who told the Father, "You gave Me the authority to give eternal life to all who believe in My name."

Bill and I peeked repeatedly at each other while Sam poured out his heart to the Lord. I guess I was praying that no leader in my church would pop his head in and see his new pastor on his knees with a renegade who didn't know how to pray properly!

But the power and presence of the Spirit of the Living God was in that place!

On Wednesday evening our church had a prayer rally in the dining hall. At the end of the meeting, I stood on the platform and, perhaps in an effort to impress all the new church members, asked if there was anyone who wanted to bring a short "word of testimony" before I closed the evening.

Heart attack of all heart attacks! This big old man stands up in the back row and begins to amble his way down to the front of the hall and up onto the platform. With my heart pounding in my chest, Sam Rhodes leaned forward on the small lectern and said, "Monday this preacher here and Bill Adams over there come walking into my place over there and told me about Jesus. I want y'all to know I took Jesus into my heart, and I want y'all to know I have never felt so "blankety-blank" in all my life!" I felt as though I would be the shortest serving pastor in the history of this great church! But not so! The people broke out in spontaneous applause!

One year later Sam Rhodes lay dying from cancer. Just moments before he died, he said to Bill Adams, "Bill, I want you to tell that preacher just how much I thank him for coming to ask me to give my heart to Jesus. I'm fixing to die! But don't worry about me 'cause I'm going to heaven to be with Jesus!"

And he died!

What joy!

The Response

We have considered five foundational aspects of the sending out of the Christian disciple. They are the wait, the issue, the power, the scope, and the joy. The final foundation upon which the sending out of the believer is laid is the response. It causes me to think about a special song that carries a significant question. The youth in our church spend all year preparing to sing in prisons across America as a part of the Mirror Image Choir Tour. Before I stand to speak to these people who are incarcerated for crimes against humanity, the young people sing a song that stays with me all year round: "Will You Be the One?"

I truly believe Jesus was not asking this in question form when He prayed to the Father. What He was doing was making a statement that is inextricably intertwined into the nature of Christian discipleship. Jesus does not say, "I plan on asking a few of these believers if they would be so kind as to consider My offer to send them out into the world with the gospel message." No, rather He was saying, "Because you have been sanctified by My Spirit, you are being sent into the world to be My witnesses."

The confusion over this matter is alarming in today's world and is the cause for much of the stress, despondency, sickness, and even death among so many of God's people. This call is God's call in the life of every believer. And His call is our mission!

A PERSON WHO IS TOTALLY HATED

My mother always had an aversion for the word *hate*. My brothers and I knew this to be true, especially when we used the term on one another, even in our childlike context. To hate someone literally means to have an extreme aversion for a person to the point of open hostility and passionate antagonism.

This is exactly what the Lord Jesus was saying to the Father when He said, "The world hated them because they are not of the world" (John 17:14).

What Jesus was referring to on the eve of His departure from them was the future volatility of their relationship with the world. They already knew this was true. It would seem every step they had taken alongside the Messiah had borne witness to anger and hostility of the highest order. The world was out to get Him, and His life and ministry were one continual call for His blood! But things were about to go from bad to worse. Jesus was about to leave them. And He was not about to leave them in a comfortable situation. The opposite was true. Their world was about to explode in fury. They would be surrounded by antagonists who would threaten them at every turn with the worst kinds of antagonism.

The word *hate* here is used as a general term to describe all people who do not believe Jesus was the Messiah. It could not be a reference to things, time, and space because none of these things have the capacity to express hate. Hate is a distinctively human trait; it can only express the animosity of one person toward another person he or she vehemently opposes. In practical terms hate is not only something *opposite to* but it is *in opposition to* people toward whom the hatred is directed. Being opposite to someone does not necessarily mean action is taken against that person, because silence can often be the expression of mere difference of opinion. The kind of hatred Jesus was talking about in His prayer is more the *action* of hatred, the kind that carries the worst consequences for the victim.

Because we have the advantage of the Scriptures, we know that the believer in Jesus' day faced the most awful expressions of practical hatred. Look at what happened to Peter. After he had denied the Savior at the foot of the cross, the resurrected Lord confronted him on the shore of the Sea of Galilee with a major prediction of Peter's own death at the hand of the world haters: "I assure you: When you were young, you would tie your own belt and walk wherever you wanted. But when you grow old, you will stretch out your hands and someone else will tie you and carry you where you don't want to go" (John 21:18).

Jesus was preparing Peter (and all believers), ultimately, for long periods of systematic and relentless hate that would culminate in death. Later on, long after the Lord Jesus had been exalted at the right hand of the Father in heaven, Peter wrote to encourage the believers in the provinces of Pontus, Galatia, Cappadocia, Asia, and Bithynia to hold onto their "living hope" in Christ Jesus, "though now for a short time you have had to be distressed by various trials" (1 Pet. 1:6). He concludes by pointing out that the believers would be able to "rejoice with inexpressible and glorious joy" (v. 8) despite the hateful attitudes that would surround them.

When Jesus talked about the hatred of the world, He was presenting the Father with the reality of a world in which the believer would have to live. The apostle John did not mince his words about the kind of world Jesus was referring to: "Do not love the world or the things that belong to the world. If anyone loves the world, the love for the Father is not in him. Because everything that belongs to the world—the lust of the flesh, the lust of the eyes, and the pride in one's lifestyle—is not from the Father, but is from the world. And the world with its lust is passing away, but the one who does God's will remains forever" (1 John 2:15–17).

The contrary attitude of the world toward the righteousness of God in the person of the Lord Jesus was so intense that they crucified Him instead of Barabbas; and if this is what they would do to Him, how much more vulnerable would the disciples be without Him present to watch out for them.

The fact is, every believer is a candidate for the "roaring lion" who is actively engaged in seeking out believers to devour (see 1 Pet. 5:8). The thief is the prince of this world and is out to destroy and kill with a hatred so intense it would be impossible for the disciples to cope without the Lord's protection.

A Person Who Is Spiritually Connected

I love America! This is the land that adopted me, has loved me, and has become my true home. All three of our children—Rob, Greg, and Shelley—are grown now, but all three were born in New Orleans, Louisiana. The people of America are my people, and I am one of them. I am an American who has great difficulty accepting the way some people talk about this country! I have a hard time accepting news broadcasts, especially overseas, that seem bent on breaking down everything about the United States of America. I am so proud and grateful for our brave men and women who have worn the uniform of this nation and have sacrificed so much for the freedoms we enjoy today. I cannot tell you just how proud and grateful I am for men like Marine Lieutenant Andrew Kinard who served with such distinction in Iraq and paid a high price with the loss of both of his legs in a bomb blast! The list goes on and on!

Most normal, family-oriented people want to belong. This is natural and perfectly good in every way. The need to belong is important and carries feelings that are hard to describe at the best of times. In the United States of America it seems everyone is either an African American, a Polish American, a Chinese American, an Italian American, a Spanish American, a Southern American, or a Northern American. Nationalities from all over the world have aligned themselves with the United States. Even the American constitution is a reminder that all people are created equal. Everybody belongs to somebody, even the nobodies. The very heart of gangsterism is based on the basic need of people to belong. Being a part of a group brings certain benefits that make life easier, including identity, protection, security, status, reference, and opportunity—all basic human needs.

But no matter how much I love America, Jesus reminds me that "they are not of the world, as I am not of the world" (John 17:16). The follower of the Lord Jesus Christ is not a member of any nation, creed, or culture. Just as the Lord Jesus Christ was from heaven above, so it is that He reminds us of our standing in Him. We, too, belong to our Father in heaven.

When the Lord Jesus prayed to the Father about this matter of citizenship, He was truly leveling the playing field for all who believe in His name for two reasons:

Because of Who He Was

The Son connects the citizenship of the believer to His own citizenship. Because the disciple is a follower of Christ, the believer literally treads in His footsteps. Jesus was never of this world, yet now was at the point of leaving it. He was never the world's favorite, and He never accepted the ways of the world. He didn't even have a place to lay His head down. Not one thing in this world had any hold over Him, and He was never mastered by anything in the world. The Savior made Himself no reputation and was rejected and despised by all who refused to believe He was the Messiah.

Because of Who They Were

True Christians are not of this world, and the Son was making this clear in His prayer. No believer can be in favor with man on every issue. Many times there is an unquestionable call on the believer to take a stand for the things of God. Numerous times the clarion call to follow the Lord Jesus is not the most popular thing to do as far as man is concerned. Believers will be delivered from the world, and their prevailing business ought to be about things that are from above the world. Perhaps the words penned by Mary Slade put the issue of the believer's citizenship in a rightful perspective.

> *Sweetly, Lord, have we heard Thee calling, "Come, follow Me!"*
> *And we see where Thy footprints falling, Lead us to Thee.*
>
> *Tho' they lead o'er the cold, dark mountains, Seeking His sheep,*
> *Or along by Siloam's fountains, Helping the weak.*

If they lead thro' the temple holy, Preaching the Word,
Or in homes of the poor and lowly, Serving the Lord.

Then at last, when on high He sees us, Our journey done,
We will rest where the steps of Jesus end at His throne.

Footsteps of Jesus that make the pathway glow;
We will follow the steps of Jesus where'er they go.

Believers are no ordinary people. They are the people of God! And as the people of God who are not of this world, they receive all the wonderful things the Lord has for His own.

We have taken a good look at the portrait of the Christian disciple. Although this is not an exhaustive list, it is taken from the spoken words of our Savior as He looked up to heaven and spoke to the Father. It most certainly is a prayer directed at an exclusive group of people, who by definition are the ones who "believe You sent Me" (John 17:21). This is what the Son has to say about them, and it is what the Son tells the Father He is going to continue to do for them.

A Practical Application

Before we turn our attention to the inclusive prayer, I want to present you with one practical application. It has often been said that it is one thing to understand words that are spoken, but it is another thing to apply those same words in the reality of life. Everything the Lord Jesus placed before the Father can be applied to daily life and function.

Every church is led by leaders. The question is, what qualifies them to be leaders in the church? In many instances people are placed in leadership positions in the local church for all the wrong reasons. Contrary to public opinion, neither the ability to give money nor the length of time a person has been a member is sufficient to qualify one for leadership in the church. With all due respect, I believe many of the problems in local churches are caused by leaders who, though they may occupy positions of respect and leadership in the world, are not spiritually qualified to make decisions in concert with the will of God for

His church. How is it possible to call upon such people when their own relationship with Him is not what it ought to be—let alone, perhaps, nonexistent?

Many years ago a group of godly men and I gathered together and determined to know the pleasure of the Father concerning the election of deacons in our church. After much prayer and study, I presented to them the eighteen qualifications for leadership directly from the Word of God. The decision was made to ask every man nominated by the church for possible election to the office of deacon to come to a two-hour seminar led by me. Our men responded in a wonderful way. During this seminar I presented them with the eighteen biblical qualifications for church leadership and suggested they answer each mandate with a simple yes or no. Their answers would be personal and kept private and were designed for their eyes only. Each qualification was dealt with in some detail, and each candidate was asked to examine himself in the light of God's Word with the full realization that none are perfect, and the only thing that separates the leader from all others is the grace of God.

At the conclusion of the biblical mandates, I included a practical application related specifically to the life and ministry of our church. Each church has unique areas of service and ministry. The biblical requirements cannot be changed, but the practical application certainly will change from one church to another. Here's the outline:

The Deacon—Scriptural Qualification

ACTS 6:3

"Therefore, brothers, select from among you seven men of good reputation, full of the Spirit and wisdom, whom we can appoint to this duty."

Are you a man of good report?	____Yes	____No
Are you full of the Holy Spirit?	____Yes	____No
Are you full of wisdom?	____Yes	____No

ACTS 6:5

"The proposal pleased the whole company. So they chose Stephen, a man full of faith and the Holy Spirit, and Philip, Procorus, Nicanor, Timon, Parmenas, and Nicolas, a proselyte from Antioch."

Are you full of faith?   ____Yes ____No

1 TIMOTHY 3:8

"Deacons, likewise, should be worthy of respect, not hypocritical, not drinking a lot of wine, not greedy for money."

Are you seriously minded?   ____Yes ____No
Are you double-tongued?   ____Yes ____No
Are you given to much wine?   ____Yes ____No
Are you greedy of money?   ____Yes ____No

1 TIMOTHY 3:9

"Holding the mystery of faith with a clear conscience."
Are you a holder of the faith?   ____Yes____No

1 TIMOTHY 3:10

"They must also be tested first; if they prove blameless, then they can serve as deacons."

Are you tested and proved?   ____Yes ____No
Are you blameless?   ____Yes ____No

1 TIMOTHY 3:11–12

"Wives, too, must be worthy of respect, not slanderers, self-controlled, faithful in everything. Deacons must be husbands of one wife, managing their children and their own households competently."

Do you have a Christian family life?   ____Yes ____No
Are you the husband of one wife?   ____Yes ____No
Are you ruling your children and household well?   ____Yes ____No

1 Timothy 3:13

"For those who have served well as deacons acquire a good standing for themselves, and great boldness in the faith that is in Christ Jesus."

Are you bold in the faith?   ____Yes ____No

1 Timothy 3:2

"An overseer, therefore, must be above reproach, the husband of one wife, self-controlled, sensible, respectable, hospitable, an able teacher."

Are you hospitable?   ____Yes ____No

Are you self-controlled?   ____Yes ____No

Are you able to teach?   ____Yes ____No

1 Timothy 3:3

"Not addicted to wine, not a bully but gentle, not quarrelsome, not greedy."

Are you contentious?   ____Yes ____No

The Deacon—Practical Qualifications

I am willing:

To attend deacon meetings   ____Yes ____No

To attend specially called meetings   ____Yes ____No

To attend church business meetings   ____Yes ____No

To be faithful in church worship service attendance   ____Yes ____No

To be faithful in special assignments   ____Yes ____No

    (Sunday offering, committees, Lord's Supper service, prayer room)

To be faithful in deacon family ministry   ____Yes ____No

To be faithful in giving   ____Yes ____No

To pray for my church   ____Yes ____No

To pray for and support my pastor publicly and privately

                                          ____Yes ____No

Only a visit to our church will bear testimony to the manner with which the Lord has chosen to bless the application of His Word in this vital aspect of the life and ministry of the local church. Today I am privileged to serve alongside the most unified group of men. Our deacons meetings are more like worship services. The business of the church is discussed in an atmosphere of mutual interest and desire to know and do the will of the Savior. For many years I have been privileged to sit in deacons meetings where not one ugly word has been said. Nobody gets bent out of shape because they did not get their own way, and even on points of difference there is a keen sense of mutual submission to the will of God. Every man is valued, and servanthood is the order of the day.

No wonder the Lord is blessing His church!

Chapter 9

Jesus Announces the Practice of Intercession

In this final chapter of this exclusive prayer, I want us to focus on one statement made by the Lord Jesus. This short but powerful utterance will carry us naturally from this section into the final part of Jesus' prayer, which takes us into the heartbeat of our mission to all the world. Jesus looked up to heaven and said, "I pray for them." This is Jesus' intercessory prayer for all believers, so this is not a prayer for salvation. When He prays "I pray not only for these, but also for those who believe in Me through their message" (John 17:20), He is praying for the salvation of those who were yet to believe in His name.

The fact that the Lord Jesus prays for us is both marvelous and remarkably special at the same time. This is a most precious thing to know and contemplate. There are three by-products of Jesus' statement about praying for believers that form the concrete into which our own prayers are built:

1. Jesus prays to God for us.
2. We can pray to God through Him.
3. We can pray for others through Him.

One can only imagine the frustration on the part of the Old Testament saints who wanted to approach Jehovah. You might recall Aaron, the high priest and brother of Moses. His parents, Amran and Jochebed, were from the tribe of Levi. Aaron had four sons: Nadab, Abihu, Eleazar, and Ithamar. The first two perished when they offered sacrifices with fire that God had not commanded them to make. In Exodus 28–30:10, we learn about Aaron and his sons.

Aaron and his sons were separated and consecrated by God to the office of high priest. Aaron, in fact, started the divine call of Israel's formal priesthood. From Exodus 28:2–43, we get a description of the first priestly garments worn by the high priest. These clothes included breastplates, girdles, linens, and fabrics in purple, gold, and scarlet, with jewels of onyx, topaz, emeralds, sapphire, diamonds, amethyst, and jasper! Sounds spectacular!

Along with this fine wardrobe, Aaron had the responsibility to go into the holy place God had set apart, behind the curtain and in front of the atonement cover on the ark of the covenant. It was there that Aaron, in obedience, initiated the sacrificial system designed to atone for the sins of the children of Israel.

But the story of the high priesthood is fraught with disobedience, frustration, and even bad behavior. The law became "only a shadow of the good things to come" (Heb. 10:1). These worshippers continually had to offer sacrifices over and again and could only deal with one sin at a time. Their efforts to gain access to God must have been tiring, time consuming, and extremely tense because they never really knew where they stood with God.

This frustration even carried through into the church age. Religious groups of all kinds were created by self-styled prophets who based all they did on their claim to be God's right hand on earth. The sale of indulgences and the corruption of the church led Martin Luther to begin the Protestant Reformation in 1517 with the nailing of his Ninety-five Theses to the door of Wittenberg Castle Church. Justification for sin, he discovered from God's Word, came only by God's grace through faith in the Lord Jesus Christ who gave His life for the redemption of humankind.

Jesus came and died on the cross because "it is impossible for the blood of bulls and goats to take away sins" (10:4). Through the man Christ Jesus "we have been sanctified through the offering of the body of Jesus Christ once and for all" (10:10).

He is our high priest "over the house of God" (10:21), making intercession for us because He offered one sacrifice for our sins forever and is now seated at the right hand of the Father (see 10:12).

And so the Lord Jesus Christ arrived in Bethlehem to begin His life and ministry on behalf of those who would believe in His name. As He taught His disciples, they heard Him lay out the principles of prayer on many occasions. He gradually impressed them with the indispensable mandate of prayer. They responded and became inquisitive about prayer. "Teach us how to pray," they asked Him.

And He did.

But Jesus went even further in His teaching on prayer. He gave them the model for His own manner of praying. It was a servant model in which the humble servant comes in humility before the Master to present petitions for Him to consider:

> Whenever you pray, you must not be like the hypocrites, because
> they love to pray standing in the synagogues and on the street corners
> to be seen by people. I assure you: They've got their reward! But when
> you pray, go into your private room, shut your door, and pray to the
> Father who is in secret. And your Father who sees in secret will reward
> you. When you pray, don't babble like the idolaters, since they imagine
> they'll be heard for their many words. Don't be like them, because
> your Father knows the things you need before you ask Him.
> (Matt. 6:5–8)

And so Jesus said, "I pray for them" (John 17:9).

I can personally testify to the power of prayer. I know the Lord has prayed for me time and time again. And He has used those who are closest to me. My wife has prayed for me ever since she first met me. And that took some praying!

I even remember an incident in my young life when I know someone must have been praying for me!

My earliest recollection of someone significant interceding on my behalf involved my mother. I guess many of us can look back at our younger days and wish things could have been a little different. The passing of time produces much reflection, great healing, and, of course, deep gratitude for those who never let go when life was tough and mean and hard to understand.

"There but by the grace of God" has particular significance for me. And I must confess it is difficult for me not to use my own life as a testimony because I do believe I have a testimony to the grace of God. And so do you, by the way.

My younger days were a little tumultuous, to say the least. Dad had come to know the Father only after his three sons were born. The Lord Jesus rescued him from who knows what had he not confessed his sin and trusted Jesus as his personal Savior and Lord. Mom's life changed forever, too. Although we will never know, my brothers and I may have grown up in a broken home. By all accounts Mom and Dad were headed in that direction when the Lord intervened.

My problems began with Dad's inevitable moves around the country. I found myself shunted from one school to another before the age of eight, at which point I headed to boarding school in Zululand. Don't misunderstand me at this point. Some of my greatest and most cherished memories in life were produced during these years. I have fond memories of riding horses, open spaces in the African countryside, negotiating rapids down the Mooi River, playing rugby, playing cricket, and even winning the hop, skip, and jump event on athletic day. We traveled and sang all over the country as members of the select choir and climbed every part of the mighty Drakensberg mountain range feasible, or so it seemed to me at that young age.

But boys will be boys, and boarding school will always be a place where the survival of the fittest is the order of the day. Fending for myself and fighting for survival became part and parcel of what I had to do.

I even remember when the choirmaster woke me up after lights-out and invited me to accompany him to the Johnson Memorial Chapel to rehearse my solo part for the upcoming boys choir tour to the city of Durban (ironically to sing in my Dad's church on the bluff). No one else was around at that time of the night, and so this nine-year-old did what he was told to do. I can still remember sitting on the second row of the pews and this man beginning to unzip his trousers in front of me. The fear I experienced that night was something hard to describe. For some unknown reason I took flight back to the Chicken Run dormitory where I hid under my bed for the rest of the night hoping the choirmaster would not come after me. Within the next week his evil pursuits were uncovered, and I can still remember the inquest that was conducted in light of all he had done to many of the boys on that campus. I had personally escaped, but many had not. I sure needed someone to pray for me.

From there I went to a prestigious all-boys school where I ended up failing the eleventh grade outright. Although my life was going to turn around, I was an angry young man. I did not like myself at all, certainly did not have the time of day for the things of the Lord, and must have caused my parents all kinds of grief. To this day I cannot imagine how difficult it must have been for my Dad to have preached the Word of God with such power and to have loved on a people as their shepherd with a son at home who seemed bent on traveling down a broad road that could only lead to destruction.

Although I still had a road to travel, I cannot blot out of my memory the sound of my mother praying for me. From my adult vantage point, I absolutely believe the prayers of my mother protected me from the choirmasters of my life. Her passionate imploring before the Father gave a nine-year-old child the ability to bolt and run from the outstretched paws of a roaring lion! On many occasions I would find myself walking (or storming) past her bedroom only to be stopped dead in my tracks by the sound of her groanings before the Lord on my behalf. I know the Lord was listening to her. In fact, He answered her prayers!

I must leave the final word to my favorite hymn. It goes like this:

> *What a friend we have in Jesus, All our sins and griefs to bear!*
> *What a privilege to carry everything to God in prayer!*
> *Oh, what peace we often forfeit, Oh, what needless pain we bear,*
> *All because we do not carry everything to God in prayer!*
>
> *Have we trials and temptations? Is there trouble anywhere?*
> *We should never be discouraged, Take it to the Lord in prayer:*
> *Can we find a friend so faithful Who will all our sorrows share?*
> *Jesus knows our ev'ry weakness, Take it to the Lord in prayer.*
>
> *Are we weak and heavy laden, Cumbered with a load of care?*
> *Precious Savior, still our refuge; Take it to the Lord in prayer:*
> *Do thy friends despise, forsake thee? Take it to the Lord in prayer;*
> *In His arms He'll take and shield thee; Thou wilt find a solace there.*
> —Joseph Scriven

Conclusion

This exclusive prayer has revealed so much concerning the source, nature, character, and function of the believer. In a general sense, the Lord Jesus has incorporated the lifeblood of salvation in His conversation with the Father. In an effort to try to harness a bird's-eye view of these fourteen verses, I want to list the ten functional elements of salvation included in Jesus' words. These elements are all crucial to our understanding of this great miracle called salvation. Conversion is, indeed, the greatest miracle that can ever take place, especially when one considers that the heart of man is exceedingly wicked. Even the psalmist made this point when he stated, "Salvation is far from the wicked because they do not seek Your statutes" (Ps. 119:155).

As we listen to God praying, we overhear the essential ingredients that make up this phenomenal happening called salvation. To be a Christian and a follower of the Lord Jesus Christ is the most wonderful thing that can ever happen to any person at any time. This conversation lays back the cover of salvation and provides us with the twelve functional elements of salvation. I simply list them because each element has been drawn directly from the words of the Son of Man, and we have already considered them in the text of our discussion.

The Twelve Elements of Salvation

1. The plan of God
2. The purpose of man
3. The selection of man
4. The revelation of God
5. The mediation of the Son
6. The necessity of faith
7. The exclusivity of believing man
8. The nature of submission
9. The portrait of the disciple
10. The sanctification of the believer
11. The intercession of the exalted Son
12. The glory of the Father

And so, as we transition into the inclusive prayer of our Savior, we will hear the Son establish an essential pattern of behavior for all who come to know Him through the testimony of their message. Jesus, after all, was about to leave them. And His destination was to be our destination. His life was to be our life. And His desire was that all who follow Him, throughout all the generations to come, may know the fullness of His indwelling presence.

Part III

The Inclusive Prayer

Introduction

Have you ever felt left out? God will never leave you out!

It may, perhaps, be a great asset to our understanding of these final words of our Savior to take a look at the church at Ephesus for a moment. This fledgling church was not unlike many of our churches today. Despite all they had been taught about the truth of God in Christ Jesus, this group of believers had, evidently, stopped praying for the lost. Their community of faith had become infiltrated by Judaistic false teachers who had seriously perverted and twisted the gospel message to suit their own ends. One of the hallmarks of their perverted teaching was the contention that salvation be restricted only to Jews and some of the Gentiles who had converted to Judaism. Needless to say, this kind of false teaching can only result in a narrow definition of salvation and, most certainly, would seriously impede any effort on the part of the believers to pray evangelistically.

It sounds similar to a church I was told about that enjoyed many years of wonderful growth as the Lord brought more and more people into His church through salvation. The members of the congregation prayed continually for the lost and were even more serious about bringing their lost family and friends to hear the message of salvation. Sadly, when the pastor left for another church, the search committee recommended a man who was totally incompatible with the evangelistic heartbeat and fervor of this New Testament church. Soon after his arrival the new pastor began to teach the congregation "another gospel," which placed all the emphasis on congratulating the saved to the exclusion of inviting the lost. It did not take long before the pastor had surrounded himself with his band of followers, and the church began to die. And why would anyone bother to come to a church that believed and practiced religious exclusivism?

I believe these kinds of churches have the potential to attract two kinds of Christian people. First, they attract those who have grown tired of all the time and effort required to grow a church that reaches out to a lost and dying world. Many pastors fall into this category. They have served the Lord faithfully in small, dying, struggling churches and have seen little for their gallant effort. They have grown weary in well doing. Oftentimes they have been subject to the most ruthless and godless kinds of behavior from established power brokers inside these churches. Many of these pastors have been terminated with little reason following meetings called by these godless men and women, many of whom firmly believe they own the church of God. And so along comes a theological excuse for them to back away from the hard sell of evangelism and soul-winning, a theology that erroneously teaches that God has predetermined some for salvation and some for damnation!

A second reason some people fall into the trap of religious exclusivism is because they are deep theological thinkers. The trend is for persons who are academically inclined and theologically astute to become engaged in something with a little more meat in it! This is one of the reasons so many bright students have attached themselves to leaders who espouse a nonevangelistic practice of theology. It suits such people to sit and talk about the deep things of God rather than be engaged in the disciplined activity of reaching out to the lost. Many of these people would rather travel across the country to attend conclaves of spirituality than walk across the street to tell a lost man about the wonderful saving grace of God in and through the sacrifice of the Lord Jesus Christ!

This is why this prayer of the Lord Jesus is so significant.

You have not been left out! No one has been left out or abandoned by God before you were born!

Zacchaeus was one such lost man! When the Lord Jesus was passing by, he climbed up a tree to see the Lord. Jesus stopped and called him down from the tree and came into his house and his heart and said, "The Son of Man has come to seek and to save the lost" (Luke 19:10).

And so back to the church at Ephesus, which became a prime example of a people who would have had great difficulty accepting this spoken word of the Son of Man concerning those who would come to believe in His name after His death, burial, and resurrection. They were no different. False teachers had crept in among them and had taught them to stop worrying about lost people. So they did! Read what Paul had to say to them:

> First of all, then, I urge that petitions, prayers, intercessions, and
> thanksgivings be made for everyone, for kings and all those who are in
> authority, so that we may lead a tranquil and quiet life in all godliness
> and dignity. This is good, and it pleases God our Savior, who wants
> everyone to be saved and to come to the knowledge of the truth.
>
> For there is one God and one mediator between God and man, a
> man, Christ Jesus, who gave Himself—a ransom for all, a testimony at
> the proper time.
>
> For this I was appointed a herald, an apostle (I am telling the
> truth; I am not lying), and a teacher of the Gentiles in faith and truth.
> (1 Tim. 2:1–7)

The urgency with which Paul calls on these believers to pray for everyone is because the lost have great need to be saved. Believers should always be asking God to intercede and save unbelievers from eternal damnation. Even the word *intercessions*, which means "to fall in with someone," accentuates the need to have compassion for the lost to the point that an intimate conversation takes place with the only One who can save them from their sin. Paul was calling on the Ephesian Christians to pray and petition God with an urgent compassion in their hearts. The reasons for this are based on the reality that all believers were, themselves, once without Christ. Paul makes this point clear.

> We too were once foolish, disobedient, deceived, captives of vari-
> ous passions and pleasures, living in malice and envy, hateful, detest-
> ing one another. But when the goodness and love for man appeared
> from God our Savior, He saved us—not by works of righteousness
> that we had done, but according to His mercy, through the washing
> of regeneration and renewal by the Holy Spirit. This Spirit He poured

out on us abundantly through Jesus Christ our Savior, so that having been justified by His grace, we became heirs with the hope of eternal life. (Titus 3:3–7)

With the conscious mind-set of a sinner saved by the grace of God, Paul exhorts the Ephesian Christians to plead with God for the souls of everyone, including kings and all who are in places of authority. This reference to "everyone" is a reference to the lost in general and not the elect of God only. God's sovereign decree concerning the elect is His business alone. No believer can possibly know who God's elect are until they respond to the invitation to accept Him as Savior. The vast extent of God's grace reaches to the ends of the earth and defies any human attempt at definition! Any person who determines to deny God's call to go into all the world on the basis of their predisposed theology sets themselves up as God because they have determined who God's elect are in place of God!

Because so many powerful kings and queens are opposed to the Savior, Paul urges believers to be passionate about interceding for them. Needless to say this was a bitter pill to swallow for the Christians of Paul's day because of the unmitigated terror they faced from many of the Roman emperors. But no one was left out!

In short, this discourse is a reference to the divine purpose for which Christ died. His divine purpose was His saving purpose. It was the purpose for which God sent Him to this earth. It was the purpose for which He labored in human flesh on this earth. It was the purpose for which He died on the cross. It was the purpose for which He rose triumphantly from the grave. And through His death and resurrection, Jesus became the One and only mediator between God and man. He became the only One who had God's complete authority "over all flesh; so He may give eternal life" (John 17:2). This authority carried with it the right to intervene between two conflicting parties. In the course of intervention, the conflict is resolved and a covenant of agreement is ratified. Jesus Christ went to the cross to accomplish exactly this state of affairs between man and God. As mediator He was able to restore peace because He was the only perfect God-man who could bring both God and man together.

This inclusive prayer is the climactic moment of His purpose-driven life on earth. It is the defining moment. It is the announcement the disciples had been waiting for. It validated their mission. It compelled their determination to go into all the world. It provided the sanctuary in which they could operate with confidence and boldness in a lost and dying world. It allowed them to understand they would not be alone. It made them see the sovereign work of God being carried out through the ages. It motivated them to keep on keeping on even when persecution reached the point at which they could not keep on! It bolstered their faithfulness even when pain and suffering were the order of the day. It sharpened their strategy and gave them meaningful direction as they sought to tell the good news. It emboldened their proclamation and drove them to stand up and be counted even when the crowds howled for their blood.

From this moment on every believer would know forever that no person was left out of the reach of God's amazing grace. They would know that God's business is God's business! They would know that their business was to be obedient and do what God had told every believer to do—go and tell the good news!

Jesus came to this earth and became our high priest! This is the main point.

> Now the main point of what is being said is this: we have this kind of high priest, who sat down at the right hand of the throne of the Majesty in the heavens, a minister of the sanctuary and the true tabernacle, which the Lord set up, and not man. For every high priest is appointed to offer gifts and sacrifices; therefore it was necessary for this priest also to have something to offer. Now if He were on earth, He wouldn't be a priest, since there are those offering gifts prescribed by the law. These serve as a copy and shadow of the heavenly things, as Moses was warned when he was about to complete the tabernacle. For He said, Be careful that you make everything according to the pattern that was shown to you on the mountain. But Jesus has now obtained a superior ministry, and to that degree He is the mediator of a better covenant, which has been legally enacted on better promises. (Heb. 8:1–6)

Chapter 10

Jesus Celebrates His Mediatorial Function

Jesus' hour was fast approaching, and He knew it well. The agony of the cross loomed over the place where He stood looking up into the heavens. He could see the Father seated on the throne of His kingly rule over the universe. He could see Himself seated at the right hand of the Father. And He could hear His eternally established plea of intercession for all those who would still come to believe in His name through the message preached by those who believe in His name.

He could see the desperate plight of man thrashing about in the imprisonment of his self-imposed exile from the loving embrace of the Father. He could see their faces. He could hear their pathetic cries. He could see their futile efforts to find peace and joy and meaning in life. He could watch them as they wallowed about in their own orchestrated brilliance brandishing their own humanly devised methods of soul-satisfaction. He could hear the eulogists sounding forth from one funeral to another the virtues of dead people whose lasting contribution had been all the things they had done and had given and had established while on this earth. Yes, the Son could see Jerusalem.

There they were. All the people. All the people of the world! Men, women, boys, and girls of every description and from every segment of society! And He wept! And now He found Himself about to go out with the disciples across the Kidron Valley where there was a garden! Lying in wait for Him there would be someone who had walked with Him in the garden before. Hiding anxiously behind a tree would be someone who had looked the part, played the part, and spoken the part. Waiting to pounce on the Savior would be one who always looked like one of them but was never one of them.

But Jesus knew! He had always known. He could never be fooled or distracted. He never let on but He knew. He had the amazing capacity to see through all the outer garments. He had the ability to listen to the heart that sang the song and not the mouth that expressed the words.

For He was God. He had always been God and was there from the beginning. He had not abdicated His right as God but had simply laid down His rightful privilege as God.

And now that rightful privilege was about to be restored. The glory that was His from before the world began was about to be His at the right hand of the Father.

He was about to do His divine duty. His mission was about to be accomplished. This was the time when Jesus would "set the seal" on His right to act as mediator between God and man and to function as the eternal intercessor. When the Son of Man spoke the words "I pray for them. I am not praying for the world" (v. 9) in the exclusive prayer, He was announcing His role as intercessor. When He spoke the words "I pray not only for these" (v. 20), He was announcing His role as mediator.

As mediator He was sealing the nature of His God-ordained role as mediator between God and man. His assignment was to broker the agreement God had put in place that was the new covenant through the blood of Jesus. This was God's plan for the redemption of sinful man. There was no other way and no other person who could ratify this treaty. This role and function incorporated a number of indispensable dynamics, all of which are vital components of the means by which man is restored in his severed relationship with God.

While the prospect of the cross was cause for pain and agony, the thought of the nature of His mediatorial function as high priest was cause for great celebration. Jesus' function as mediator was accomplished in two ways:

1. By means of a designed act of obedience
2. By means of an eternal prayer with the Father

In the first He set Himself to be crucified on the cross. In the second He reaped the rewards of His obedience. In the first He took on Himself the sins of the world for an unrighteous man. In the second He carried the sins of the world to a righteous Father. In the first He conquered sin and death and the grave. In the second He presented His victory over sin and death and the grave. In the first He ascended to be seated at the right hand of the Father. In the second He prayed continually to the Father. In the first He acted with the complete authority of the Father. In the second He offered eternal life with the complete authority of the Father.

This is why He prayed, and still prays, not only for all believers but for all who will still believe! The prayer with which God prays is the prayer with which the Son prays. This Godhead prayer serves several important functions:

1. It presents God as God.
2. It demonstrates the love of God.
3. It speaks as God.
4. It proves the genuineness of God.
5. It petitions God.

Remember that the Lord Jesus had yet to go to the cross at the time this prayer was prayed. With this in mind, the final part of God's prayer is nothing short of a celebration. This celebration confirms a number of things:

1. It is a confirmation of the nature of God.
2. It is an affirmation of the work of God.
3. It is a presentation of the sacrifice of God.
4. It is an anticipation of the exaltation of God.
5. It is a portrayal of the eternal glory of God.
6. It is an acceptance of the divine will of God.

In short, when Jesus said He was praying "not only for these" (v. 20), He was making a twofold acceptance of His divine assignment from God.

He Was Accepting His Divine Responsibility to Discharge His Duty to God

This was the Father's will from before the foundation of the world. This was not an afterthought or an emergency plan that God came up with to bail out the children of Israel who had messed up so badly in their efforts to earn their salvation. No, this was a better covenant, designed by the foreknowledge of God, to redeem man for all time and for all eternity.

To discharge one's duty is to carry out an accepted responsibility regardless of personal consequence. Lieutenant Andrew Kinard could have chosen to become a medical doctor, an engineer, or just about anything he wanted to become in his professional life. He had the ability and the personality to do anything his heart desired. But he wanted to become a soldier and serve in the United States Armed Forces. I remember the day he graduated from Dorman High School and went off to the United States Naval Academy in Annapolis, Maryland. He looked so dapper and was so determined to do his best. And he did! Those years in Annapolis were marked by the highest achievements and by excellence in every imaginable way. This young man was headed for the top, without a doubt. In his final year as a midshipman at the Naval Academy, Andrew was appointed to serve on the brigade staff, one of the highest honors. He became the brigade training officer in charge of all the training for members of the fourth class.

He graduated with all the pomp and fanfare afforded the best of the best this nation has to offer, accompanied by the handshake of the commander in chief of the United States of America. When the announcement was made, caps flew into the air. The country cheered in appreciation and adoration of these brave men and women who were so dedicated to their country. Andrew could have chosen any branch of service he so desired. Commanding a submarine, special intelligence, nuclear arms, a fighter pilot were just a few of the options he could have taken and risen to the highest rank without a doubt. But he chose to don the uniform of the Second Light Armored Reconnaissance based in Camp LeJeune, North Carolina. Shortly thereafter he found himself in Alpha Company, First Platoon on assignment in the Anbar Province of Iraq.

His training involved light armored vehicles that had a human cargo of seven soldiers and carried a 25 mm canon accompanied by a 7.62 mm machine gun.

On October 29, 2006, Andrew led some of his men on a patrol. When the bomb exploded, the young lieutenant found himself lying in a massive pool of blood. His men reported that their seriously wounded leader made certain they were all well stationed for action and protection before he literally succumbed to the massive loss of blood. Only a miracle from the Lord could have saved Andrew's life!

By the time he reached Germany, he had received more than eighty units of blood and had gone into cardiac arrest on at least two occasions.

I shall never forget the day I stood at his bedside with his father in Bethesda, Maryland. I cannot describe looking down on the legless body of this young man. His face was torn to shreds with shrapnel, and his head was swollen out of proportion. His fingers were blackened by the combination of congealed blood and dirt. Pipes and tubes came out of his body from everywhere. The attending physician was extremely cautious about Andrew's chances of survival.

We all wept.

Thousands of people were praying!

Sometime later Andrew's father asked his son the most searching question any father could ever ask of a son. "Son, " Harry asked, "during all of this pain, all this you have endured, has there ever been a time you have wondered if it was all worth it?"

Only one statement came from Andrew's heart and soul.

"Giving up is not an option!"

Even without legs, Andrew will rise to the top.

How much more so the Lord Jesus Christ, who was about to lay down His life a ransom for many. Jesus knew what lay ahead of Him as He anticipated the agony of the cross. He knew the suffering and shame associated with such an inhumane death at the hands of the Romans. But He accepted His divine responsibility to discharge His duty to the Father.

Giving up was not an option for the Savior! He was just doing His job. He was simply accepting His responsibility to discharge His duty!

He Was Accepting His Divine Responsibility to Give an Account of His Discharged Responsibility to God

There is a sense in which "I pray not only for these" is the Lord Jesus affirming His continual debriefing of the Father until He comes to receive His own into glory. His death on the cross and His glorious resurrection marked the beginning of His ability to report back to the Father concerning the continuing redemption of God's created man. The reconciliation of alienated man and his restoration with a righteous God would continue until the return of Christ to this earth to set up His millennial reign. The means by which this continual restoration would take place was about to be accomplished through the work on the cross. This is why the Son was able to say, "It is finished" (John 19:30). But His work of mediatorial intercession on behalf of those who had yet to believe would continue throughout the ages.

I have had the privilege of visiting the White House on two occasions. It is hard to imagine the power housed in this magnificent house. The Oval Office is where the President of the United States of America finds the symbolic and practical expression of his responsibility to lead the greatest nation the world has ever known. One cannot even begin to imagine the discussions that must have taken place around that table in that room. Some have said it is the absolute seat of power and influence. Basically three things happen, or should happen, in the process of making decisions that affect so many people in America and the world. First, issues are discussed, analyzed, and presented to the president. Second, decisions are made. These decisions are certainly made in concert with his top advisers, but ultimately the president is the one who makes the final decision. Third, his top advisers continually come back to him with reports on the progress and outcome of every decision made. The president is given a briefing every day by his counsel on matters of importance, and he is debriefed every day on decisions that were made earlier and are being carried out according to the instructions of the commander in chief. I am sure many secretaries of state, defense, or treasury has heard the president call out something like this:

"Morning, Karl."

"Morning, Mr. President. You get your latte this morning OK?"

"Certainly did, Karl. It's sitting on my desk in the Oval. Thanks, man. Appreciate you slipping out to Starbucks for me!"

"Sure thing, Mr. President. Glad to do it. I get myself one on the corner of Washington, so it's no sweat picking you up one as well."

"Oh, by the way, Karl. Got a word on the project in Africa?"

"Yes, sir. If you've got a minute, I'll bring you up-to-date. I think you'll love what we've done for those folks. Thousands of lives have been saved as a result of your initiative to go in and help them. They just couldn't do it for themselves. They were powerless to take care of their own misery. More than ten thousand of them had died of starvation. Your plan was outstanding. It looks like we're the only ones who have the means and the authority to go in and offer them the kind of help that would rescue thousands more from certain death. Word is out, and there is a buzz in the international community. Reporters are going berserk on this one! They want to know more. Our ambassadors are doing a good job of spreading the good news. Of course, there are the naysayers and critics. In fact, one group wants to have you impeached for the gross interference in the plight of a starving nation. They are really mad because it has upset their own plans and initiatives to gain a pat on the back from the international community. But you know their plans to help themselves could never work. They never worked before, and they never will work now. We are the only ones who could do what needed to be done, and you are the only commanding officer who could have devised a plan such as this. It's working, Mr. President. It's sure working!"

"Thanks for the debriefing, Karl!"

I realize this sounds somewhat simplistic, but I can see the Savior engaged in a constant debriefing of the Father. The Bible tells us that the angels are delighted when sinners come to put their faith and trust in God. It conjures up this picture in my mind. Each time someone is born of the Spirit and believes that God sent Jesus to this earth to die for their sins, there is an eruption of joy in heaven. I can see the millions of angels gathered around the throne of God, watching, waiting, serving, and listening for every announcement that comes from the mouth of the Savior.

"Father," the Son says with a smile on His lovely face, "Sue Ellen has come to believe in Your name and is now one of Your children. I have just written her name in the Lamb's book of life!"

And with that the whole chorus of the heavenly hosts erupts with unspeakable joy! "Worthy is the Lamb," they shout.

> Then I looked, and heard the voice of many angels around the throne, and also of the living creatures, and of the elders. Their number was countless thousands, plus thousands of thousands. They said with a loud voice:
>
> The Lamb who was slaughtered is worthy
> to receive power and riches
> and wisdom and strength
> and honor and glory and blessings!
>
> I heard every creature in heaven, on earth, under the earth, on the sea, and everything in them say:
>
> Blessing and honor and glory and dominion
> to the One seated on the throne,
> and to the Lamb, forever and ever!
>
> The four living creatures said, "Amen," and the elders fell down and worshiped. (Rev. 5:11–14)

We are reminded of the meaning of intercession in many ways. I remember a man calling me on the telephone one day to tell me his marriage was in serious trouble. He and his wife had been married for twenty years, and things had evidently developed to the point his wife had left him. He was heartbroken, to say the least. Of course I realize it takes two people to make a marriage work the way a marriage ought to work, and so I listened to him with as much empathy as I could, realizing I had not heard from his wife. She, however, would not meet with me. When, finally, I did manage to talk to her on the phone, she admitted she had been unfaithful to her husband and claimed she did not want to be married to him anymore. Because I believe divorce is not an option except in the case of adultery, I shared with the husband that he had biblical grounds for divorce but soon came to discover he was willing to forgive his wife because he loved her so much.

I can still remember his pleadings with me to act as an intercessor, a media-tor, between him and his wife. I did so but sadly to no avail. She had determined to go her own way, and I pray for her in the consequences she will have to deal with as time goes by.

And so it is evident that Jesus' two references to prayer in our study are intended to highlight His activity of intercession when in heaven.

The Activity of Intercession

This wonderful practice carries two distinct possibilities:

INTERCESSORY PRAYER FOR THE BENEFIT OF BELIEVERS

The intercessory prayer we read about in verse 9 is Jesus' representation of the acts and activities of believers that still need to be accomplished. This is why we are able to approach God's throne with confidence and boldness. Here we hear the Son anticipating what He will be able to do for all believers once He has finished the work God had assigned Him to do on the cross. He sees Himself in heaven at the right hand of the Father "making intercession for us." He is petitioning our every circumstance and our every need before our heavenly Father. He is assuring every believer of His constant and continual prayer for them. He is encouraging every believer to stand strong in the knowledge of a Savior who loves without ceasing and who is praying without ceasing. And the cherry on the top is the power and presence of the Holy Spirit who indwells every believer. The Holy Spirit groans for us when we are unable to make sense of our own lives. The Holy Spirit communes with God on our behalf even when we do not know what to say to God or how to approach Him with our own needs and circumstances.

INTERCESSORY PRAYER FOR THE SALVATION OF SINNERS

The intercessory prayer of the Lord Jesus in verse 20 is the representa-tion of an act already accomplished. It finds our Savior asking the Father to give Him more of "the men You gave Me from the world" (John 17:6). This petition would result in the salvation of those "who [will] believe in Me" (v. 20) through the message of those who were sent "into the world" (v. 18). The first intercessory prayer comes from the heart of the exalted Savior as He sits at the right hand of the Father praying for believers because His ministry continues. The second intercessory prayer comes from the heart of the glorified Savior as He sits at the right hand of the Father praying for the salvation of sinners because His work is complete!

The very nature of Jesus' ministry of intercession incorporates several significant ingredients.

It Is Highly Exclusive

Jesus' intercession on our behalf is our guarantee that God really cares for us. No disciple of Christ is ever alone. We are never abandoned. God is praying for us because He loves us and gave us the Lord Jesus Christ, who, having died for our sins, now makes intercession for us. Everything about the believer is eligible to be brought before the Father by the Son. Membership in God's family has many blessings. We are forgiven of our sin. We have our names written in the Lamb's book of life. We have an abundant life given to us through our Lord Jesus to all His children. But surely the most wonderful thing to contemplate in the journey of life is that He never leaves us and never forsakes us! He is always praying for us, every moment of every day! And we can bring every petition to Him with absolute confidence and great boldness because we have an advocate with the Father!

It Is Highly Inclusive

This is the greatest incentive to pray for those who have not yet come to know the Lord Jesus as their personal Savior. It is one thing to be engaged actively in soul-winning and witnessing, but it is entirely another to know that our Savior is praying for the souls of those who have yet to believe in His name. It is truly an amazing thing to think that we have such an ally as the Savior of the world. The burden of every believer's heart for the salvation of sons and daughters, parents and grandparents, neighbors and friends, business associates and strangers is shared with the heart of a Savior who is actively engaged in praying for them.

What's more, every believer's message has been ordained to be an instrument in the hands of a loving God in the wonderful work of salvation. Every time we preach the Word of God, every time we teach others about Jesus, every time we go on a mission trip to some strange land, Jesus is praying that the message we bring would result in the salvation of many people. My work for Christ and your work for Christ is not in vain. And because of this, all believers are reminded that their responsibility is to go and tell and leave the results up to God!

It Is Highly Personal

The personal nature of Christ's intercession is one of the distinguishing features of the Christian faith. I know of no other religion or deity that prays for his own. Every religion I know demands a high price of continual sacrifice and work that leaves a person with nothing but an empty dream. Not so with the Lord Jesus Christ and His followers! I love to tell people that I have a real relationship with a real Lord Jesus Christ, who died on a real cross and came back to life by the power of God and then went back to a real heaven where He sat down and now prays for me (and you)! He's alive! He's a living God and a wonderful Savior. And He prays continually so that all people will have a personal relationship with Him.

It Is Highly Purposeful

The purpose for which the Lord Jesus Christ died and rose again did not come to an abrupt end with His ascension. His praying for every believer is based on His desire that all would be sanctified through Him in order to be sent out into the world with the message of the gospel. We may well talk about the purpose for which all people have been created, which is to fellowship with our Creator and worship Him, but God is at work in every circumstance, bringing His purpose to bear on the lives of those who love Him. Jesus is actively engaged in praying for the fulfillment of that purpose in every believer's life. Above all, He is praying that we would follow His every command and be completely obedient to His will.

It Is Highly Detailed

Listen, again, to what Paul had to say to the Christians at Philippi when he gave them a practical guide to their daily living. Most of what the apostle had to say had to do with theology and doctrine. It was important for believers to know who God is. But the importance of good doctrine had a direct bearing on practical living.

It has been said, "A weak theology will result in a weak lifestyle," and I think that is true. Many of the greatest tragedies of the modern era have been the result of self-styled men who set themselves on a higher plane than God. In a sense they gave themselves permission to behave badly by justifying what they did outside the parameters set by God. The beauty of Jesus' intercessory prayer is that the details of our lives are never excluded. God is not interested in certain things while not in others. Nothing is too simple to bother Him with, and there is nothing that pertains to our lives that falls outside the scope of His prayers for us. Many believers find themselves wondering whether or not the Lord would be interested in the smaller things of their lives. Paul gave a wonderful perspective when he wrote, "Don't worry about anything, but in everything, through prayer and petition with thanksgiving, let your requests be made known to God" (Phil. 4:6). This means we can place before Him everything and anything because He is praying for us about everything and anything!

It Is Highly Informative

Almost every time I find myself praying for someone in need, I try to mention that Jesus prays for us. Think about this for a second. Jesus not only hears our prayers, but He answers them too! Even silence, sometimes, is an answer. He always opens and closes doors, and He always responds to us because He is actively engaged in interceding for us. This is one of the many reasons it is good to wait on the Lord because He will renew our strength!

It Is Highly Loving

How can we ever describe the love of our Savior at this point? One would think He had every right to sit down and forget about us. His work was done, after all, and He had paid a high price for every believer! The fact that He prays for us is such a powerful statement about the love He has for us. Perhaps the hymn writer has put this into a better perspective than I can.

> *Sweet hour of prayer, sweet hour of prayer,*
> *That calls me from a world of care*

And bids me at my Father's throne,
Make all my wants and wishes known!
In seasons of distress and grief,
My soul has often found relief,
And oft escaped the tempter's snare
By Thy return, sweet hour of prayer.

Sweet hour of prayer, sweet hour of prayer,
Thy wings shall my petition bare to Him,
whose truth and faithfulness
Engage the waiting soul to bless:
And since He bids me seek His face,
Believe His word, and trust His grace,
I'll cast on Him my ev'ry care,
And wait for thee, sweet hour of prayer.

Sweet hour of prayer, sweet hour of prayer,
May I Thy consolation share,
Till, from Mount Pisgah's lofty height,
I view my home and take my flight:
This robe of flesh I'll drop and rise
To sieze the everlasting prize;
And shout, while passing through the air,
"Farewell, farewell, sweet hour of prayer!"
—William Walford, 1772–1850

It Is Highly Instructional

The more the Lord Jesus prays for us, the more we learn about Him. This is a major function of the Holy Spirit, who declares the glory of the Lord to us. Jesus told His disciples about the significance of the work of the Holy Spirit in this regard: "I still have many things to tell you, but you can't bear them now. When the Spirit of truth comes, He will guide you into all the truth. For He will not speak on His own, but He will speak whatever He hears. He will also declare to you what is to come. He will glorify Me, because He will take from what is Mine and declare it to you" (John 16:12–14).

The instruction we receive from the Spirit is that which the Son presents to the Father, certainly about the Father and from the Father, but also from every believer to the Father as the Son intercedes on our behalf. We are instructed in His ways as a result and have become equipped to serve Him.

It Is Highly Continual

There is not one word in the Scriptures that tells us Jesus will ever stop interceding for us. Until He comes back again to receive us to Himself forever, the Lord Jesus will be praying for us and for all those who will come to believe in His name.

It Is Highly Satisfying

All believers have reason to be highly satisfied because Jesus is praying for them. When Paul encouraged believers to be anxious for nothing (see Phil. 4:6), he concluded by telling them that "the peace of God, which surpasses every thought, will guard your hearts and minds in Christ Jesus" (v. 7). Here we have the wonderful benefit of intercessory prayer. What can we say about the search for peace in the world in which we live? Every believer has peace with God and, through the continual prayers of the Savior, has peace through God. This is what all people strive for and every Christian has received. And this peace is directed at the heart and the mind, the two areas of greatest turmoil and tension in the human disposition.

What does this all mean for us? Jesus is praying for you, and He is praying for me. He is also praying for all who have yet to believe in His name. He created you, He understands you, and He feels for you; He intercedes for you and me and every person in this world because He came to "seek and to save that which was lost"!

Chapter 11

Jesus Calls for
Unprecedented Unity

The matter of unity occupies a significant place in the words of our Savior in this final prayer. This call for all believers to be unified leaves the distinct impression that Jesus was not simply making a request. He was asking the Father to enforce this as a mandate for all believers. It is also vitally relevant to the constitution of the body of Christ. The functionality of the church is connected with the functionality of the triune God. And this interconnectedness becomes manifestly evident in all the Savior has to say to the Father in this inclusive prayer.

This is the point at which the Savior begins to focus attention on our future. And because our future is inextricably intertwined with His future, it stands to reason that our behavior must be a mirror reflection of all that He is as God. This final word of prayer allows believers throughout the ages to gain an insight into the reality of God's great expectation for the church. Jesus has already prayed about security and sanctity. He has already outlined the deeper meaning of the character of the Christian disciple. He has already established the basic premise of the Christian faith and the pillars of our salvation.

Now the burden of His prayer is unity. His central and overriding concern for all the children of God is that they experience the practical outworking of the oneness of the Godhead. This would ultimately bode well for the church throughout the ages because spiritual unity highlights the fact that all believers belong to the Lord Jesus Christ and to one another.

We will make an effort to understand what Jesus was saying by looking at two aspects of unity. They are the basis of Christian unity and the face of Christian unity.

The Basis of Christian Unity

What is the essential basis for true Christian unity? Is this something the church strives for because it provides for easier living or perhaps because it allows leaders to go unchallenged? Needless to say, the Lord Jesus points to the essential nature of the triune God when He says, "May they all be one, as You, Father, are in Me and I am in You" (John 17:21). He goes on to add, "May they also be one in Us," "May they be one as We are one," and "May they be made completely one" (vv. 21–23).

Read the words of Paul to the church at Ephesus. In this passage we hear the apostle pleading with the believers at Ephesus to conduct themselves in a manner well-pleasing to the Lord. And the basis of his plea finds ground in the person and work of the Lord Jesus Christ: "I, therefore, the prisoner in the Lord, urge you to walk worthy of the calling you have received, with all humility and gentleness, with patience, accepting one another in love, diligently keeping the unity of the Spirit with the peace that binds us. There is one body and one Spirit, just as you were called to one hope at your calling; one Lord, one faith, one baptism, one God and Father of all, who is above all and through all and in all" (Eph. 4:1–6).

One can hear the apostle changing gears from doctrine to duty, from principle to practice, and from position to practice. His use of the word *walk* carries with it the idea of daily conduct and matches the theme of the rest of His pastoral letter. The worthiness with which they are admonished to walk is an instruction. Paul encouraged them to have their talk match their walk.

And the basis of the call to Christian unity is identical to Jesus' presentation to the Father in the inclusive prayer. The Spirit bestows oneness on all believers, creating a bond of peace that surrounds God's children in everything they seek to accomplish for His sake. Even in his instructions about sexual purity, Paul points to the oneness between the believer and the Lord as a sure hallmark of protection against immorality: "But anyone joined to the Lord is one spirit with Him" (1 Cor. 6:17).

Just as the Lord Jesus refers to His oneness with the Father, so Paul refers to the spiritual cord that binds God's people together. He lists specific areas of oneness that demonstrate unity: body, Spirit, hope, Lord, faith, baptism, and God the Father. His focus is on the Trinity. Paul emphasizes their complete unity in every aspect of their divine nature and plan even though they have unique roles as the members of the Godhead.

ONE BODY

Since the coming of the Holy Spirit at Pentecost, the body of Christ is united without distinction. This is made possible by means of the work of the Holy Spirit.

ONE HOPE

Herein lies the pledge and promise of eternal life through Jesus Christ, the Lord. Every believer, without distinction, is given this guarantee by the seal of the Holy Spirit, by whom we "were sealed with the promised Holy Spirit. He is the down payment of our inheritance, for the redemption of the possession, to the praise of His glory" (Eph. 1:13–14).

ONE LORD

Jesus is the only way to the Father and the only means by which reconciliation can take place. Because of Him "there is no distinction between Jew and Greek, since the same Lord of all is rich to those who call on Him" (Rom. 10:12).

ONE FAITH

Here we find the body of doctrine taught throughout the New Testament. Jude, one of the four half brothers of the Lord Jesus, wrote, "Dear friends, although I was eager to write you about our common salvation, I found it necessary to write and exhort you to contend for the faith that was delivered to the saints once for all" (v. 3). Unity in doctrine is an essential ingredient to the body of Christ.

ONE BAPTISM

The reference here is to the unity demonstrated by the believer as he passes through the waters of baptism. This signifies the common identification of all believers as they publicly profess their faith by virtue of their identification with the death, burial, and resurrection of the Lord Jesus Christ. The spiritual baptism of all believers who are baptized by the Holy Spirit unto faith in Christ may also be implied at this juncture.

ONE GOD

Ultimately all believers in Christ are born again in and through one God, who is none other than the God and the Father of our Lord Jesus Christ. The Corinthian Christians were reminded of this as they struggled with the issue of idols: "For even if there are so called gods, whether in heaven or on earth—as there are many 'gods' and many 'lords'—yet for us there is one God, the Father, from whom are all things, and we for Him; and one Lord, Jesus Christ, through whom are all things, and we through Him" (1 Cor. 8:5–6). These are the essentials of the basis of spiritual unity for all believers, essentially because all believers are "one in Us."

The life of Christ demonstrates a spiritual act of God whereby the believer has been immersed with the Spirit into unity with all other believers. As such, all believers are immersed into the body of Christ to the point at which they cannot be believers if they have not been born again of the Spirit of God. It follows that there cannot be more than one Spirit baptism. If there was an alternative, then the whole point of unity made by the Lord Jesus in His prayer has no grounds. Jesus' statement in this regard, just hours before His work is complete, is not a call for sinners to clamor after an experience that is designed to produce unity but rather because salvation is rooted in the fact of the Godhead, it is a reality to acknowledge and live out.

The Face of Christian Unity

In John 17:23 the Lord Jesus pleads that "they may be made completely one" so that the world may come to believe that God sent Him to die on the cross.

In essence, the Savior is establishing the face of unity. Herein lies the accountability that is produced by the action of unity. Jesus is referring to the outward manifestation of unity, not unlike the many references to "fruit" in the Scriptures. Unity is a "doing" word that, by implication, has a face that must be seen by a lost and dying world. If we refer back to Paul's wonderful admonition to the church at Ephesus to walk in unity, it will quickly become clear that unity has a practical product. Paul points to four faces of unity, all of which serve as prime examples of the completeness referred to by our Savior.

HUMILITY

The word *humility* was not a word readily found in the Greek culture of Paul's day and age. This was no wonder, considering the haughtiness of the Romans. Even the religious sects and the Jews had a religious arrogance, considering themselves superior to all others. According to James, "God resists the proud, but gives grace to the humble" (4:6). The only hope man has in the context of his dismal failures and sinfulness is the grace of God.

James reminds believers that God gives grace as a demonstration of His power over sin, flesh, and even Satan himself. This quote from the Old Testament book of Proverbs reveals not only the object of God's grace but also the objective of God's grace. The object of His grace is the one who has humbled himself in the presence of a righteous and holy God. The objective of His grace is the encompassing of all believers to the point of completion so that all may see the demonstration of God's grace.

Jesus makes this point clear. In this prayer, He does not refer only to an exclusive or select few who are especially endowed with the gift of humility and lowliness. Rather He refers to one of the essential marks that must encompass all who believe in His name. Humility is the ultimate face of unity in Christ because it speaks most eloquently to the submissiveness of the believer to the lordship of Jesus Christ. It is the greatest and most identifiable testimony to the willing and conscious submission to God's divine authority over all things. It is the ultimate mark of the true servant of God and lies at the heart of Paul's repeated emphasis on being a bond slave of God.

Humility is the most foundational of all the Christian virtues. It is the quality of character commanded in the first beatitude (see Matt. 5:3) and describes the noble grace of God in and through the Lord Jesus Christ.

GENTLENESS

If humility is the foundation of Christian character, then gentleness is the product of humility. It refers to that which is mild of spirit and bears witness to a believer who is under major self-control. An illustration often used of gentleness is that of a fine stallion under the control of the master who sits on his back. The bit in his mouth keeps him under pressure to hold back until the master releases him to gallop away and demonstrate his full potential. Gentleness is such an admirable indicator of complete unity in that it puts on public display the willingness of might and power under control. Few people in the local church do not recognize leadership, status, and power. They know what a man has in his hand. They see the accomplishments. They feel the power of character. And yet, when such a person behaves in a gentle manner despite these things, great witness for the cause of Christ is seen and heard. This is why the Lord Jesus repeatedly refers to the resulting testimony of true Christian unity.

Jesus said, "All of you, take up My yoke and learn from Me, because I am gentle and humble in heart, and you will find rest for yourselves" (Matt. 11:29). In Galatians, gentleness is listed as a key fruit of the Spirit (see 5:23). In speaking of the essentials of the Christian life, Paul reminds the believers at Colossae to "put on heartfelt compassion, kindness, humility, gentleness, and patience," as well as love, which is "the perfect bond of unity" (Col. 3:12–14). The act of "putting on" is an appeal to the seat of emotions because it represents the completeness of one who is unified in Christ. Gentleness is a vital part of the character of the new man in Christ and carries with it the idea that the believer would be willing to suffer injury or insult rather than to inflict such pain on others.

PATIENCE

The original language literally translates *patience* as "long tempered" and conveys an understanding of a resolved patience that is an outgrowth of humility and gentleness. Even in his exhortation to pastors in 1 Thessalonians,

Paul reminds them to be patient in their dealings with people. This applies especially to the weak and those without moral and spiritual strength to do what is right in the eyes of God. This characteristic of the face of unity is the opposite of quick anger, resentment, or revenge. As such it epitomizes the life, ministry, and testimony of the Lord Jesus and validates His demand for unity on the part of all those who would believe in His name through the message of the saved. While patience speaks more to the manner with which believers endure difficult circumstances, longsuffering looks more at the manner with which believers endure difficult people. Both are synonymous in function but apply in differing arenas of life and ministry.

The ultimate application of patience belongs, once again, to our Savior. Peter asks us to "regard the patience of our Lord as an opportunity for salvation" (2 Pet. 3:15). Having previously explained that the Lord's patience was the reason He delays ultimate judgment. Here Peter adds that during the time of His patience, Christians should engage in seeking the salvation of souls.

ACCEPTANCE

This fourth characteristic of unity is another hallmark of the Lord's practical expression of unconditional and continuous love. The means by which acceptance is carried is love, which is the greatest of all Christian virtues. This was the foundation of Christ's sacrifice on the cross, the love of God! This kind of love produces acceptance and must be applied with great fervency according to Peter. This means that the kind of love that produces acceptance is a love that is stretched to the maximum. Such an expression of Christian unity requires the Christian to put another's spiritual good ahead of his own desires, even if he is treated with hostility for doing it. The end result of acceptance is forgiveness and restoration. It provides a key means by which the church is built and people are blessed.

DILIGENCE

I am going to add a fifth characteristic of unity because it completes the picture presented by the Lord Jesus. Diligence is applied unity. *Webster's* defines *diligence* as "the constant and earnest effort to accomplish what is undertaken." Paul's appeal for unity in the body of Christ culminates with the exhortation to "diligently keep the unity of the Spirit with the peace that binds us." Diligence drives the application of unity. It takes humility, gentleness, patience, and acceptance to the drawing board.

Without diligence, unity will not be accomplished or, at the least, be sustained. For it is one thing to foster and promote unity but another thing entirely to sustain it over a long period of time. People grow weary in well doing. They end up taking leadership and excellence for granted. Sometimes they just forget who they are in Christ. And many times the "old man" rears his head, and behaviors emerge that are not at all pleasing to the Lord. It is amazing how large a forest fire can be set ablaze by just a small slip of the tongue! Diligence keeps unity on the front burner and is a constant reminder to the believer of his call and obligation to be unified in the Spirit of the living God.

The Purpose of Christian Unity

Jesus' prayer not only points to the basis of Christian unity and the face of Christian unity but also to the purpose of Christian unity. Without a doubt Jesus knew that divisiveness among believers would be one of the single most damaging things for the cause of Christ. Without having any way to back up this statement, I heard a man say that the famous Indian leader Mahatma Ghandi was heard to say that the only reason he would not become a believer in the Lord Jesus Christ and become a Christian was because of other Christians. What a tragedy!

The church, in today's world, suffers from this curse as much as any other. Stories abound of congregations fighting with one another. I have heard of people who come to church business meetings literally armed and prepared for the fight. Staff members spend major time and effort discrediting one another while gossip wreaks havoc knowing no boundaries. Many church congregations revolve around powerful people who own the actions and activities of their churches because of money they have given, status they have, or the length of time they have been involved.

One thing that impresses the world is the way Christians love one another and live together in harmony despite differences of opinion. My father always taught me, "You can disagree without being disagreeable!" The witness of unity is an indispensable mandate from the heart of our Savior. "May they also be one in Us, so the world may believe You sent Me." Could this be any more direct? Is there any part of what Jesus is praying that is not clear?

Perhaps an illustration would be helpful. I am privileged to serve the Lord Jesus together with a most remarkable group of people. Some may consider me obviously biased, and I can certainly understand, but the Lord has allowed me to assemble the most precious group together in the country! We love together, laugh together, play golf together, cry together, dream together, and work extremely hard together! But it certainly was not this way when I first began my ministry. Staff members had built their own empires, jealousies existed, a spirit of noncooperation was emerging, and some actually believed they were the "divine alternative" to the pastor. This was not good and was symptomatic of a major problem that still exists across the board in most denominations and churches.

After much prayer the Lord impressed this inclusive prayer on my heart, and I heard what the Lord Jesus was saying to the Father with fresh ears. Something had to be done. I realized some would have to go! And when they went, some would be unhappy in the church because "their possession" had been touched. But I soon came to realize that church growth is not just about adding people to the church. It is as much about losing people from the church.

Based on God's divine call and purpose for unity among believers, He gave me a five-point covenant designed for our staff. We gathered up in the mountains over two full days. I shared these five points in detail with all the staff. We knelt and prayed together and bound ourselves to strive to live by, operate through, and conduct ourselves according to these principles.

1. We are militantly and fiercely loyal to our Lord and Savior Jesus Christ.
2. We are militantly and fiercely loyal to our own families and to one another's families.
3. We are militantly and fiercely loyal to one another.
4. We are militantly and fiercely loyal to our pastor.
5. We are militantly and fiercely loyal to our church.

Each one of these issues can only be accomplished as a result of unapologetic unity! And, as I am sure you can appreciate, every point can take an entire day to explain and expound.

I cannot tell you the blessing this has been to all of us. It reminds me of the ultimate gift parents can give to their children. Provisions, security, and everything else we do for our children are extremely important if you want to put a smile on your child's face like none other, let him or her see you as parents truly loving each other in mutual love, loyalty, and unity.

The lost world cannot see God, but they can see Christians. Someone has said, "The only Bible some will ever read is you!" Others have commented, "The greatest testimony for the world to see is the testimony of a changed life!" And it all comes together, in practical reality, in unity!

Chapter 12

Jesus Looks Toward His/ Our Future Glory

The final cry of the Son's heart endears the heart of man like no other. Our journey through this prayer has allowed us to hear the Savior talk about where He came from. It has reminded us why He came to this earth and the purpose for which He would die. We have been taken back to our point of origin and have been reestablished in our faith and understanding. We have heard the joyful news that many will believe in the Lord through the message He has given us as believers.

And now it is time for the Son of Man to die! But before He journeys to the cross, the Lord Jesus puts the cherry on the top for all of us when He says, "Father, I desire those You have given Me to be with Me where I am" (John 17:24). This echoes His precious and endearing words of comfort to the disciples when He told them:

> "Your heart must not be troubled. Believe in God; believe also in Me. In My Father's house are many dwelling places; if not, I would have told you. I am going away to prepare a place for you. If I go away and prepare a place for you, I will come back and receive you to Myself, so that where I am you may be also." (John 14:1–3)

This is the ultimate eschatological statement! This is the finest moment of any consideration of the doctrine of last things! Regardless of what we believe concerning the timing of the Lord's coming or the order in which these things will occur, Jesus makes the most reassuring of all statements when He tells the Father of His innermost desire that all who love Him will be with Him forever! What more assurance do we need?

It is necessary to contextualize Jesus' promise of our eternal home. Needless to say, any study of last things is enormous and exciting. It is not my intention to do a detailed analysis of all the issues that I have done in other contexts but rather to take a cursory glance at the issues invoked by Jesus' passionate plea with the Father. I propose to do this in four segments: the anticipation of His return, the promise of His return, the timing of His return, and the events surrounding His return.

The Anticipation of His Return

Jesus will return to earth! Most believers refer to this event as the "second coming." This momentous event will by no means go unnoticed because "every eye will see Him" (Rev. 1:7), and "every knee will bow" to Him (Rom 14:11). My denomination, the Southern Baptists, refers to this in their official document called *The Baptist Faith and Message:*

> God, in His own time and in His own way, will bring the world
> to its appropriate end. According to His promise, Jesus Christ will
> return personally and visibly in glory to the earth; the dead will be
> raised; and Christ will judge all men in righteousness. The unrigh-
> teous will be consigned to hell, the place of everlasting punishment.
> The righteous in their resurrected and glorified bodies will receive
> their reward and will dwell forever in heaven with the Lord.

The first time Jesus was on this earth, He was condemned to death as He stood before Pilate. The second time, Pilate will be judged by Him. The first time Jesus was crucified. The second time, He will be crowned as King of kings and Lord of lords. The fact that He is coming back to receive all believers to Himself in heaven is a constant source of hope, joy, and comfort to all believers.

Jesus' plea to the Father is simply an affirmation of His factual return for this stated purpose.

The Promise of His Return

The expectation of Jesus' return is based on the promise He made while on earth: "Your heart must not be troubled. Believe in God; believe also in Me. In My Father's house are many dwelling places; if not, I would have told you. I am going to prepare a place for you. If I go away and prepare a place for you, I will come back, and receive you to Myself, so that where I am you may be also" (John 14:1–3).

Two basic points need to be noted about Jesus' promise to return. First, the value of the promise depends totally on the value of the person who made the promise. The One who made this promise is none other than the "faithful and true Witness" (Rev. 3:14), the same precious Savior who makes certain all believers hear Him assures them once again just hours before His final act on the cross. Jesus also promised that He would rise from the grave. Trustworthy witnesses verified that He did (see 1 Cor. 15:6), and His witness within our hearts continues to verify that truth. Jesus promised that those who accept Him will receive eternal, abundant life (see John 10:10), and the Holy Spirit continually testifies to that truth within our hearts. We can trust God to keep His promises.

Second, when Jesus promised to return, He was not talking about His resurrection from the dead. Nor was He talking about the coming of the Holy Spirit at Pentecost (Acts 2:1–4). Clearly He was referring to His personal, bodily, literal return to this earth after His resurrection and after the coming of the Holy Spirit at Pentecost.

Two passages of Scripture forcefully verify Jesus' personal return. The first is found in the book of Acts. As Jesus' disciples watched Him ascend into heaven after His resurrection, two angels standing beside them said: "Men of Galilee, why do you stand looking up into heaven? This Jesus, who has been taken from you into heaven, will come in the same way that you have seen Him going into heaven" (Acts 1:11). Paul stated that "the Lord Himself will descend from heaven with a shout, with the archangel's voice, and with the trumpet of God"

(1 Thess. 4:16). Paul and the other apostles confidently declared that Jesus would return to the earth.

Praise the Lord! Jesus is not sending a representative or a deputy. He will appear in person. We will see Him face-to-face.

The Timing of His Return

In light of Jesus' words of assurance, it is reasonable to ask when these things would occur. The apostles of the New Testament era had every reason to believe the Lord Jesus would fulfill His promise to them in their lifetime. They were a people suffering under great oppression, and the ruthless dictates of Emperor Nero and others added to their desperation. Declining eschatological expectation over the generations is widely believed to be a contributing factor in the decline of the vigor of the church through the Dark Ages and other periods of history. Theologians, by the thousands, have speculated and sermonized with great vigor concerning the timing of Jesus' return. This is usually heightened whenever crises arise in the world, and speculation can even get out of control.

Over the years many so-called prophets have tried to set the exact date for Jesus' return, but they have always been wrong. Why? Because God has not revealed to anyone the exact time of His return. Jesus Himself stated that even He did not know the time of His return to the earth: "Now concerning that day or hour no one knows—neither the angels in heaven nor the Son—except the Father" (Mark 13:32). Jesus also stated that His return would be sudden and unexpected, like a thief in the night (see Matt. 24:43).

Even though Jesus said we will never know the exact time of His return, the curiosity and debate continue about the timing of the events surrounding His second coming. Much of the discussion relates to the millennium. Put simply, *millennium* means "a thousand years." It refers to the period in the last days when Christ rules on the earth and Satan is bound (see Rev. 20:2).

One point of the debate about the millennium centers on when it will take place. Historically, three major views related to the millennium have been proposed. They are identified with these big words: *postmillennialism, amillennialism, and premillennialism,*. Quite a mouthful to say, let alone understand. Let me try to help you a little.

POSTMILLENNIALISM

The prefix *post* gives a clue to the viewpoint of this group. *Post* means "after," thus postmillennialists believe Christ will return *after* the millennium. Those who hold this view propose that the world will get better and better as Christians win the world to Christ. Ultimately a period of peace and justice will develop that continues for one thousand years. During this time, Christ will rule the world through Christians. At the end of the millennium, Christ will return to the earth to establish a new heaven and a new earth. In connection with Christ's return, a general resurrection of the dead will take place, followed by the judgment of those who rejected Christ while on earth.

PREMILLENNIALISM

The prefix *pre*, which means "before," points to the meaning of this viewpoint. Premillennialists believe Christ will return *before* the millennium begins. This viewpoint has two distinct expressions: dispensational premillennialism and historical premillennialism. Both of these views hold that Jesus will return to the earth at the beginning of the millennium and will then rule for a thousand years while Satan is bound.

A major difference between these two premillennial views relates to an intense, seven-year period of suffering called the "great tribulation" (Rev. 7:14). Dispensational premillennialism proposes that the church goes to heaven with Christ during the tribulation while non-Christians experience the tribulation on the earth. Historical premillennialism holds that the church is not taken out of the world during the tribulation. They believe Christians, too, experience the turmoil of the tribulation period. Both premillennial views believe a literal antichrist will appear in the last days and that there will be a literal battle of Armageddon. Perhaps a brief description of these two views will be helpful as we celebrate Jesus' encouraging words.

Those who hold to the dispensational premillennial view believe the seven churches addressed in Revelation 2–3 represent seven church ages. The last church age is marked by apostasy and is the present time. According to this view, the church is taken up or "raptured" after the seventh church age (end of Rev. 3).

Based on this view, the church remains above the earth with Christ while the great tribulation is taking place on earth. During this time the raptured body of Christians will receive ruling assignments that they will carry out during the millennium following the great tribulation. The antichrist appears during the tribulation. At the end of this period of suffering, the Lord Jesus will return to the earth in great triumph (the second coming), accompanied by all believers, followed by the battle of Armageddon (see Rev. 16:16; 19:19–21). When all the battling forces are defeated by the spoken word of the Savior (see 19:21), Satan is bound, and Christ begins His thousand-year reign. Nonbelievers face the great white throne judgment at the end of the thousand years (see 20:11) and are cast away from His presence into eternal hell forever.

Those who hold to the historical premillennialist viewpoint believe the first three chapters of the book of Revelation apply specifically to first-century churches and also to churches throughout the centuries. They do not separate history into different ages. According to this view, chapters 4–22 of Revelation cover the time from Christ's crucifixion to His return and into eternity. As noted already, this view believes Christians will be on earth during the tribulation period. Thus, they will face the antichrist. At the end of the tribulation period, the battle of Armageddon takes place (see Rev. 16:16; 19:19–21); Satan is defeated and bound. All Christians then will meet Christ in the air (see 1 Thess. 4:17). At that time the wicked are judged, and Christ begins His thousand-year reign on the earth. A new heaven and a new earth will be established.

AMILLENNIALISM

The prefix *a* means "no" or "non," referring to the fact that this group does not believe Christ's reign on earth is a literal thousand years. Rather, they believe the thousand years, the millennial reign, symbolically pictures the rule of God in the hearts of believers throughout history. They interpret the revelation symbolically as the ongoing struggle between God and Satan. This is seen in the conflict between the forces of good and evil and the church and the world. For them the tribulation period represents the suffering and persecution Christians endure individually and as a body of believers. They believe Jesus' return is certain but not connected to a literal thousand-year period of time.

A difference in viewpoints about the millennium and the end-time events certainly should not cause us to fall out of fellowship with one another. In fact, all the viewpoints just described are represented among most evangelical Christians. What is vitally important is that most agree about the critical things related to the second coming. In light of Jesus' desire for all believers to "be with Me where I am," it may be useful to list some of the important areas of common agreement found generally among evangelical Christians in the world. Among these are (1) the fact of Christ's future return; (2) God's purpose for the world; (3) the resurrection of the dead; (4) the future judgment for all people; (5) the reality of heaven and hell; and (6) the absolute certainty of life after death.

The Events Connected to His Return

As emphasized already, Jesus did not give us a detailed account of the timing of the events surrounding His return. He did, however, give us a general look into the events connected with His appearance. A brief look at these events is important because of the significance they have in every believer's life.

One day, all those who have accepted Jesus Christ as their personal Lord and Savior will be gathered unto the Lord Jesus Christ forever. There will be a glorious meeting in the air. Christians who die before Jesus' return will meet Him first, followed by those who are alive when He returns (see 1 Thess. 4:15–17).

This is how Paul described the meeting with Jesus: "Then we who are still alive will be caught up together with them in the clouds to meet the Lord in the air" (1 Thess. 4:17). A close look at 1 Thessalonians 4:13–18 will help us picture and better understand the meaning of this meeting.

In verse 13, Paul told the Thessalonian Christians, "I would not have you to be ignorant" (KJV). The word *ignorant* is a translation of the Greek word *agnoeo*, from which we get the word *agnostic*, which means "not to know." An agnostic is always doubting, never able to come to the knowledge of the truth. The agnostic will perish in his sins. In contrast, believers can know and understand what God reveals. Specifically, the Holy Spirit tells us that we are not ignorant about the future. We know where we are going. We know our salvation is secure.

A second point Paul brought out in these verses is that "God will bring with Him those who have fallen asleep through Jesus" (v. 14). Those who have "fallen asleep through Jesus" are Christians who die before Jesus' second coming. The dead in Christ are now with the Lord and will come with Him on that day.

The third point Paul made is in verse 15: "We who are still alive at the Lord's coming, will certainly have no advantage over those who have fallen asleep." Believers, whether dead or alive when Christ returns, are equal before the throne of God.

"The Lord Himself will descend from heaven" (v. 16) was Paul's fourth point. Just as Jesus ascended to heaven following the resurrection, He will descend to the earth to enforce His power across the universe. Note the double emphasis, "the Lord Himself." This emphasis echoes Acts 1:11, "This same Jesus . . . shall so come in like manner" (KJV). Let there be no mistake. It will be our Lord personally and in reality.

A fifth observation Paul made in this passage is that Jesus will "descend from heaven with a shout" and will be accompanied by the voice of the archangel and "with the trumpet of God" (1 Thess. 4:16). A shout of command will summon God's people upward.

Sixth, Paul affirmed that "we . . . will be caught up . . . to meet the Lord in the air" (1 Thess. 4:17). The word *rapture* has been coined to describe this ascent to meet Jesus in the air. This word is actually an interpretation, rather than an exact translation, of the Greek term that is translated "caught up" by a number of Bible versions (HCSB, KJV, NASB, NIV, RSV, NEB). The Greek word has several meanings: (1) "To catch away speedily": The ascent will happen fast, in the twinkling of an eye. (2) "To seize without resistance": We will gladly be snatched away from under the nose of our enemy, Satan. (3) "To rescue from danger": We are saved from the wrath that is to come by Him who loved us. (4) "To move to a new place": Earth is not our permanent home. This meeting marks the point when all believers will be with the Lord forever.

Dispensational premillennialists believe the meeting described in 1 Thessalonians 4:16–17 takes place before the great tribulation. According to this view, Christians are taken out of the world into heaven and remain there until the tribulation is over. They then return to the earth with Jesus, and His thousand-year reign begins.

Historical premillennialists believe the meeting in the air takes place after the great tribulation, immediately before Jesus' return to earth. After this meeting, Jesus takes the believers back to earth to establish His thousand-year reign. Christians will reign with Christ during the millennium (see Rev. 20:6).

Both dispensational and historical premillennialists believe Satan will be bound during Christ's thousand-year reign on earth. At the end of this period, Satan will be set free, then he will be "tormented day and night forever and ever" (Rev. 20:10).

Jesus' return is certain. The exact time and the exact details are for God alone to know.

Summary of Views on Three End-Time Events

Amillennial

Tribulation: Symbolic of suffering

Millennium: Undetermined length of time between Jesus' first coming and His second coming

Jesus' Return: Definite historical event

Historical

Tribulation: End-time suffering that Christians go through

Millennium: Thousand-year reign of Christ after tribulation

Jesus' Return: Takes place at beginning of millennium

Dispensational Premillennial

Tribulation: End-time suffering only non-Christians go through

Millennium: Thousand-year reign of Christ after tribulation

Jesus' Return: Before tribulation, Christians taken above the earth

Postmillennial

Tribulation:	Symbolic of suffering
Millennium:	Thousand-year reign of Christ through Christians
Jesus' Return:	Takes place after the millennium

The bottom line of all of this remains the fact of Jesus' marvelous final word of assurance to all believers. This was always part of the plan of God before the world's foundation (Matt. 25: 34). What love indeed!

All that remained was the cross!

Conclusion

God prayed: "It is finished!" (John 19:30).

A Final Word

When the Billy Graham Association gave me the wonderful privilege of teaching this subject at The Cove, I had little idea of the impact it would have on my own personal life and ministry. Having been raised in a Christian home, I have always been surrounded by people of prayer. My earliest recollections often include the sound of my father's voice calling out to the Lord in prayer from within the confines of his pastor's study. As a rebellious teenager there were many times I would pass by my mother's bedroom to hear her pleading with the Father on my behalf. My wife, Karyn, has a passion for prayer—something passed on to her by her father, who is a man of deep and abiding prayer.

But prayer has always been something I have struggled with throughout my life and ministry. It is not that I have neglected to seek God's leadership continually in my life through prayer. It is not that I have failed to pray for my family, my church, and just about everything and everyone imaginable. It is not that I do not believe in the power of prayer. I have just struggled. When I pray, my mind often wanders very quickly. My life seems to get so busy that prayer is frequently relegated to a few desperate moments just before I have to be somewhere or do something.

But this study has taken me to a new and fresh level. I feel as though I have had a fresh encounter with my Heavenly Father because I have heard Him pray. As I watched my Savior pour out His heart to the Father as He began His journey to the cross, I realized I was listening to my sovereign God cry out for the souls of every person ever created in His image. I now see my Savior taking on Himself my sin so that I might find myself acceptable to my Father who is holy and righteous. I have come to understand that I can talk to Him as did my Savior.

He is listening!

God is praying!

STEPS TO PEACE WITH GOD

1. RECOGNIZE GOD'S PLAN—PEACE AND LIFE

The message in this book stresses that
God loves you and wants you
to experience His peace and life.

The BIBLE says ... For God loved the
world so much that He gave His only Son,
so that everyone who believes in Him may
not die but have eternal life. John 3:16

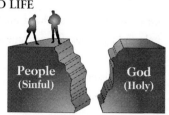

2. REALIZE OUR PROBLEM—SEPARATION FROM GOD

People choose to disobey God and go
their own way. This results in
separation from God.

The BIBLE says ... Everyone has sinned
and is far away from God's saving
presence. Romans 3:23

3. RESPOND TO GOD'S REMEDY—THE CROSS OF CHRIST

God sent His Son to bridge the gap. Christ
did this by paying the penalty of our sins
when He died on the cross and rose from
the grave.

The BIBLE says ... But God has shown
us how much He loves us—it was while we
were still sinners that Christ died for us!
Romans 5:8

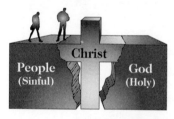

4. RECEIVE GOD'S SON—LORD AND SAVIOR

You cross the bridge into God's family
when you ask Christ to come into your life.

The BIBLE says ... Some, however, did
receive Him and believed in Him; so He
gave them the right to become God's
children. John 1:12

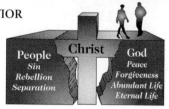

THE INVITATION IS TO:
REPENT (turn from your sins), ASK for God's forgiveness, and by faith RECEIVE
Jesus Christ into your heart and life and follow Him in obedience as your Lord
and Savior.

PRAYER OF COMMITMENT
"Dear Lord Jesus, I know that I am a sinner, and I ask for Your forgiveness. I believe
You died for my sins and rose from the dead. I turn from my sins and invite You to
come into my heart and life. I want to trust and follow You as my Lord and Savior.
In Your Name, Amen."

If you are committing your life to Christ, please let us know!

Billy Graham Evangelistic Association
1 Billy Graham Parkway, Charlotte, NC 28201-0001
1-877-2GRAHAM (1-877-247-2426)
billygraham.org/Commitment